THE
IRISH BECKETT

JOHN P. HARRINGTON

SYRACUSE UNIVERSITY PRESS

First Edition 1991
    91 92 93 94 95 96 97 98 99   6 5 4 3 2 1

Permission to quote from the following sources is gratefully acknowledged:

The works of Samuel Beckett. By kind permission of Grove Press.
"The Big House," by Elizabeth Bowen. Reproduced by permission of Virago Press. Copy-
        right © 1986 by Curtis Brown Ltd London, Literary Executors of the Estate of the late
        Elizabeth Bowen.
"Young Beckett's Irish Roots," by J. C. C. Mays. By kind permission of *Irish University Review*
        14, no. 1 (1984): 18–33.

The paper used in this publication meets the minimum requirements of American National
Standard for Information Sciences — Permanence of Paper for Printed Library Materials,
ANSI Z39.48-1984. ∞™

Library of Congress Cataloging-in-Publication Data

Harrington, John P.
        The Irish Beckett / by John P. Harrington. — 1st ed.
            p.   cm. — (Irish studies)
        Includes bibliographical references and index.
        IBSN 0-8156-2528-6
            1. Beckett, Samuel, 1906–   —Criticism and interpretation.
        2. National characteristics, Irish, in literature. 3. Ireland in
        literature. I. Title. II. Series: Irish studies (Syracuse, N.Y.)
        PR6003.E282Z6678   1991
        848'.91409—dc20   90-23476
                                                                CIP

Manufactured in the United States of America

For all the good that frequent departures out of Ireland had done him, he might just as well have stayed there.

— Watt

I began at the beginning, like an old ballocks, can you imagine that? Here's my beginning. ... I took a lot of trouble with it. Here it is. It gave me a lot of trouble. It was the beginning, do you understand? Whereas now it's nearly the end. Is what I do now any better? I don't know. That's beside the point. Here's my beginning.

— Molloy

JOHN P. HARRINGTON is Associate Professor of Humanities at The Cooper Union for the Advancement of Science and Art, which is in New York City. He has also compiled a collection of travelogues, *The English Traveller in Ireland,* and edited an anthology of plays, *Modern Irish Drama*.

CONTENTS

THE IRISH BECKETT

INTRODUCTION

WHEN SAMUEL BECKETT was announced winner of the Nobel Prize in Literature in 1969, there was an interesting sort of confusion in the press. As the *New York Times* reported in "Beckett Wins Nobel for Literature,"

> It was not immediately clear whether Mr. Beckett should be regarded as an Irish or a French winner, although Nobel officials recognize the country of work and residence. Mr. Beckett has lived in Paris since 1937, and has written mostly in French.
>
> The only Irish Nobel winner in literature was William Butler Yeats, the poet, in 1923. George Bernard Shaw, born in Ireland, was honored a few years later, but as a British author. (3)

It was implied in this manner in New York that Beckett might be mostly French, as Shaw was mostly British. The French press, however, preferred to refer to Beckett as *un inconnu célèbre*. Some European news agencies contacted the *Irish Times* for information about the winner, but the Dublin paper expressed surprise that it should be considered in any way knowledgeable about Beckett. James Mays, in an essay on "Beckett and the Irish" in press at an Irish journal at the time of the announcement, added for publication the observation that he "was interested to note that while the English news on the evening of October 23rd described Beckett as 'the Irish writer,' [Irish news] called him 'Dublin born'" (14). Beckett himself, secluded in Tunisia, was studiously unhelpful. He would accept the award, but not personally, a situation in which protocol specifies that the award be ac-

1

cepted by the winner's ambassador. Although he held an Irish passport, Beckett informed Dublin that he did not wish to be represented by their Swedish ambassador, Tadgh Seosamh O'Hodrain. Nor did he wish to be represented by the French ambassador. Instead, he chose Jerome Lindon, his French publisher. At the banquet following the presentation ceremony, Beckett's representation was ambiguous: Lindon and O'Hodrain were seated side by side.

There was no parallel confusion, though much ingenuity, in regard to the sort of work for which Beckett was being honored. Alfred Nobel's stipulation that literature deserving of his prize be "uplifting" required special grandiloquence from the academy for justification of its choice of an author popularly notorious for absolute pessimism. The academy resolutely cited Beckett for "a body of work that, in new forms of fiction and theater, has transmuted the destitution of modern man into his exaltation." The *New York Times,* however, like virtually all the international press, remained skeptical. It described Beckett's novels as "a search for the self and an achieving of nothing," it referred to *The Unnamable* as "a novel about a blob," and it summed up the plot of *How It Is* as follows: "a humanoid looks for meaning while crawling through primeval ooze and discovers another creature, called Pim. Each may be the other's victim" (3). Karl Ragnar Gierow, secretary to the academy, offered a radio commentary as counteraction to establish the uplifting aspects of Beckett's work. As his words were reported by the *New York Times*:

> "The degradation of humanity is a recurrent theme in Beckett's writing," Dr. Gierow said, "and to this extent his philosophy, simply accentuated by elements of the grotesque and of tragic farce, can be said to be a negativism that knows no haven."
>
> But, using a photographic analogy, Dr. Gierow said that when a negative was printed, it produced "a positive, a clarification, with black proving to be the light of day, the parts in deepest shade, those which reflect the light sources. . . ."

> Praising Mr. Beckett for "a love of mankind that grows in understanding as it plumbs further into the depths of abhorrence," Dr. Gierow concluded rhapsodically:
>
> "From that position, in the realms of annihilation, the writing of

Samuel Beckett rises like a miserere from all mankind, its muffled minor key sounding liberation to the oppressed and comfort to those in need." (3)

Twenty years later, these particular sentiments surely seem jejune. But they were repeated in virtually unchanged form on the occasion, twenty years later, of Beckett's death. Moreover, the thrust of this exposition—Beckett's transcending humanism and his cleverly indirect optimism — has remained the thrust of most criticism of Beckett's work from 1969 to 1989.

Beckett criticism, during and since the 1960s, by virtue of the Beckett works that first attracted its attention and by virtue of its own historical moment in literary criticism, has almost invariably adumbrated a Beckett that is, as in the title of one of Richard Ellmann's last works, a "Nayman From Noland" and a Beckett whose salience is the construction of elevating artistic images out of elemental and so universal materials. In the chapters that follow, I detail specific examples of this fairly uniform approach to what is, now at least, more generally appreciated as a rather varied body of work. The humanistic quality of his work is by no means a self-evidently inappropriate approach, especially as generated by a perception of Beckett's work provoked by *Waiting for Godot* or *How It Is*. But it is a singular approach and, as uniform, a somewhat programmatic approach. The tendency of Beckett criticism to operate in singular ways has been pointed out before. In a 1981 piece Michael Wood saw Beckett criticism as uniform enough to warrant collective criticism of itself: he commented on its tendency, lacking thorough examination of its own language or methodology, to base astonishingly broad generalizations on quite specific and quite minimal Beckett texts. Wood's generalization is itself fairly broad, and more specific consideration is given to individual cases in the course of my study. But it is worth mentioning here that this uniform bloc of "Beckett Studies," as epitomized by *The Journal of Beckett Studies,* has varied little over some time and has stood impervious to such criticism of itself as Wood's. At this later date it is interesting to note that a number of collections of critical essays about Beckett's work released around the time of the author's eightieth birthday, most boasting a multiplicity of perspectives, tended to reprint easily available essays from the 1960s and in some cases to reprint well-known essays which had just been reprinted in other new collections. It is of some interest here, too, that none of the multiplicity-of-perspectives collections offered anything devoted to the Irish contexts of Beckett's work.

In one recent study, *Ascendancy and Tradition in Anglo-Irish Literary History from 1789 to 1939,* W. J. McCormack took occasion to survey the general thrust of Yeats studies. As he saw two "movements" in Yeats's work, local and universal, so he saw two dangers in Yeats criticism. The first was reduction of Yeats "to dextrous celebrant of Irish 'realities'" and the second was "Platonizing him out of existence": "What is of genuine interest is the historical conjuncture of these rival possibilities" (296). The tendency in Beckett criticism is solely the latter, Platonizing him out of existence. I certainly hope to avoid reduction of Beckett to dexterous celebrant of Irish "realities." However, I also hope to give Beckett studies the interest of rival possibilities. Beckett criticism has been of immeasurable benefit to me in preparing this study, as my critical references should make clear. Nor are the conclusions drawn here wholly incompatible with existing criticism. My intention is to supplement the ways in which Beckett has been read by paying greater attention to Irish contexts than to humanistic traditions. Irish contexts are most explicit in Beckett's early work, and so I shape his *oeuvre* rather differently than is customary in Beckett studies. Here, closest attention is devoted to Beckett's miscellaneous criticism, to *More Pricks Than Kicks,* to *Murphy,* and to *Watt;* and then the paradigm of local dialectics extracted from those works is applied in provisional, abbreviated form to the trilogy of novels, to the major plays, and to later works. I treat Beckett's work as an *oeuvre* whose consistency emerges most clearly by consideration of texts commonly marginalized by an impression of Beckett's work derived from its shape in the 1960s. His work has been periodized in the course of Beckett studies since the 1960s. Beckett and Beckett critics have in more recent years usefully complicated that periodization by publishing "trunk manuscripts" and by reprinting unavailable texts. These factors have abetted my study, and so this topic, at least, may be considered a likely historical extension of Beckett studies.

There are two obvious objections to the construction of an Irish Beckett. The first is the adjective. Derek Mahon, no completely disinterested observer of the phenomenon, has noted that "the time is coming fast, if it isn't already here, when the question, 'Is So-and-so really an *Irish* writer?' will clear a room in seconds." Though principally concerned with Louis MacNeice, Mahon further notes a comparable absence of recognizable Irish settings in the works of MacNeice and Beckett. "Yet it would take a lot of obtuseness," he adds, "to deny that some sort of Irish sensibility is frequently discernible in the work of both" (113). In place of *sensibility,* or any approximation of an essentialist criteria for nationality, my study takes a rough definition of the Irish writer from Conor Cruise O'Brien: "the condition of being involved in the Irish situation, and usually of being mauled by it" (99). In this study, I rest the adjective of the title on the comprehensive attention in Beckett's work, from early to late, to matters specifically Irish. As has been noted many times, Beckett's explicit references to Ireland are frequently antagonistic: a condition of being mauled by what O'Brien euphemistically terms the "situation." However, Beckett is scarcely singular among Irish writers for being antagonistic. Indeed, as documented here, his ridicule and denunciation of Ireland puts him in good and plentiful company of Irish writers. Further, on examination, Ireland in Beckett's work often proves an equivocal rather than a categorically hostile presence. In individual cases and in all his work, Ireland—abstracted but never replaced by anyplace else — is a complex of attraction and repulsion, a syndrome already documented in the work of other Irish writers, including MacNeice.

A second objection to the Irish Beckett may focus on the noun. With appreciable salience, and in general configuration with its own historical moment, Michel Foucault's essay "What Is an Author?" has exposed the limitations of a privileged conception of author as organizing principle of textual examination. Moreover, Foucault did that with a "direction" supplied by Beckett: the passage from *Stories and Texts for Nothing* that reads, "What matter who's speaking, someone said, what matter who's speaking." But in that essay, Foucault mentioned and put aside "numerous questions that deserve attention in this context," including how an author is individualized in a culture, what status has been given an author, what systems of valorization have affected an author, and what conditions foster "the formulation of the fundamental critical category of 'the man and his work'" (115). These are the questions that this book asks of the Beckett *oeuvre.* I address, for example, the conditions that create a sense of such a text as

Foucault quotes, "Texts for Nothing 3," in studied indifference to its reference to Duggan's pub and to the local suggestions of its observation that "we have no political opinions, simply limply republican ones" (88). These are the sorts of contexts that *The Irish Beckett* hopes to add to general appreciation of Beckett's work.

An Irish place such as Duggan's pub and the Irish import of a term such as *republicanism* are, of course, references to local knowledge, a different problem, though by no means an insignificant problem, from universal humanism. As Clifford Geertz, who has given the term *local knowledge* some currency, puts it, "To turn from trying to explain social phenomena by weaving them into grand textures of cause and effect to trying to explain them by placing them in local frames of awareness is to exchange a set of well-known difficulties for a set of largely uncharted ones" (6). Beckett's humanism is a rather well-charted problem, while Beckett's Irishness is a rather uncharted one. As this book presents a relatively new problem, my approach is necessarily inductive, though I do indeed make occasional use of theory. The result is a report on suggestive local contexts as an initial charting of the territory. The material, as it is diverse, is also less manageable than conveniently familiar material. I note in closing Seamus Heaney's observation on the neatness of sanitized formalism. And so it is of interest to note in opening an observation by Terence Brown on "Edward Dowden: Irish Victorian," who, as an unhappy contemporary of the Irish literary revival and as the brunt of Yeats's antagonisms in an Irish "situation," figures slightly here. "Throughout his career," Brown writes of Dowden, "there seemed something verging on the neurotic in his commitment to a universal and therefore sanitized and severe version of literary culture over against the offensive demands of the local, with all the risks involved of parochialism and misjudgement" (43). I take on those risks of charting a local territory that as presently constituted makes no more than very occasional and impressionistic references to Samuel Beckett.

Seamus Heaney and Terence Brown are also interesting participants in a major reassessment in Ireland of its own cultural identity, particularly as formulated by its writers, including Beckett. At the present moment, this reassessment, or revisionism, of a long-standing national ethos, or revivalism, has taken on virtually institutionalized forms of its own. Revisionism began with aggressive critique of Yeat's revivalist "fictions" of a still-vigorous Celtic nobility and a much-neglected Anglo-Irish ascendancy of grandeur and grace and selfless-ness. The most formidable spokesperson for this new, revisionist factor in the Irish "situation" has been Seamus Deane, who challenges Ireland's cultural complacency after the revival and some degree of political autonomy, and who laments, in *Celtic Revivals: Essays in Modern Irish Literature 1880 – 1980,* that "the best poets after Yeats quickly learned that the local and the ordinary defined the horizon for literature as it did for politics" (37). Samuel Beckett's works have become revealing data in this current Irish debate: as the local revivalists once excluded Beckett from the national literary canon for lack of local interest, so revisionism would now include Beckett for universalist reconfiguration of the horizon — or include Beckett specifically for his lack of local interest. Thus, establishment of the local contexts of Beckett's work in these chapters likely upsets the respective compartmentalizations of Beckett by revivalists and by revisionists. The interest of the Irish Beckett, at present, in Ireland and elsewhere, lies in these offensive demands of the local.

1

 EARLY CRITICISM IN CONTEXT

SAMUEL BECKETT IS THE MOST INTERESTING of the younger Irish writers. He is a graduate of Trinity College, Dublin, and has lectured at Ecole Normale Supérieure in Paris. He has a great knowledge of Romance literature, is a friend of Rudmose-Brown and of Joyce, and has adapted the Joyce method to his poetry with original results. His impulse is lyric, but has been deepened through this influence and the influence of Proust and the historic method. He has recently won the Hours Press prize with a poem *Whoroscope;* has contributed to *transition* and *This Quarter,* and to the examination of Joyce's "Work in Progress." This interesting exercise in self-definition and self-advertisement was written by Samuel Beckett to accompany four poems included in *The European Caravan,* an anthology assembled by Samuel Putnam in 1931 (475). For Samuel Beckett, in 1931, the exercise certainly is notable for arrogance, even if the "younger Irish writers" are presumed to be those born after 1900, even if James Joyce had authorized the use of his name and reference to *the* method of Joyce, and even if Trinity College's Professor of French Thomas B. "Ruddy" Rudmose-Brown had agreed to accept from wayward students encomium in lieu of academic emulation. But his contributor's note is also remarkable for prescience. Before his death in 1989, when the younger Irish writer had become *éminence grise,* many would agree that Samuel Beckett was the most interesting of the living Irish writers. That case needed to proceed no further than the collateral evidence of the singular interest *of* his work and the extraordinary critical interest *in* his work: the tired witticism, of course, is that as Beckett's works get shorter the commentaries on them get longer. Indeed, even if Beckett's intention in a poetry anthology in 1931 was to position himself among the younger Irish poets (i.e., everybody younger than Yeats), even then the presumptuousness of his assumption of the role of poet ("his impulse is lyric"!) came to seem more than bluster. His work may be found to be poetry on internal evidence, as Marjorie Perloff has on examination of a late piece of apparent prose, *Ill Seen Ill Said*. His work also may be found to be poetry on contextual evidence, as W. J. McCormack has on choosing to end *The Battle of the Books: Two Decades of Irish Cultural Debate* with a comparison between Beckett and Seamus Heaney.

Of course, it is possible to read Beckett's self-identification of 1931 as one in which being Irish is advanced as a liability, like being young: hence, Beckett's first distinctly not-Irish publications are listed proudly as early transcendence of an inherited liability. When Beckett advertises the Irish connections, Trinity (not University College, Dublin), Rudmose-Brown (cosmopolitan), and James Joyce (anathema), he refers to an Ireland that is not what Daniel Corkery, also writing in 1931, on *Synge and Anglo-Irish Literature,* imperiously called "the Ireland that counts" (23, 24). One wonders how well Beckett knew Corkery's rhetoric of 1931, but he was, inevitably, familiar with the general political position. Fifteen or so years later, on the way to *Godot,* Beckett produced in *Watt* a rather different version of "the Ireland that counts" in the form of Nackybal, Celticomathematical idiot savant. By *Watt,* Beckett the novelist's programmatic ridicule of all things distinctly Irish was fully operational; but in 1931, Beckett the author of a contributor's note was rather more aloof to the matter of local origins. "The most interesting of the younger Irish writers" effectively qualifies even the Joyce connection. Quantitatively, Joyce references outnumber Proust references in *The European Caravan* note, but, qualitatively, Proust (then the topic of an unmentioned, commissioned monograph) is accounted an influence, while Joyce remains the friendly mentor whose "method" is in need of adaptation. Further, the Joyce here is the Joyce of *Work in Progress* and not the Joyce of, say, *Dubliners,* which held some influence over literary Dublin. Finally, Beckett's 1931 inventory of achievements points away from Ireland. *Whoroscope,* of course, is a ninety-eight-line annotated poem derived from Adrien Baillet's 1691 life of Descartes. Beckett's contributions to *This Quarter,* edited by Edward Titus and funded by his American heiress wife, Helena Rubenstein, were English translations of the work of three contemporary Italian poets. In 1932, Beckett would contribute translations to *This Quarter* again, to a number on surrealism that was edited by André Breton and that Enoch Brater accounts "Beckett's opportunity to play a minor part in the Paris avant-garde" (*Beckett at 80: Beckett in Context* 8). *Transition* had already printed Beckett's first journal publications in essay ("Dante . . . Bruno . Vico . . Joyce"), story ("Assumption"), and poem ("For Future Reference"). The intellectual differences between most of Dublin and *transition* can be judged by the editorial response of *T.C.D.: A College Miscellany* to another of Beckett's first publications. "The Possessed" had been published anonymously in *T.C.D.* in 1930. Soon after, *T.C.D.* observed of its own recent contents that, "In the Joyceian medley, *The Possessed,* its anonymous author performs some diverting verbal acrobatics, but in the manner of a number of *transition*'s offspring, is too allusive to be generally comprehensible" (Bair 131). Thus, one could use *transition* and the late Joyce to establish that one had transcended being Irish.

But association with *transition* was not entirely incompatible with conception of oneself as "the most interesting of the younger Irish writers." The journal and its circle was of no known nationality and resisted affiliation despite its physical locations. According to Stuart Gilbert, writing in a *transition Workshop,* edited by Eugene Jolas, which reprinted two of Beckett's early pieces, "to the very end —the last of its twenty-seven numbers appeared in 'thirty eight—it remained the *International* Workshop for Orphic Creation it had set out to be" (22). So, enlistment in *transition* did not alter or cancel national identity; it was an affiliation that left nationality unaffected. Just so, the representation of reality in Beckett's most influential prose and drama avoided localization without affecting nationality. As Theodor W. Adorno puts it in "Trying to Understand *Endgame,*" "In the act of omission, that which is omitted survives through its exclusion, as consonance survives in atonal harmony" (125). Though principally concerned with formalist aesthetics, Adorno's observation of this dimension of *Endgame* is wholly relevant to the conception of precedence and tradition central to Beckett's *oeuvre,* including those works most celebrated for innovation. Further, Adorno's paradox is not contingent on the whole field of Marxist theory. Lionel Trilling, without reference to Beckett, found the same phenomenon characteristic of modernity. In *Beyond Culture: Essays on Literature and Learning*, he notes that "when a person rejects his culture (as the phrase goes) and rebels against it, he does so in a culturally determined way: we identify the substance and style of his rebellion as having been provided by the culture against which it is directed," and that "the belief that it is possible to stand beyond the culture in some decisive way is commonly and easily held. In the modern world it is perhaps a necessary belief" (xii).

The Irish devotees of Orphic creation were a well-defined subset of *transition*'s offspring, perhaps because of a charm or a stigma carried by the Joyce association, perhaps because of clannishness or even hidden agenda. Samuel Putnam's memoir, *Paris Was Our Mistress: Memoirs of a Lost and Found Generation*, was published in 1947, well before Beckett came into literary vogue. At that time, Putnam recalled the Irish associates of *transition* as virtually distinct from the rest of the group and Beckett as a member of that Irish clique. Speaking of the area around Silvia Beach's bookshop, Putnam wrote,

> This was the quarter frequented by Eugene Jolas, Eliot Paul, and the *transition* group, and by certain young Irishmen, friends and admirers of Joyce: Thomas McGreevy [*sic*], Samuel Beckett, George Reavey, and others, the Dublin intellectuals being in the habit of gathering at the Ecole Normale, where McGreevy and Beckett were instructors. Beckett and Reavey were often seen on the boulevard du Montparnasse, Jolas and his American associates very seldom, for they were workers rather than cafe sitters. (97)

There is much of interest here about Beckett's beginnings. One is company. In 1980, in *Company,* Beckett's narrator speculates that "the lower the order of mental activity the better the company. Up to a point" (12). In the early 1930s, MacGreevy and Reavey were precedent as aspiring literati from Ireland who had arrived before Beckett in Paris, where they were company, as Putnam remembered, up to a point. MacGreevy, of course, is generally credited with introducing Beckett to Joyce. MacGreevy later repatriated himself and became director of the National Gallery; he wrote a book about the national importance of Jack Yeats that Beckett found difficult to praise, but, out of obligation, he tried to do so. Reavey, who had already left Ireland to study at Cambridge, later more emphatically expatriated himself from Ireland and Irish letters and turned instead to Soviet literature. Only Beckett, the youngest of these "Dublin intellectuals," chose — or at least followed — a middle course between the divergent directions of MacGreevy and Reavey. There is, too, tradition: John Millington Synge, Oscar Wilde, George Bernard Shaw, Joyce, even W. B. Yeats, and others, had set the example of Irish writers establishing their literary credentials outside of Ireland; two of them, Synge and Wilde, after Parisian interludes had pursued directions comparable, respectively, to MacGreevy and Reavey. These all complicate the idea of standing beyond culture.

Purpose helps gather company; and by being in Paris in the 1930s, Beckett was not so much without purpose (like the Oblomov figure in Peggy Guggenheim's memoir, *Out of This Century,* or like Didi and Gogo in *Godot*) as he was adopting, or perhaps "adapting," ones not by omission or exclusion but by explicitness. Suspicions of a hidden agenda of the Dublin intellectuals are not absurd. Writing on "Young Beckett's Irish Roots," James Mays locates in MacGreevy the collective purpose of Irish intellectuals of the 1930s, including Beckett and a range of other Irish poets, artists, and teachers:

> MacGreevy's argument was politically inspired, but it amounted to depreciating Yeats's example. Yeats was classed as Anglo-Norman, alien; the whole Celtic Revival was deplored as a phase in English literature, an aspect of English colonialism foisted on a gullible native talent. And the same argument elevated the later Joyce, and the example of French and European models, conceiving that, with national independence, Ireland had rejoined a concert of European culture after being divided from it for centuries. Whereas the dominant model in Irish literary history linked the idea of Irishness with place, and assumed literature should be mimetic, this alternative, which is no less nationalistic, linked Irishness with an attitude towards European traditions in all the arts. It was consciously open to experimental techniques, less interested in realism; it looked more to the Joyce of *Ulysses* (as a book, not just as local history) and *Finnegans Wake* than of *Dubliners* and *A Portrait.* (27 – 28)

The interesting reminder here is that relocation outside Ireland was not especially unusual or divisive in the late 1920s or early 1930s. Rather, all the interesting Irish writers were drawn to Europeanism and to relocation there, less as exile than as expedition. One useful witness is an Irish writer not remarkable for sympathy with Beckett, Sean O'Faolain. Writing in *Commonweal* in 1929, O'Faolain asserted that all Anglo-Irish literature from 1875 to the establishment of the Free State, a "period [which] might be said to open with Yeats . . . represents the Europeanization of the Irish literary man" (751). Writing in 1932, also in *Commonweal*, O'Faolain further observed that "only those writers who have idealized Irish life, or whose orbit of interest is limited, or who treat of Irish life idylically by a gentle process of tactful omission, are really happy at rest at home" (215). These — idealization, limitation, tactful omission — are, of course, intended by O'Faolain as counterproductive to a writer's happy rest at home. By being in Paris, Beckett joined with, rather than fled from, the interesting Irish writers. By the 1980s, the centrality of that position for an Irish writer, that depreciation of Yeats and appreciation of Europeanization, came around again in a general program of revisionism of local literary and cultural history.

The early evidence might seem to place Beckett as far as possible away from Ireland and to indicate a susceptibility to Orphic excess. Beckett's first work for *transition* was decidedly experimental, alternative to realism, and oriented to a significant degree toward European culture. The "Poetry is Vertical" manifesto, which was signed by Beckett and others for publication in *transition* in 1932, prescribed "a-logical movement of the psyche" and "hallucinatory irruption of images" (148). Both the poem "For Future Reference" (a stream of images of a boy being bullied off a diving board) and the story "Assumption" (a surrealistic narration of high romantic suicide) followed those prescriptions. This brand of Europeanism also abrogated any special emphasis on the sense of place so fundamental to the Irish literary revival. "Dante . . . Bruno . Vico . . Joyce" approached Joyce through just those titular points of reference, and, according to Ruby Cohn, its extended commentary on Vico earned Beckett an enduring place in European bibliographies of Vico studies (*Disjecta* 8). As Vivian Mercier, an acquaintance of Beckett and estimable commentator on Irish literature, put it in 1977, in unintentional concurrence with *T.C.D*'s rebuke of "*transition*'s offspring" in 1931, Beckett was "caught up in the international avant-garde on his first flight. . . . His greatest folly consisted in attempting to imitate James Joyce: not the earlier work, either, but *Work in Progress*, the drafts of *Finnegans Wake*" (36).

But even these first works reveal engagement in local issues and specifically Irish interests, both personal and literary. The bully in "For Future Reference" is grounded in Beckett's experience at Portora Royal School in Fermanagh and W. N. Tetley, science teacher and swimming coach (Bair 32–34). "Assumption," published in the same issue of *transition* as "Dante . . . Bruno . Vico . . Joyce," adumbrates the metaphor of an easily influenced man, "not such a man, but his voice was of such a man" (268), for whom not "the least apostolic fervour coloured what was at its worst the purely utilitarian contrivance of a man who wished to gain himself a hearing" (269). Joyce described the twelve contributors to *Our Exagmination Round His Factification for Incamination of Work in Progress,* the book that included Beckett's essay, not as apostles but as "marshals." He did so in a letter that mentioned Beckett as one of two "riotous Irishmen," and he did so in a letter that could have been dictated to Beckett (*Selected Letters of James Joyce* 344–45). But Beckett's essay found occasion to depart from apostolic fervor by digressing from *Work in Progress* and the prescribed European and historical references to refer to Joyce's earlier work, and not to *Ulysses,* either, but to "The Day of the Rabblement" and *A Portrait of the Artist as a Young Man.* Those are only preliminary indications of the extent to which Beckett's early work was engaged in specifically Irish contexts.

Far from being solely *transition*'s offspring, Beckett's earliest criticism, poetry, and *obiter dicta* are profoundly entangled in Irish literary issues, including both literary precedence and consequent literary agenda. Between 1929 and 1938 he produced an eclectic body of periodical publications with one interest clearer and more consistent than any other: Irish literature and culture. His references to Ireland are sarcastic and his commentaries on most Irish writers are antagonistic, but those were his subject more often than not. Indeed, Beckett's criticism between 1929 and 1938, in which the salient works are "Dante . . . Bruno . Vico . . Joyce," "Recent Irish Poetry," and long-unpublished "Censorship in the Saorstat," is representative of a large part of his entire *oeuvre* in reduced scale. Had he subsequently only written in what has been called "Beckett's French period" (Gontarski, *On Beckett* 8), it might have been plausible to insist that the trilogy of novels and *Waiting for Godot* were made possible by what Beckett managed "to unlearn" (Mercier 36). However, the more pronounced autobiographical vein of the Beckett works from the 1980s (often written in English, the change that makes it possible to refer to a "French period") demands treatment of continuity in the Beckett *oeuvre*, which is the continuity suggested by the narrator of *Company:* "Having covered in your day some twenty-five thousand leagues or roughly thrice the girdle. And never once overstepped a radius of one from home. Home!" (60).

"Dante . . . Bruno . Vico . . Joyce," published in 1929 in *transition* and in the collection of essays *Our Exagmination,* is frequently described as an act of literary devotion and as an overture to a personal and artistic relationship with a father-mentor figure (Fitch 278; Gontarski 210, n9). Though often mined for apothegms of some relevance to Beckett's later work, the essay usually is represented as a succinct exposition of a predicament: the formidability and the anxiety of influence concerning what Beckett in "Home Olga," a poem for Joyce, called "the sweet noo style" (*Collected Poems* 8). Criticism does not present predicament without concomitant solution, of course, and such readings are based less on the essay itself than on "the sweet noo style" of Beckett's own later work. But despite the constraints placed on the essay by Joyce, "Dante . . . Bruno . Vico . . Joyce" propounds a plausible aesthetic for immediate use by Beckett himself and for the Irish literary associates in Paris and of his age who may or may not have been, in Noel Riley Fitch's phrase, "the Irish mafia" (258).

Our Exagmination was conceived, according to Richard Ellmann, as "the first apologia for *Finnegans Wake,*" a defense against "the chief critics of the book, at that time Sean O'Faolain, Wyndham Lewis, and Rebecca West" (Ellmann, *Joyce* 626). Given the opportunity, Beckett did indeed counterattack Lewis and West, Joyce's chief English critics. He did not address O'Faolain's unhappiness with *Work in Progress,* which, at least in "Style and the Limitations of Speech" of 1928, was only relative to O'Faolain's happiness with Joyce's other works. According to Ellmann, Beckett's opportunity may have stemmed from being "fresh from Dublin" (626); according to Ruby Cohn, "since Beckett had studied Italian, and particularly Dante, at Trinity College, Joyce proposed that the 22-year-old student trace *Work's* debt to the Italian trinity of Dante, Bruno, and Vico" (*Disjecta* 8). The manner in which the young Irish literary cosmopolitan was to deal with the assignment was negotiated, according to Deirdre Bair, as follows:

"Many of the ideas contained in the essay, particularly the interpretations of Bruno and Vico, came directly from his conversations with Joyce, who was eager to guide his protégé to the correct version, but the language and structure of the essay are Beckett's own" (76). The structural configuration of the essay, presumably Beckett's own, was the presentation of the Italian trinity in reverse of the chronological order indicated by the title, including interior punctuation in reference to gaps of centuries. In that presentation, far more space was given over to the "correct" ideas of Vico than to the "correct" ones of Bruno or Dante.

Beckett's aesthetic in "Dante . . . Bruno . Vico . . Joyce" focuses on liberation of content from form, and that focus is consistent in several of Beckett's other essays of the 1930s that have nothing to do with Joyce. The opening of the essay is far less concerned with tallying Joyce's structural and metaphysical exploitation of Dante, Bruno, and Vico than with liberating the text from those exemplars. Beckett's oft-cited opening sentence, "The danger is in the neatness of identifications" (*Disjecta* 19), is a warning ignored by a great deal of subsequent criticism of Joyce and of Beckett that has dwelled on their works as Vico reified or, in the case of Beckett, Arthur Schopenhauer or Ludwig Wittgenstein reified. However respectable the essay may have become as a commentary on Vico, it is rather more assertive about the reductive consequences of just that systematic interpretation: "The conception of Philosophy and Philology as a pair of nigger minstrels out of the Teatro dei Piccoli is soothing, like the contemplation of a carefully folded ham-sandwich" (19). Whatever the instructions from Joyce, Beckett is intent on rescuing Joyce's work from just those contexts mentioned in the title of the essay. "This social and historical classification," according to Beckett, "is clearly adapted by Mr Joyce as a structural convenience—or inconvenience. His position is in no way a philosophical one" (22). In just such a way, one assumes, Beckett "adapted," as he claimed in *The European Caravan*, "the Joyce method to his poetry"—as a structural convenience or inconvenience. What Beckett, about twenty years before *Molloy, Malone Dies*, and *The Unnamable*, elevates above such classification is "direct expression":

> Here Vico, implicitly at least, distinguishes between writing and direct expression. In such direct expression, form and content are inseparable. . . . On turning to *Work in Progress* we find that the mirror

is not so convex. Here is direct expression—pages and pages of it. And if you don't understand it, Ladies and Gentlemen, it is because you are too decadent to receive it. You are not satisfied unless form is so strictly divorced from content that you can comprehend the one almost without bothering to read the other. (25–26)

Beckett, of course, would labor mightily before he could approach direct expression in these terms. The forms of context directly addressed in all his work through *Molloy, Malone Dies,* and *The Unnamable,* are philosophy, history, tradition, and nationality. Beckett's work, from "Dante . . . Bruno . Vico . . Joyce" onward is intent on negotiation of those contexts and qualified liberation of self and content from context and form. The last of those contexts—tradition and nationality—are the principal topics under study here.

Beckett's contribution to *Our Exagmination* testifies to the context of being, as Ellmann observed, "fresh from Dublin." Beckett's frame of reference in his contribution to *Our Exagmination* was more explicitly Irish than that of fellow contributor Thomas MacGreevy, who was not quite so fresh from Dublin. Certainly, some of the specifically Irish references in the essay are a result of the text under examination, as in Beckett's commentary on Joyce's numerology: "Why, Mr Joyce seems to say, should there be four legs to a table, and four to a horse, and four seasons and four Gospels and four Provinces in Ireland?" (32). However, other introductions of Ireland into this most cosmopolitan discussion of Italian influences on Joyce are more clearly Beckett's own, such as his own Anglo-Irish dialect in reference to "the river puffing her old doudheen" (29) or in allusion to "the world's Portadownians" (30) without gloss of local associations. In praise of Vico's preference for the mythic power of the particular, Beckett itemizes local references in a fashion central to his own *oeuvre:* "We have Type-names: Isolde — any beautiful girl; Earwigger — Guinness's Brewery, the Wellington monument, the Phoenix Park, anything that occupies an extremely comfortable position between the two stools" (29). Joyce's exploitation of the mythic power of a particular emblem, for example phallic and imperialist associations of the Wellington monument, is operative in Beckett's own early works: for example Swift's tower in *More Pricks Than Kicks* or Sheppard's statue of Cuchulain in *Murphy.* But subsequent Beckett works move away from that comfortable position between the stools of particular and general and move toward the general: canal, or hill, or place on a road. Beckett's work never completely frees itself from the type names: Connolly's Stores in *Company*, for example, or Croker's Acres in *Not I*. But his work quite gradually and quite studiously does complicate the pride of place fundamental to the project of establishing a national identity in the Irish literary revival. That complication is gradual enough and studious enough to suggest revision of previous ideals. As Beckett in "Dante . . . Bruno . Vico . . Joyce" was as prone as most commentators on *Finnegans Wake* to lift from context any bit of prose ripe for extrapolation, one might as well say that Beckett's own movement from particular to general in the use of specifically Irish placenames or type names could be construed as fulfilling Joyce's own surmise in *Finnegans Wake* that may or may not constitute literal reference to Beckett: "Sam knows miles bettern me how to work the miracle. . . . He'll prisckly soon hand tune your Erin's ear for you" (467).

Beckett's attention to *Work in Progress* is apparent in texts other than "Dante . . . Bruno . Vico . . Joyce," such as in "Sedendo et Quiescendo" or in the prose "Text," both published in 1932. But that attention, even in the *Our Exagmination* essay, hardly warrants charges of Beckett's great folly in imitating Joyce's last work or of the essay as the "least rewarding" piece of Beckett's criticism, in J. Mitchell Morse's words, because it "deals with a work whose purposes and methods are from their foundations different from his own and with which he was constitutionally out of sympathy" (24). In 1929, of course, Beckett had no method, other than his adaptation of Joyce's, and "Dante . . . Bruno . Vico . . Joyce" shows awareness of and attention to more than one work of Joyce. In explication of *Work in Progress,* Beckett twice refers to and directly quotes *A Portrait of the Artist as a Young Man.* Furthermore, as a parenthetical anecdote, he adduces "The Day of the Rabblement." In fact, young Beckett's knowledge of young Joyce's critical proclamations may have been more thorough than he explicitly acknowledged. Melvin J. Friedman has pointed to similarities between Beckett's *Our Exagmination* essay and Joyce's "Ibsen's New Drama" on the basis of "blind dedication" (47) of author to subject. But the similarity may derive more from Beckett's appropriation of the rhetoric of Joyce's early essay. "But in dealing with the work of a man like Ibsen," Joyce wrote in 1900, "the task set the reviewer is truly great enough to sink all his courage. All he can hope to do is to link some of the salient points together in such a way as to suggest rather than to indicate, the intricacies of the plot" (*Critical Writings* 49). "And now here am I," Beckett wrote in 1929, "with my handful of abstractions, among which notably: a mountain, the coincidence of contraries, the inevitability of cyclic evolution, a system of Poetics, and the prospect of self-extension in the world of Mr Joyce's *Work in Progress*" (19).

Beckett was not alone in using Joyce's early work to address *Work in Progress*. English critics, such as Wyndham Lewis, relied heavily on *Ulysses* in explaining *Work in Progress*. Irish writers, however, looked to the earlier work of Joyce, and, in citing *Portrait* and "The Day of the Rabblement," Beckett was in company with them. In the final 1930 issue of the *Irish Statesman*, Frank O'Connor took the opportunity of *Work in Progress* to formulate his thoughts on all of Joyce, which he divided into three periods marked by *Portrait, Ulysses,* and *Work in Progress*. Also, having at hand *Our Exagmination*, O'Connor observed in "Joyce: The Third Period" that "two or three of these essays—I am thinking in particular of Samuel Beckett's, Eugene Jolas', and Thomas MacGreevy's — are very interesting, and, with a little detachment would have been first rate criticism" (115). Other Irish writers' awareness in the early 1930s of "The Day of the Rabblement" is also apparent in miscellaneous articles by Sean O'Faolain, whose objections to *Work in Progress* were limited to fairly esoteric matters of linguistics. Writing on "Literary Provincialism" in *Commonweal* in 1932, O'Faolain spoke of "weariness with the provincial rabble—I use Joyce's word" (215); and writing on "Emancipation of Irish Writers" in *Yale Review* in 1934 he called for "another day of the rabblement" (498). It was this company that Beckett joined when he enjoyed his own sneer in "Dante . . . Bruno . Vico . . Joyce." "For the benefit of those who enjoy a parenthetical sneer, we would draw attention to the fact that when Mr Joyce's early pamphlet *The Day of the Rabblement* appeared, the local philosophers were thrown into a state of some bewilderment by a reference in the first line to The Nolan. They finally succeeded in identifying this mysterious individual with one of the obscurer ancient Irish kings" (29–30).

Joyce, of course, had intended just that sort of bewilderment, at least according to his younger brother Stanislaus's account, which was published much later as *My Brother's Keeper: James Joyce's Early Years*

(146). But in this particular sort of sneer about new rabble, Beckett had more company than O'Connor, O'Faolain, and other near contemporaries. The matter of iconoclastic proclamation around the age of twenty puts him in the local company of W. B. Yeats and also, by virtue of just that particular pamphlet, Joyce himself. What these writers had in common at very early stages of their careers was not just blind devotion to singular elder writers but also fomulation of their own projects in contempt for the prevailing critical consensus, which seems to have neglected to improve itself despite successive reprimands from Yeats, Joyce, and Beckett. This exercise was performed by Yeats in 1886, when he exalted Samuel Ferguson at the expense of Edward Dowden of Trinity College. For Yeats, at this early point in the Irish literary revival, the rabble was "the shoddy society of 'West Britonism'" (*Uncollected Prose* I, 104), epitomized by Dowden, "with its ears to the ground listening for the faintest echo of English thought" (88). By Joyce's turn, in 1901, the rabblement was the Irish Literary Theatre, which "gave out that it was the champion of progress, and proclaimed war against commercialism and vulgarity. It had partly made good its word and was expelling the old devil, when after the first encounter it surrendered to the popular will" (*Critical Writings* 70). In 1929, Beckett took up the themes of both retrograde English and complacent popular taste. Like Thomas MacGreevy elsewhere in *Our Exagmination,* Beckett in "Dante . . . Bruno . Vico . . Joyce" singled out the "eminent English novelist and historian" (27), unnamed but clearly Wyndham Lewis, for his essay on Joyce in *Time and Western Man,* as proof that even an opponent of Joyce could grasp the project of *Work in Progress.* Beckett reserved personal abuse for Rebecca West, who, like most English writers, including Lewis, perceived Joyce almost exclusively in terms of *Ulysses.* In *The Strange Necessity: Essays by Rebecca West,* she accused Joyce in *Ulysses* of confidence "in his own revolutionary quality, because his sentences wear the cap of liberty" (9) and, with some irony, compared that liberty unfavorably with the "victory of comprehension over the universe" (70) in Pavlov's *Conditioned Reflexes.* West, retorted Beckett, "might very well wear her bib at all her intellectual banquets, or alternatively, assert a more noteworthy control over her salivary glands than is possible for Monsieur Pavlov's unfortunate dogs" (26). To the popular will, Beckett offered Joyce's direct expression: "And if you don't understand it, Ladies and Gentlemen, it is because you are too decadent to receive it."

Beckett's first essays are informed by contemporary Irish literary issues, precedents set by Yeats and by Joyce, and by perceptions, particularly of the early Joyce, also articulated by close Irish literary contemporaries, such as O'Connor and O'Faolain. Though that association may seem predictable and even inevitable, it is a dimension of Beckett's work that needs to be reclaimed because of the critical perception of Beckett formed by later works that seem entirely ulterior to local contexts. The evidence of Beckett's contributions to *T.C.D.: A College Miscellany* further demonstrates that Beckett's earliest occasional pieces were not aberrations irrelevant to his later work, not solitary exercises irrelevant to other Irish writers of his generation, and, indeed, not positions irrelevant to current issues in Ireland.

"Che Sciagura," published in *T.C.D.* in 1929, is a satire on the Irish ban on contraceptives. The title is an allusion to a eunuch's exclamation in *Candide*, "What a misfortune to be without balls." The piece was published as a response to the recommendations of the Committee of Enquiry on Evil Literature established by the Free State in 1926 that resulted in the Irish Censorship of Publications Act of 1929. The target of the legislative regulation was both obscene literature and literature advocating artificial birth control. The legislation of Catholic morality for all citizens of the Free State was denounced repeatedly by Yeats, who in 1928 addressed the question of obscene literature in "The Censorship and St. Thomas Aquinas," published in the *Irish Statesman,* and the question of artificial birth control in "The Irish Censorship," published in the *Spectator*. Beckett, too, would address censorship of literary publications on a different occasion, but in "Che Sciagura," wholly consistent with his allusion to a Continental writer, he focused on the condemnation of prophylactic birth control as a misguided attempt to isolate the newly autonomous and predominantly Catholic state from corruption by outside influences. The dialogue of "Che Sciagura" centers on a tangled geometry of routes out of the Free State, such as via the Antrim Road to partitioned Northern Ireland or the British and Irish packet service to Liverpool:

Abstract the Antrim Road, Carrickarede Island, and the B. & I. boat threading the eye of the Liffey on Saturday night.
And you will allow coincidence?
Absolute coincidence.
Mode, then.

.

Mode.
I propose the uncompromising attitude as advocated by the Catholic Truth Society.
Though unfamiliar with the publications of that body, I understand that the bulk of their pronouncements is of a purely negative character.
Maximal negation is minimal affirmation. (42)

The allusion here to the Bruno paradox is indicative of Beckett's characteristically equivocal use of philosophical conceptions. Though presented here as sophistry of an unidentified speaker, the same paradox of Bruno was ingenuously elaborated by Beckett earlier in 1929 in "Dante . . . Bruno . Vico . . Joyce."

All of Beckett's work can be treated as an implicit response to Ireland's agenda for *cultural exclusivism,* the useful term used by Terence Brown in *Ireland: A Social and Cultural History: 1922–85* (68). Beckett's explicit attacks on that exclusivism in the form of prohibition of information and embargo on means to artificial contraception continue after "Che Sciagura." In "Censorship in the Saorstat," his other piece on the censorship act of 1929, Beckett's commentary on banned authors included the observation that, if Ireland should be "found at any time deficient in Cuchulains, at least it shall never be said that they were contraceived" (*Disjecta* 87). About a decade later, writing *Watt* in France during World War II, he offered the embargo on contraceptives, for rhetorical purposes depicted as an aphrodisiac called Bando, as an introduction to a digression on grant-funded searches for unspoiled Gaelic Ireland. "The unfortunate thing about Bando," says Arthur in *Watt,* "is that it is no longer to be obtained in this unfortunate country. For the State, taking as usual the law into its own hands, and duly indifferent to the sufferings of thousands of men, and tens of thousands of women, all over the country, has seen fit to place an embargo on this admirable article, from which joy could stream, at a moderate cost, into homes, and other places of rendezvous, now desolate. It cannot enter our ports, nor cross our northern frontier, if not in the form of a casual, hasardous and surreptitious dribble" (170).

Soon after the composition of *Watt,* Beckett reiterated this point in another work, written in the the mid 1940s but not published until much later, *First Love.* "What constitutes the charm of this country, apart of course from its scant population, and this without help of the meanest contraception, is that all is derelict, with the sole exception of history's ancient faeces. These are ardently sought after, stuffed and carried in procession. Wherever nauseated time has dropped a nice fat turd you will find our patriots, sniffing it up on all fours, their faces on fire. Elysium of the roofless" (21). As Ireland was not officially proclaimed a republic until 1949, the reference in *Watt*, completed by 1945 though not published then, to the Free State is not anachronistic. Seamus Deane, in *Celtic Revivals*, has written of this passage from *First Love*, "repudiation of Ireland is of a piece with [Beckett's] repudiation of history" (130). In Beckett's work, however, that repudiation of Ireland, or history, is never wholly free of its object of scorn. The historical dimension of *First Love*, for example, is apparent in the word *derelict* in Beckett's own translation of his French text, for derelict means "destitute" and also "abandoned by owner." The passages relevant to contraception from "Che Sciagura," "Censorship in the Saorstat," *Watt*, and *First Love*, texts across fifteen years in Beckett's work, are all severe critiques of the Irish Free State, specifically its intention to be culturally unified and culturally remote from the modern world.

Beckett's attack on cultural exclusivism is compatible with his earliest attacks on literary complacency, as in "Dante . . . Bruno . Vico . . Joyce," and with his much later critique of identity in narrative fiction. The contraception issue, especially in relation to the censorship act of 1929, is relevant because, as Terence Brown argued in *Ireland: A Social and Cultural History*, it was to protect a "supposedly distinctive Irish religious life and practice that, sometimes associated with the Irish language and the Gaelic way of life, comprised national identity" (70). "Che Sciagura," with its direct address to the issue, is preliminary to less direct and more fundamental examination of literary forms of identity in Beckett's later work. Further, "Che Sciagura" retains relevance to contemporary Ireland. In reference to "Che Sciagura" and the Bando passage from *Watt*, Eoin O'Brien has observed, "Whatever the sadness of the nation's shortcomings may have been in the 'thirties and 'forties, the tragedy is that Ireland in the 'eighties has changed but little. It took a high-court action to enshrine the individual's right to use contraception, and a referendum to change the ridiculous law that placed the distribution of contraceptives in the hands of the medical profession" (261). In addition, in the 1980s a referendum to relax divorce law was firmly rejected by the republic.

T.C.D.'s own commentary on "Che Sciagura" was that it was "extremely clever, though fortunately a trifle obscure for those who did not know their Joyce and their Voltaire" (Bair 92–93). This obscurity was fortunate, presumably, because negative critique of Free State policy was bad manners. But *T.C.D.*'s association of Beckett with Joyce, in reference to a text with little stylistic debt to any of Joyce's work, indicates Beckett's notable company in this position of dissent. Opposition to the censorship act and related legislation was of course central to Yeats's political work in the 1920s and 1930s; on occasion, for example, an objection to compulsory Gaelic printed in the *Irish Statesman* in 1924, Yeats favored the dialogue form used by Beckett in "Che Sciagura" and his next contribution to *T.C.D.*, "The Possessed." "The Possessed" largely reiterated opposition to cultural isolation though on more aesthetic terms than in "Che Sciagura." "The Possessed," published in 1931, was Beckett's riposte to an unfavorable review in *T.C.D.* of a Trinity Modern Languages Society parody of *Le Cid,* called *Le Kid.* The production, written by Beckett and by George Pelorson, was produced at the Peacock Theatre in early 1931. "The Possessed" again adverted to less restrictive formulas outside the Free State.

> I am from the North,
> from Bellyballaggio
> where they never take their hurry
> minxing marriage in their flaxmasks
> omygriefing and luvvyluvvyluvving and wudiftheycudling
> from the fourth or fifth floor of their hemistitched hearts
> right and left of the Antrim Road.
> That's why I like him
> Ulster my Hulster!
>
> (*Disjecta* 99– 100)

The other speaker in this dialogue is an obsequious reviewer, likely of *T.C.D.,* reporting to a professor, likely Rudmose-Brown, that

> A production, Professor,
> from every centre of perspective

> vox populi and yet not
> platotudinous
> cannot entertain
> me.
>
> (100)

The gist of "The Possessed" is that such Continental literature as can be imported into the Free State must be platitudinous and sufficiently respectable to please just that "popular will" ridiculed by Joyce in "The Day of the Rabblement" and Beckett in "Dante . . . Bruno . Vico . . Joyce." *T.C.D.'s* own response to "The Possessed," previously cited, was that it was a "Joyceian medley" much in "the manner of a number of *transition's* offspring." The Joyce association certainly was useful to Beckett in Paris, but the Joyce association could also be useful to others as a form of disparagement. However, even in Dublin, being placed by local authorities in the camp of Joyce and of *transition* did not leave one an outcast. When Denis Devlin and Brian Coffey, soon members with Beckett of the "Irish mafia" in Paris, published *Poems* in 1930, the *National Student,* UCD's equivalent to *T.C.D.,* offered its response in the form of parody.

> We are the Mystics, the Dark Ones!
> Let none understand us.
> We are the Writers of Modern Verse!
> Let none reprimand us. Etc.
>
> (Mays, "Introductory Essay" 13)

Hence, these early pieces by Beckett did not separate him from literary aspirants in Dublin at this time; they placed him in an active faction of Free State literary reorientation.

Of all the "Dark Ones," Beckett may have been the most forthcoming and the most explicit about his own sense of the priorities of modern verse. At the moment of his planned return to Dublin from his appointment at Ecole Normale Supérieure, Beckett garnered, by chance, by virtue of his poem *Whoroscope,* and by connections with MacGreevy, a commission for an English-language study of Proust. Quite apart from its merits as an analysis of Proust, Beckett's monograph offers the premises of his own poetry from this time in a form that encourages extrapolation to his later work.

Proust, certainly, is read by more students of Beckett than by students of Proust. Though the topic of *Proust* left Beckett the critic at some remove from local Irish context, the aesthetic formulas in *Proust* are wholly consistent with those expressed earlier in "Dante . . . Bruno . Vico . . Joyce" and later in "Recent Irish Poetry." A monograph on Proust no doubt had a certain cachet for one of the Dark Ones because of its cosmopolitan topic and likely local disapproval; *Proust* did become an item for which Beckett was reprimanded during the Henry Sinclair libel action around the time of the publication of *Murphy.*

Beckett's essay on Joyce begins with the sentence, "The danger is in the neatness of identifications"; his monograph on Proust begins with the sentence, "The Proustian equation is never simple" (1). The danger of neatness or simplification, in this argument, is convention: Proust "is aware of the many concessions required of the literary artist by the shortcomings of the literary convention" (1). Beckett's principal point about Proust is that his work describes relief of habit in a form that is itself relief from literary convention.

> Habit then is the generic term for the countless treaties concluded between the countless subjects that constitute the individual and their countless correlative objects. The periods of transition that separate consecutive adaptations (because by no expedient of macabre transubstanstiation can the grave sheets serve as swaddling clothes) represent the perilous zones in the life of the individual, dangerous, precarious, painful, mysterious and fertile, when for a moment the boredom of living is replaced by the suffering of being. (8)

In light of Beckett's other pieces from this time, habit may also be said to be the generic term for maintenance of fixed, chosen, defensive, and even reactionary identity, personal or national. Habit as *treaty* (hardly an innocuous word in Ireland in 1930) between subjects and objects reappears in "Recent Irish Poetry" as the flight from self-awareness, as antiquarianism, as conventionality in specifically Irish literary forms. This passage from *Proust* is provocative in regard to Beckett's later work as well: it suggests the proximity of cradle and grave in the famous "birth astride of a grave" passage in *Godot* (57) and also the many narrators of Beckett's later fiction in perilous zones of life and identity. This passage also includes a clear statement of one well-known eccentricity in Beckett's work: his elaboration of a poetics of suffering. The assumption that suffering is the only alternative to habit is an arbitrary one and an especially peculiar one in reference to Proust. It is reiterated elsewhere in *Proust:* "Suffering — that opens a window on the real and is the main condition of the artistic experience" (16).

From that scarcely examined proposition follow well-known corollaries in Beckett's work: its poetics of experimentation and its poetics of futility. In *Proust,* habit is synonymous with adaptation; habits are "separate consecutive adaptations" relieved by transitions. Beckett used the word in "Dante . . . Bruno . Vico . . Joyce" to describe Joyce's use of social and historical classifications, and he used the word in *The European Caravan* to describe his own use of the Joyce method. These adaptations must be momentary, experimental, and ultimately futile, all qualities for which Beckett successfully developed a newer vocabulary of deliberate inadequacy in his art criticism after World War II. But for Beckett in *Proust* and in "Recent Irish Poetry," suffering, experimentation, and futility were deemed the only apparent alternatives to complacency, repetition, and positivism. These afflictions were presented even in *Proust* as especially endemic to Ireland. "In fact," the monograph argues in a passage on the superiority of involuntary to voluntary memory, "if Habit is the Goddess of Dulness, voluntary memory is Shadwell, and of Irish extraction" (20). That is, the emblem of voluntary memory, barely discernible from habit, is that unfortunate Irish writer, traveler, and Jesuit, Richard Flecknoe, whom John Dryden, in 1682 in "Mac Flecknoe," charged as responsible for Thomas Shadwell's legacy of stupifying literary habit.

Given its unusual level of generality, *Proust* lends itself to application to Beckett's later work. The emphasis in *Proust* on involuntary memory, for example, can be presented by a chiefly formalist critic like Melvin J. Friedman as a "psycho-literary device" (50) or presented by a neo-Marxist critic like Jan Bruck in unfavorable comparison with Walter Benjamin's conceptions of potential productivity. Friedman's application places Beckett in a linear modernist tradition of Proust and Joyce, while Bruck's application places Beckett in a kind of terminal meaninglessness that remains "a political act, a warning of a danger of which we have to be aware" (170). It is always difficult to

find positivistic import in Beckett's major works: that is well known
to parties as different as Theodor W. Adorno and the Nobel Prize committee. Bruck politicizes "warning" in Beckett's major works on
purely aesthetic grounds: "to reach that position [of complete si-
lence], he is compelled to write, to express his traumatic experience
of shock, to use words which contain the very *angst* of which he is a
victim" (168).

The extraction of Beckett's "position" from specifically Irish
terms of angst can be observed in "Recent Irish Poetry," a review essay
first published in *The Bookman* in the summer of 1934 under a pseudonym of unknown origin, Andrew Belis. At this time, Beckett was
writing reviews for various periodicals, for example, of MacGreevy's
Poems for the *Dublin Magazine* or of Proust criticism for *Spectator. More
Pricks Than Kicks* had been published on 24 May 1934 (Bair 179). In
the July issue of *The Bookman*, Francis Watson had written of it: "The
influence of Joyce is indeed patent in 'More Pricks Than Kicks' but
Mr. Beckett is no fashionable imitator. Like Joyce he is a Dubliner and
an exile, and Dublin has for him that peculiar compulsion which it
exercises upon all Irishmen except Bernard Shaw" (219–20). The idea
of *exile* may have been a matter of book jacket or other publicity, for
the term is far too unequivocal for Beckett in 1934. But the idea of a
Dublin-specific compulsion is prescient if that compulsion be male-
diction, for given an opportunity, no doubt at least in part because of
Watson's entirely positive review, Beckett vented displeasure on fellow Irish poets that was wittier but otherwise quite consistent with
the contemporary critical consensus on the poetic prospects of Ireland.

The issue of *The Bookman* in which "Recent Irish Poetry" appeared was an "Irish Number" with contributions by Stephen
Gwynn, Lennox Robinson, Frank O'Connor, and Sean O'Faolain.
Robinson and O'Connor, especially, represent the Irish Academy of
Letters formed, largely owing to W. B. Yeats, two years earlier in
1932, according to Liam Miller, to "consolidate the image of a cul-
tured Ireland" (292). That consolidation was at least conceived and
intended as opposition to the program of social exclusivism evident in
the Free State. One oddity of the academy was its distinction between
members and associate members. As Yeats described the project to
Joyce, the distinction was between those who wrote "creative work
with Ireland as subject matter" and those Irish writers who did some-

thing else: "The creators Academicians, the others Associates" (Ellmann, *Joyce* 672). Some, including Joyce and Sean O'Casey, declined membership because the affair seemed too provincial; others, including Daniel Corkery, declined because it was not provincial enough. Out of context, "Recent Irish Poetry" may seem the work of an angry young man repudiating his elders. In the essay, it is true, Beckett sneers at the "academic" function of "our lately founded Academy" (*Disjecta* 71). But only by virtue of the ingenuity of his invective does Beckett manage to separate himself from the other stalwart commentators on Irish letters in *The Bookman*'s "Irish Number." On this occasion, Gwynn was apologetic about the Gaelic revival and opposed to mandatory Gaelic. Robinson, a founding member of the academy, joked to its expense about the full and associate membership distinction. O'Connor, also a founding member, lampooned the Free State's predicament of wanting to offer literature in the Irish language, while wanting to protect its people from evil literature, and, consequently, banning writers like O'Faolain and Liam O'Flaherty while offering Irish readers Gaelic translations of Charles Dickens and Joseph Conrad.

"Recent Irish Poetry" was no solitary act of romantic rebellion against uniformity. Critiques of the Irish literary revival or dispirited apologies for it were the preoccupation of the time for the literary intelligensia not employed by the Free State. Beckett's choice of pseudonym may suggest fear of scandal and libel. But a simpler rationale for using the pseudonym was that Beckett had a short story, "A Case in a Thousand," in the same issue and reserved his own name for that. O'Connor was the only other contributor of two pieces. He, too, signed them differently, using his well-known pseudonym, Frank O'Connor, for his story, "The Man That Stopped," and his real name, Michael O'Donovan, for his essay, "Two Languages." As printed, O'Connor's two contributions are all that separate the pages of those by Andrew Belis and Samuel Beckett.

Because there have been reprintings, the argument of "Recent Irish Poetry" is fairly well known. Andrew Belis's premise is "the new thing that has happened, or the old thing that has happened again, namely the breakdown of the object, whether current, historical, mythical, or spook" (*Disjecta* 70). As a consequence, one may neatly sort by awareness or unawareness of the new thing all "younger Irish poets" (70), including James Stephens (then aged fifty-two, as old as Joyce, Beckett's senior by twenty-four years). Those unaware of the new thing, the "antiquarians," "continue to purvey those articles which, in Ireland at least, had ceased to be valid even before the literary advisers to J. M. Synge found themselves prematurely obliged to look elsewhere for a creative hack" (70). The articles purveyed by those advisers, certainly including W. B. Yeats, are "an iridescence of themes — Oisin, Cuchulain, Maeve, Tir-nanog, the Táin Bo Cuailgne, Yoga, the Crone of Beare — segment after segment of cut-and-dried sanctity and loveliness" (71). These are the specie of the antiquarians, who deliver "with the altitudinous complacency of the Victorian Gael the Ossianic goods" (70). Those aware of the new thing, known only as the "others," celebrate instead "the cold comforts of apperception" (70), demonstrate that "it is the act and not the object of perception that matters" (74), and so "constitute already the nucleus of a living poetic in Ireland" (76).

A principal interest of "Recent Irish Poetry" is its proof of Belis's awareness not of the new thing but of the old things. Vivian Mercier has observed that the "rescue from pseudonymity" of the essay by *Lace Curtain* in 1971 "revealed that Beckett knew enough about the Gaelic tradition to mention Oisín, Cuchulain, Maeve, *Tír na nOg*, the *Táin Bó Cuailgne*, and 'the Crone of Beare.' Prompted by a reference in Thomas MacGreevy's poetry, he even quoted the opening words of Egan O'Rahilly's most famous poem, 'Gile na Gile' ('Brightness of Brightness') in Irish. He was also aware of Arland Ussher's *The Midnight Court*, translated from the Irish of Brian Merriman" (22). Of course, many of these references are prominent in Anglo-Irish literature, especially the work of Yeats, and, indeed, as Andrew Belis admits, most of the Victorian Gaels dealt in such goods. But one important indication of Beckett's fundamental involvement in Irish literary culture, an involvement usually ignored in treatment of the early Beckett as formed by Dante or Descartes or even the Joyce of *Work in Progress,* is this awareness in "Recent Irish Poetry" of the working antiquarians, as well as of the "others." In Beckett's fairly comprehensive roll call, the principal antiquarians are James Stephens, Austin Clarke, F. R. Higgins, and Monk Gibbon. Clarke and Higgins were founding members of the Irish Academy of Letters, which may have been a greater offense to Andrew Belis than flight from self-awareness. They are presented in "Recent Irish Poetry" as successors to Padraic Colum, Yeats, and AE (George Russell)—member, vice-president, and secretary, respectively, of the academy. In "Recent Irish Poetry" the "others" are a union of Irish mafia and Dark Ones: MacGreevy, Devlin, Coffey, and Ussher. Though their predecessors are vaguer than those of the antiquarians, Beckett states their prospect in terms distinctly local and consistent with "Dante . . . Bruno . Vico . . Joyce": "The issue between the conventional and the actual never lapses, not even when the conventional and the actual are most congruent. But it is especially acute in Ireland, thanks to the technique of our leading twilighters" (70 – 71). The sentiment, at least as phrased, puts Beckett in good company. Chief academician, Yeats, would four years later attribute *Purgatory* to a problem that "is not Irish, but European, though it is perhaps more acute here than elsewhere" (Torchiana 358).

However acute the issue, Beckett's position had little real opposition, a further indication of his involvement in and even complicity with the Irish literary culture of the 1930s. First, his charges caricature his imagined opposition. He charges Austin Clarke, for example, with trading in "fully licensed stock-in-trade, from Aisling to Red Branch Bundling" (72). Clarke, however, certainly thought that he was liberating the "Ossianic goods," liberating them with a modern sexuality inimical to the current politics of the Free State. Indeed, Clarke's inversion of predictable "stock-in-trade," as in "The Young Woman of Beare" poem from *Pilgrimage* (1929), Beckett's principal Clarke target, is compatible with Beckett's own play with stock-in-trade in *Murphy,* which he began later in 1934 and in which he satirized Clarke. Second, the representation of Irish letters at the time as polarized twilighters and new voices was not news. An only slightly older but far more established Irish writer took up the same theme at the same time for the same topic. In "Irish Poetry Since the War," published in *London Mercury* in 1935, or in a British journal like *The Bookman* a year later, Sean O'Faolain informed his readers of the new thing, that there had been "not merely a political but a social revolution" (545) in Ireland and warned readers that, because "the Ireland of popular opinion is to-day the Ireland of the Celtic Twilight, remember that the young men I speak of represent something utterly different" (546). O'Faolain then prefaced praise of Clarke with the apology that "he was at the start very much under the influence of Yeats" (546–47). Though O'Faolain the literary realist might be expected to have little sympathy with Beckett's "others," he praised MacGreevy as one of those young men working at something utterly different. O'Faolain and Beckett even reached the same conclusion about Higgins, though Beckett's dudgeon was far higher. O'Faolain found in Higgins's *Arable Holdings* (1933) "tough strength, very different to the Celtic Twilight kind of poetry" (548). Beckett found *Arable Holdings* "most refreshing after all that attar of far off, most secret and inviolate rose" (73). The only real difference between these critics on these critical occasions was that O'Faolain resigned himself to the fact that "self-consciousness will end in intellectualism" (552), while Beckett actively agitated for just such a development in Irish poetry.

In condemning antiquarian themes as "cut-and-dried sanctity and loveliness" and in praising Higgins for refreshing departure from "far off, most secret and inviolate rose," Beckett was, of course, casting his argument in allusions of Yeats's poems. In the 1960s, when examination of Beckett's early work began, he assisted his bibliographers, Raymond Federman and John Fletcher, by describing a lost essay later revealed to be "Recent Irish Poetry" as a review of a "late work by W. B. Yeats" (Federman and Fletcher 105). The review rebukes Yeats the egregious mythologizer, but that was no more his only commentary on Yeats than "Recent Irish Poetry" was solely concerned with *The Winding Stair and Other Poems*. Beckett's allusion in "Recent Irish Poetry" to the Yeats of *Responsibilities* (1914), to "A Coat," is one of praise: "Mr. W. B. Yeats, as he wove the best embroideries, so he is more alive than any of his contemporaries or scholars to the superannuation of these, and to the virtues of a verse that shall be nudist. 'There's more enterprise in going naked'" (71–72). In this he is at one with Louis MacNeice, who, writing of the same poem in 1941, praised Yeats for his ability "to jettison his romantic bric-a-brac" (117). Beckett's critique of *The Winding Stair and Other Poems* actually excavates poems worthy of emulation from those most theme-bound, antiquarian, or steeped in ascendancy mythology. Beckett's mimic of the antiquarian position is that, according to it, "without a theme there can be no poem, as witness the exclamation of Mr. Yeats's 'fanatic heart': 'What, be a singer born and lack a theme!'" (71). However, the first allusion here, to "Remorse for Intemperate Speech," cites the Yeats unable to adhere to formulations, including those shared with antiquarians, and the second, to "Vacillation," cites the Yeats eagerly admitting impulses inimical to accredited formulations. Even Yeats's choice of theme, of "sanctity and loveliness," in "Coole Park and Ballylee, 1931," is not that insistence on Ossianic goods allegedly the danger of conventionality especially acute in Ireland. Beckett's disparagement of Yeats the mythologizer helps excavate a more problematic, more pertinent Yeats. Beckett notes that Yeats's "bequest in 'The Tower' of his pride and faith to the 'young upstanding men' has something almost second-best bed, as though he knew that they would be embarrassed to find an application for those dispositions" (72). Just so. For in "The Tower," Yeats relinquished faith and pride to compose himself of other things. Later, Beckett would return to just that proposition and apply it by allusion to "The Tower" in both the title and the text of his 1977 television drama " . . . but the clouds. . . . "

Beckett's praise in "Recent Irish Poetry" of something other than antiquarianism is less innovation than affiliation with a critique of cut-and-dried Ossianic goods virtually as old as those goods themselves. By attacking antiquarianism, Beckett did not relinquish his own involvement in local culture. Instead, he joined a dissenting faction of impeccable credentials that has been an important feature of modern Irish literature in all but its crudest revival forms or most exigent aims. Yeats himself had adopted such an antithetical position in the 1890s in criticism of Young Ireland ballads and of Charles Gavan Duffy's New Irish Library. Joyce, of course, took up a similarly antithetical position in "The Day of the Rabblement" and all his fiction. The immediate obsolescence of the antiquarian goods and endorsement of awareness of modernity is embedded in discussions of the Irish literary revival contemporary with it. A typical instance is the opening statement of John Eglinton, or W. K. Magee, in an 1899 collection of essays by himself, Yeats, George Russell, and William Larminie called *Literary Ideals in Ireland*. "The truth is, these subjects [ancient legends], much as we may admire them and regret that we have nothing equivalent to them in the modern world, obstinately refuse to be taken up out of their old environment and be transplanted into the world of modern sympathies. The proper mode of treating them is a secret lost with the subjects themselves" (11). This statement, of the necessity for a modern Irish literature to be informed by modernity, is wholly compatible with Beckett's critique of antiquarianism in 1934. The myths of the revival seem most monolithic when viewed through critiques of them. But, of course, those very critiques disprove the notion that revival mythology was ever left unquestioned.

The proposition that first or marginal work, such as Beckett's early criticism, can be considered pertinent to later or major work, such as Beckett's most influential novels and plays, was offered by Beckett himself in a review written immediately after "Recent Irish Poetry." To the final, Christmas 1934 issue of *The Bookman,* Beckett contributed three reviews, the most significant of which is a review of Sean O'Casey's *Windfalls: Stories, Poems and Plays,* "The Essential and the Incidental." it opens with the assertion that, "What is arguable about a period—that its bad is the best gloss on its good—is equally so of its representatives taken singly" (*Disjecta* 82). In its exposition of knockabout and "the principle of disintegration in even the most complacent solidities" (82), the review is a useful commentary on Beckett's own plays. Indeed, David Krause argues that the review offers a conceptual base for all modern Irish drama, including "the kind of drama Beckett himself was still twenty years away from writing" (*Profane Book of Irish Comedy* 273). In "Dante . . . Bruno . Vico . . Joyce" and in "Recent Irish Poetry," Beckett took specific writing occasions as opportunities to generalize freely about Joyce and Yeats. He did so as well for "The Essential and the Incidental." *Windfalls* was cannon fodder for a caustic and self-consciously cosmopolitan young Irish writer. The collection of stories, poems, and plays in *Windfalls* includes lyrics with such titles as "Thoughts of Thee" and "The Garland" that would hardly pacify angry Andrew Belis. In fact, Beckett dismissed O'Casey's poem "Walk with Eros" for "accredited poetic phenomena and emotions to match" (83). Nevertheless, Beckett used the occasion to praise "two one-act knockabouts" (82). The basis for praise, of course, was O'Casey's other work. In the 1920s, Beckett had seen productions at the Abbey of *The Shadow of a Gunman, Juno and the Paycock,* and *The Plough and the Stars,* as James Knowlson reports in *Samuel Beckett: An Exhibition* (22). In "The Essential and the Incidental," Beckett quotes O'Casey's reference in the book under review to the Abbey Theatre's rejection of *The Silver Tassie,* and he praises *Juno* as O'Casey's "best work so far, because it communicates most fully this dramatic dehiscence, mind and world come asunder in irreparable dissociation—'chasis'" (82).

In later exchanges, O'Casey, in reference to *Godot,* would praise the play but not the man; Beckett, on O'Casey's eightieth birthday, praised the man but no play. O'Casey's *Windfalls* was banned in Ireland very quickly after publication in 1934. Beckett's first book of fiction, *More Pricks Than Kicks,* was of more obscure authorship and so eluded vigilance until early 1935. O'Casey and Beckett acted in concert more than twenty years later when, to protest censorship of productions in the Dublin Theatre Festival in 1958, they chose to ban performances of their own dramatic works in Ireland.

The whole matter of censorship, which linked Beckett and O'Casey in the 1950s, was of particular cultural importance in the mid 1930s, when Beckett wrote "Censorship in the Saorstat." Beckett had addressed the issue in *T.C.D.* in 1929. But in the 1930s, the first years of full influence of Eamon de Valera's Fianna Fail party and Beckett's literary ambitions together mandated a more forceful statement as a matter of conscience and as a prerequisite to accredited intellectualism. The censorship act of 1929 had been enacted by Liam Cosgrave's Fianna Gael party, but implementation of the legislation took a more conservative and more threatening turn in the hands of the de Valera party in 1932 and in the following years. The turn was distinctly anti-intellectual and, to repeat Terence Brown's phrase, a form of cultural exclusivism. In 1928, soon after the creation of the Free State and partitioned Ireland and while the censorship bill was still in debate, George Bernard Shaw spoke of its apparent exclusivism in terms especially relevant to Ireland a half century later: "Since it would be in vain to appeal to the Irish people, I turn to the Church, which is not Irish, but Catholic. Is it going to submit to this amateur Inquisition which is eliciting triumphant chuckles of 'We told you so' from Ulster?" (*The Matter with Ireland* 275). Even if the original bill be accepted as reflective of the will of the people, according to F. S. L. Lyons,

> in practice it did not work out like that for long. The Censorship Board, composed of five people (intended originally to consist of a representative of the Catholic Church, a lawyer, a medical man and one representative from each of the two universities), was set up in 1930

and went to work with a will. Before long it had begun to make not only itself, but the whole country, ridiculous as its probing finger moved on from the pornography which had set the whole strange mechanism in motion to the works of eminent contemporary authors, and even to those of other authors long since dead. Nevertheless, despite the outraged protests of Irish intellectuals — and scarcely any Irish writer of note in the last fifty years has escaped condemnation — the principle of censorship was written into the Constitution of 1937 and the Censorship Act itself amended in 1946. (*Ireland since the Famine* 687)

So clear was the position of the intellectuals that Beckett's contribution to those protests had something almost obligatory about it. It may be claimed that Ireland's cultural exclusivism and anti-intellectualism, especially as represented by the censorship laws, were the primary causes of alienating Beckett from Ireland. But if that were true, Ireland would have driven more of its other writers to compositions like *The Lost Ones*. Between publication of *More Pricks Than Kicks* and *Murphy*, Beckett attacked Irish censorship less out of accumulated bile than real relish for the topic and the company that public denunciation of it brought. In discussion of the work of Sean O'Faolain in the 1930s, Maurice Harmon observes, "Censorship was certainly one of the irritating factors in Irish life, but it did not hinder any Irish writer of ability from doing whatever his artistic conscience decreed. In fact it became a kind of humorous accolade: the better the book the more likelihood there was of its being banned. Irish writers of distinction, such as Austin Clarke, Liam O'Flaherty, Frank O'Connor, and Sean O'Faolain, continued to produce work of sufficiently high caliber to merit the disapproval of the censors" (49). Though Harmon then notes less humorous ramifications, particularly in sales, Arland Ussher, witness to the 1930s intellectuals' well-rehearsed expressions of shocked outrage, offers instead, in *The Face and Mind of Ireland*, the opinion that projected Irish sales without censorship would have differed little from actual sales: censorship measures "did little more than register prohibitions that would in any case have been effective in fact if not in form" (78). It is interesting to speculate whether Lyons, arguing that the censorship measure ran away from the people's will, is apologist, or whether Ussher, arguing that the people ran with the measure, is censorious himself.

At any rate, it would be academic in Beckett's most sarcastic sense of the word to speculate about censorship and the sales of his first books: *More Pricks Than Kicks,* banned, did little better or worse than *Murphy,* which was neglected by the censors despite its strenuous efforts to rile them. Beckett's rather studied *cri de coeur* in "Censorship and the Saorstat" was no forlorn cry of a lonely protester but articulation of the intellectuals' consensus and a form of application to Dublin's literary company. In his biography of Frank O'Connor, which is not at all concerned with Beckett, James Matthews brings these two dimensions — censorship and literary associations — together at just this time and place.

> In *Guests of the Nation* O'Connor had written the hysteria of revolution out of his system, but by 1934 he felt Ireland needed another transformation. . . . He and the younger members of the Irish Academy of Letters made their objections to this act known by sending endless letters to the editors of Dublin's newspapers. Although the shadow of censorship made literary life frustrating in Dublin in 1934, it was an exciting time to be a part of that life. On the one hand, a new crop of writers had emerged to claim the ear of Irish readers. Men such as Denis Johnston, Paul Vincent Carroll, Peadar O'Donnell, Patrick Kavanagh, Austin Clarke, Francis Stuart, Liam O'Flaherty, Sean O'Faolain, and Frank O'Connor were drawn together by the belief that they held the key to Ireland's future, that the eclipse of Yeats and AE and the rest of the Olympian generation did not have to mean intellectual darkness. (109)

It is useful to recall that the priorities of the Irish Academy of Letters in regard to censorship were more than merely pedantic, as suggested by Beckett. It is also useful to observe the consistent and conspicuous absence of Beckett from these lists by Harmon and Matthews of Irish writers of the 1930s.

Beckett composed his attack on censorship and related restrictions, on Irish "sterilization of the mind and apotheosis of the litter" (*Disjecta* 87), in London, in settings he would represent in *Murphy,* though ones that did not hermetically seal the mind of Beckett like the mind of Murphy. Dating of "Censorship in the Saorstat" differs in accounts by Ruby Cohn in her edition of Beckett's *Disjecta,* by Deirdre Bair, and by Lawrence Harvey. It seems most probable that the essay was written for *The Bookman* in the fall of 1934 after "Recent Irish Poetry" and that, when *The Bookman* ceased publication at the end of 1934, the essay, revised and updated, was sent to George Reavey's new European Literary Bureau later in the next year. The essay includes the number of *More Pricks Than Kicks,* which was placed on the Register of Prohibited Publications on 31 March 1935, and it cites the register of banned books as of 30 September 1935, though that may be a projection based on the unlikelihood that any book would come off the list. There is some indication that Jolas wanted the piece for *transition* (Bair 217–18), but it remained a known though unpublished text for another fifty years.

"Censorship in the Saorstat" is a sarcastic and vituperative summary of the four parts of the censorship act of 1929. It opens with a direct quotation from the bill ("to make provision for the prohibition of the sale and distribution of unwholesome literature" [*Disjecta* 84]) and updates it with reference to more recent, increasingly arbitrary, and restrictive applications of the principle of the bill. The parts, all of which delight Beckett for bureaucratic absurdity, concern the definitions of "indecent," the constitution of an almost carnivalesque Censorship of Publications Board, the related restrictions on publication of judicial proceedings, and the "other purposes incidental," including literature endorsing contraception. To Beckett, as indeed to any literary opponent of the bill, the political liabilities of the act are self-evident: intrusion of state on art, intrusion of state on private morals, intrusion of state on plural citizenry. As evidence of the absurdity of this particular form of those liabilities, Beckett need only cite the administrators themselves. The luminary of administrators in Beckett's essay is Deputy J. J. Byrne, who is confident that "it is not necessary for any sensible individual to read the whole of a book before coming to the conclusion whether the book is good, bad, or indifferent," and who insists, "Give me the man broadminded and fair who can look at the thing from a common sense point of view. If you want to come to a proper conclusion upon what is for the good of the people in a question of this kind, I unhesitatingly *plump* for the common sense man" (85). On turning to Irish authors who had publications prohibited as of 1935, Beckett lists O'Flaherty, O'Casey, O'Faolain, Shaw, Clarke, George Moore, and, lastly, himself. *Ulysses* is the only novel mentioned by title. Among other publications banned at that time, Beckett lists by author works of John Dos Passos, William Faulkner, Colette, Boccaccio, and Bertrand Russell, and by title such magazines as *Health and Efficiency* and *Health and Strength*.

The historical moment of "Censorship in the Saorstat" offers interesting data of context, chronology, and critical assumption. In discussing Yeats and his own protest against censorship, F. S. L. Lyons, in "Yeats and the Anglo-Irish Twilight," sketches the drift of Ireland in the 1930s with these selective facts: Corkery's *Synge and Anglo-Irish Literature* in 1931, de Valera's coming to power in 1932, the death of Lady Gregory in 1932, the Eucharistic Congress in Dublin in 1932, the tax on foreign newspapers in 1933, the prohibition of importation of contraceptives in 1935, the death of AE in 1935, the new constitution in 1937 (230). Beside the facts, one can place Beckett's essay on Joyce in 1929, his bits in *T.C.D.* in 1929 and 1930, "Recent Irish Poetry" in 1934, "Censorship in the Saorstat" in 1934 or 1935, *More Pricks Than Kicks* in 1934, *Murphy* in 1938, and subsequently a progressive aloofness to specific literary or cultural issues. This is all part of a longer literary chronology as well. In *The Politics of Irish Literature: From Thomas Davis to W. B. Yeats,* Malcolm Brown points to a sequence within his own self-imposed chronological limits. Having cited the John O'Leary to Yeats succession, the aberration of George Moore, and the death of Synge, Brown continues:

> Next came a generation of writers specializing in antipatriotism. Systole, diastole — the idealist gave place to the "born sneerer." Irish writing passed into the hands of James Joyce, Liam O'Flaherty, Sean O'Faolain, Frank O'Connor, Patrick Kavanagh, and Austin Clarke. Yeats's indignation against Ireland arrived at the insult-sexual ("On Those That Hated the *Playboy*"). Joyce pushed on to the insult-carminative in the close of the "Sirens" chapter of *Ulysses,* and stands as champion of the literary method that guaranteed a tavern brawl. (10–11)

This passage is, of course, another instance of the conspicuous absence of Beckett's name from a litany of Irish writers. It is also a theory of Irish literary history that the example of Beckett qualifies. Though systole, diastole may appear to be the pattern of the early part of the century, one looks in vain for a regular replacement of sneerers by new idealists, of literary antipatriotism by new literary patriotism. Including Beckett's work in this local literature indicates a literary history of more than binary action: from insult-sexual to insult-carminative to insult-aloof. The addition of Beckett to that binary action, however, does not provide a synthesis extracted from dialectic. Rather, Beckett's work is a culmination capable of absorbing those oppositions in representation only of equivocation, inertia, and impasse.

Two additional examples of Beckett's criticism demonstrate the process in which aloofness to Ireland was constructed in relation to a particular sense of "Irishness" and not wholly apart from it. Soon after "Censorship in the Saorstat" and during the composition of *Murphy*, Beckett published in the *Dublin Magazine* an unsolicited review of Jack B. Yeats's work of fiction *The Amaranthers*. In it he rehearsed the image of the solitary romantic artist vainly offering newness to the armies of conventionality: "The Chartered recountants take the thing to pieces and put it together again. They enjoy it. The artist takes it to pieces and makes a new thing, new things" (*Disjecta* 89). The point, of course, is that Jack Yeats is an artist and that he is an artist because of the direct expression of his work, a criterion familiar from "Dante . . . Bruno . Vico . . Joyce." This form of direct expression, this form of departure from contexts of convenience or inconvenience, is defined here by Beckett in a passage of great relevance to all his later work. "The Island is not throttled into Ireland," Beckett writes of Yeats's *Amaranthers,* "nor the City into Dublin, notwithstanding 'one immigrant, in his cups, recited a long narrative poem'" (90). This definition was reiterated nearly a decade later, in 1945, when, on return to France after the war, Beckett, in the *Irish Times,* observed in the course of reviewing MacGreevy's book on Jack Yeats, that Yeats's representations, especially in painting, "are characteristic notations having reference, I imagine, to processes less simple, and less delicious, than those to which the plastic *vis* is commonly reduced" (*Disjecta* 97). This formulation suggests something of the tendency in all of the later Beckett work to represent Ireland without that specificity of place so fundamental to the literature of the revival and even after it.

Beckett's review of Denis Devlin's *Intercessions* for *transition* in 1938 is not so explicit on representation of Ireland, but it demonstrates (as do Devlin's poems) the implicit relevance of local issues on dissenting aesthetics. As he had in "Dante . . . Bruno . Vico . . Joyce," Beckett in "Denis Devlin" seized the opportunity to defend an Irish writer against English critics. In an unsigned review the *Times Literary Supplement* had dismissed *Intercessions* as "more intoxicated than intelligible" and had concluded: "There are lines here and there which rise above the gulf of turgid incoherence, but not enough of them to form a bridge between the poet and the reader" (786). In opening his review, Beckett observed with a distinctly Yeatsian hauteur that "poets have always played push-pin in the country of Bentham" (*Disjecta* 91); in closing his review, he praised a particular poem that he noted had been "adduced in the *Times Lit. Sup.*, in a tone of exhausted disapproval, as indicating mental confusion and technical ineptitude" (94). This particular antagonism survived at least ten years, for in *Molloy* the narrator to the same effect praises *TLS* for insular characteristics: "I wrapped myself in swathes of newspaper, and did not shed them until the earth awoke, for good, in April. The Times Literary Supplement was admirably adapted to this purpose, of a never failing toughness and impermeability. Even farts made no impression on it" (*Three Novels* 30). Between those gibes at the English, "Denis Devlin" offered a characteristic counterassertion on art, one that on this occasion was articulated in castigation of all forms of literary positivism: "The time is perhaps not altogether too green for the vile suggestion that art has nothing to do with clarity, does not dabble in the clear and does not make clear, any more than the light of day (or night) makes the sublunar, -lunar and -stellar excrement" (94). From such a position, it follows that art has nothing to do with the clarity of literary nationalism.

Such an application of Beckett's anticlarity generalization may seen reductive and relentless (and clear), but there is adequate evidence to substantiate the limited but significant local import of Beckett's most general statements. Though Beckett's frame of reference in "Denis Devlin" is most general, knowledge of his immediately previous criticism makes apparent the sources in specifically Irish issues of the terminology of these and later formulations. Beckett's defense of Devlin, for example, opens with praise because Devlin's work "is a relief now that verse is most conveniently to be derided (or not) at the cart-tail of faction or convulsed on the racks of disaffected metres or celebrating the sects, schisms, and sectiuncles that have had all the poets they are likely to want in this world at least. The relief of poetry free to be derided (or not) on its own terms and not in those of the politicians, antiquaries (Geleerte) and zealots" (91). It was quite obviously in Ireland that the "sects" and "politicians" were most familiar to both Beckett and Devlin, as were the "disaffected metres" of literary antiquarianism of the Celtic twilight sort. In the review of Jack Yeats, Beckett's address to Irish literary issues is explicit. In the review of Denis Devlin, it is implicit.

An alternative and fairly common counterargument about Beckett's work is that it was elaborated from a base of ideas in the abstract, that it took its form from an intellectual and philosophical erudition without evident reference to Irish culture. At this stage in Beckett's work, such an argument would point to two incidental statements of well-mined relevance to the work that brought Beckett to general attention. One is a letter written in German in 1937 to an acquaintance named Axel Kaun about the possibility of Beckett translating poems by Joachim Ringelnatz (Hans Botticher), and the other is an essay called *"Les deux besoins,"* which is Beckett's first significant composition in French. These works are now published in the collection *Disjecta:* the letter as translated by Martin Esslin, the essay in Beckett's French. The Axel Kaun letter is of interest for its prospectus on literary use of language: "And more and more my own language appears to me like a veil that must be torn apart in order to get at the things (or the Nothingness) behind it. Grammar and Style. To me they seem to have become as irrelevant as a Victorian bathing suit or the imperturbability of a true gentleman" (171). In addition, the letter indicates distance between Beckett and Joyce because in it, long before the well-known Israel Shenker interview, Beckett wrote to Kaun that, "with such a program, in my opinion, the latest work of Joyce has nothing whatever to do" (172). Having examined Beckett's earlier essays on Irish topics in some detail, however, one can detect in this comment to Kaun the familiar hostility to anything vaguely Victorian and the interest in Joyce's work before *Work in Progress.*

"Les deux besoins" offers much the same prospectus as that letter, and it may have been composed in French (more accessible to Beckett than German) to escape what he described to Kaun as that "something paralyzingly holy in the vicious nature of the word" (172). *"Les deux besoins"* offers metaphysic without proliferation of allusion or erudition; in that respect, its rhetoric effaces literary, philosophical, or cultural contexts and associations. The essay also relies to a large extent

on a diagram of overlaid triangles, with points labeled, to represent the interrelation of needs that remain ill defined. *"Besoin d'avoir besoin (DEF),"* the visual and verbal illustration runs, *"et besoin dont on a besoin (ABC),"* and so on (56). That effacement of context and association was already formulated in regard to Jack Yeats. The thought survives, however, in quite specifically Irish context in *Mercier and Camier* as among the "concepts" of the pair of wandering Irish characters: "There are two needs, the need you have and the need to have it" (72). Many of Beckett's friends thought the essay, circulated in manuscript form, a "take-off" (Bair 294) on *A Vision* by W. B. Yeats, the second version of which had been published in 1937. The similarity extends beyond the diagram, which does indeed resemble the gyres of Yeats. Beckett's labeling of the diagram is also similar to the notations by Ezra Pound described in the opening of *A Vision* (5). Finding Pound in Yeats may have interested Beckett, for he had written a review in praise of *Make It New* in 1934. But the presence of Yeats is further evident in the conception of *"Les deux besoins"* itself, for it parallels the emphasis on "desire" and the "double contemplation" in *A Vision* (94). Certainly, there is much in *A Vision* entirely different from anything in *"Les deux besoins,"* but there is some continuity between the two in premise, in terminology, in time of composition, and in problematic contemporary relation of author to nation. Hence, items like the letter to Kaun and *"Les deux besoins"* represent ideas familiar from Beckett's other criticisms of Irish writers and rely explicitly and implicitly on reference to Joyce and Yeats.

Two final comments by others, from the 1930s and from the 1970s, are helpful as a conclusion to the discussion of Beckett's criticism and prospectus for consideration of his better-known works. In January 1936, T. S. Eliot visited Dublin for the first time to lecture on "Tradition and the Practice of Poetry." Beckett's personal awareness of the lecture is not known, but he had already written positively in "Recent Irish Poetry" of *The Waste Land* and before that he had "adapted" its endnotes in *Whoroscope*. Also, Eliot's appearance in Dublin generated a great deal of interest. Long after "Tradition and the Individual Talent," Eliot returned to that topic in Dublin in special reference to Irish literature and, especially, to Yeats. At UCD, Eliot told an overflow audience, "the general situation in Ireland is so different from what it was thirty years ago that it must give rise to a new poetic impulse. . . . A new school of poetry in Ireland might well seem to conservatives, at first, to be outrageously un-Irish; and would come to be recognized as Irish, only after it has gradually become evident that it is not anything else" (879). In addition, in a sentiment that would satisfy one Andrew Belis, Eliot warned that "provincialism is not merely the absence of something, but the addiction to positive literary vice, and it is the endless task of men of letters to disturb the provincialism of their particular time and place" (882).

Forty years later, Irish novelist David Hanly reiterated Eliot's proposition with welcome humor. In his novel *In Guilt and in Glory,* two characters, Keegan and Crossan, discuss first Joyce and then Beckett. Their sarcasm is evident, but their irony is less than-complete.

"[Joyce] would be anachronistic [now]. We seem to produce men for our times. Our guru now must be Mr. Beckett."

"Ah."

"I fear his cockerel's head."

"He has nothing to say."

"Excuse me. He has plenty to say, but knows the futility of saying it."

"Mr. Beckett is an evangelical zombie, preaching for years to an empty church. Then the word gets out, the church fills to overflowing, and when they hear his sermon he is telling them that they shouldn't listen to preachers."

Crossan smiled. "A very hard thing to accept."

"Especially if you're Irish."

"It's a useful appellation."

"Do you think of Mr. Beckett as Irish?   "

"He's a Protestant of English blood, educated at Trinity, a cricket player who lives in Paris and writes in French. Of course he's Irish." (98–99)

2

 MORE PRICKS THAN KICKS,
DUBLIN, 1930S

ONE OF THE INTERESTING FEATURES of Samuel Beckett's "Irishness"
is the abruptness with which Beckett's work either became Irish or
somehow reverted to Irishness. Of course, this is no biographical
problem. Instead, it is an interesting phenomenon of recent literary
and cultural history. The early Beckett, of *More Pricks Than Kicks* or
Murphy, once seemed categorically Irish. But the later, best-known
Beckett works, *Godot* or *How It Is,* seemed and generally still seem to
most to be commendably detached exercises in textuality that are per-
tinently vague in origin and powerful enough to marginalize that
early, Irish Beckett. This remains the general condition in Beckett
studies, although there have been some adjustments, especially on
such occasions as the author's birthdays, which understandably
prompt the-man-and-the-work sort of quasi-biographical celebratory
treatment.

When newly appointed at UCD, James Mays wrote in *Hibernia*
in 1969 about his surprise at the general indifference to Samuel Beckett in Irish literary studies. In that piece, already mentioned in reference to the Nobel Prize, Mays wrote, "I have not yet reached the
point where I can see how Ireland can afford to write off the man
whom the rest of the world assumes to be the country's greatest
writer" (14). Later, in 1984, writing for a special issue of *Irish University Review* on Samuel Beckett, Mays recalled that earlier piece and updated it with observations on the intervening incorporation of Beckett
into Irish literary studies. His specific examples in that later essay,
"Young Beckett's Irish Roots," include the introduction of Beckett

into the syllabus of the Anglo-Irish Studies program at UCD in the 1970s and the inclusion of Beckett in literary reference books published in Ireland at the same time. In retrospect, Mays observed that the early "indifference had a willed quality about it": "Ignorance was compounded by defensiveness, and people didn't think much about Beckett because the word was that he didn't think much of them" (19).

More Pricks Than Kicks must have been a contributing factor to those early reactions: the volume was out of print for a long period following its publication in 1934, thus aiding ignorance, but those with excellent memories or with appetites for library research would be quite right to think that *More Pricks Than Kicks* was, to say the least, critical of Ireland. Disapproving criticism of the Irish national ideology of the 1930s has become increasingly prevalent thirty or forty years after that decade, though this new revisionism takes pride in being absolutely without precedent. Some compatibility between dissent in the 1930s and dissent in the 1980s must be at least a contributing factor in the incorporation of the disapproving Beckett of *More Pricks Than Kicks* into Irish literary studies. An additional factor is the evolution of Irish literary studies in Ireland, in part as institutionalization of higher education but also in significant part as address to social issues in a young republic that owes much to literature. W. J. McCormack noted in *Hermathena,* the TCD journal, on the occasion of Beckett's eightieth birthday, that "the Culture Industry has been thriving in Ireland with the help of a refurbished sectarianism" (39) and that "the work of Samuel Beckett is currently being more thoroughly built into the Irish culture industry than that of any writer since *Ulysses* emerged from under the counter of Hodges Figgis" (40).

But these speculations on the politics, literary and otherwise, of incorporation of Samuel Beckett into Irish literary studies are unusual. A more representative example of the manner of Beckett's readmission into Irish literary studies is Alec Reid's exasperation in his introduction to an essay on Beckett in a collection called *The Irish Short Story.* "As a people the Irish are said to have a great love of debate and, if necessary, any true-born son of Erin can sustain a worth-while argument with his own shadow. Be that as it may, we do not here propose to question the propriety of including Beckett in a book on the Irish short story. Incontestably Mr. Beckett is Irish and, equally beyond debate, he is the author of *More Pricks Than Kicks,* a collection of ten short stories about Dublin written in English and published by Chatto and Windus in 1934" (227). So, as David Hanly's character in the novel *In Guilt and in Glory* said of Beckett, "of course he's Irish." But exactly why he is now and why he was not always are penetrating questions about both Beckett's work and Irish literary studies.

This change in appreciation of Beckett has been paralleled in criticism outside Ireland. In America, the Modern Language Association (MLA) placed Samuel Beckett in its bibliography sections on French literature until recent years, at which time Samuel Beckett was transferred briefly to the bibliography sections on British literature, perhaps as a geographical compromise between Dublin and Paris, and then, in a remodeled bibliography, to Irish literature. The first placement presumably was on the basis of the language of composition of *Molloy, Malone Dies, The Unnamable,* and *Godot.* The last placement was without explanation: a matter, as for Alec Reid, self-evidently unquestionable and incontestable. Very few, of course, ever considered Beckett a significant item in specifically French literary or cultural studies, though indeed his work did once generate more attention in France than in Ireland. Rather, Beckett's placement in French literary studies seemed innocuous because, if Beckett's work was detached textuality, then it seemed an insignificant item in any specifically national literary or cultural study.

In the Beckett criticism of the 1960s, especially American and academic, the effect of reading Beckett through *Godot* and the trilogy of novels, and the effect of predominant critical formalism, was that even as socially conscious a Beckett work as *More Pricks Than Kicks* was treated in terms evasive of social context. For example, in *The Literature of Silence: Henry Miller and Samuel Beckett* of 1967, Ihab Hassan approached *More Pricks Than Kicks* with passing reference to the book's Irish setting and immediate effacement of that setting by global terms characteristic of Beckett criticism then: "the timber of the book makes it clear that Beckett wants to question social reality in middle-class Ireland by planting in its midst an absurd hero. Belacqua reflects ironically on the mediocre world about him but cannot yet escape it mentally" (126). Similarly, John Fletcher's 1964 *The Novels of Samuel Beckett* quickly reduces the specificity of *More Pricks Than Kicks* to the projects of the later, French, fiction: "Belacqua is not only a bourgeoise communicant of the Church of Ireland, he is also the first in a line of Beckettian heroes whose condition of exile becomes gradually more painful; he is in fact the natural precursor of the expulsé of the *Nouvelles*" (23). Even as important a work devoted wholly to Beckett's early fiction as Raymond Federman's *Journey into Chaos: Samuel Beckett's Early Fiction,* published in 1965, shares both Hassan's gesture toward "social reality" and Fletcher's reduction of any Beckett text to the terms of those texts judged most important for having been written about most often. Federman's book, written before *More Pricks Than Kicks* was reprinted, was an important and even now essential synoptic analysis of Beckett's early work. As editor with John Fletcher of the 1970 model work of bibliography called *Samuel Beckett: His Works and His Critics,* Federman was well aware of Beckett's essays and reviews on Irish writing. Yet, on turning to the early Beckett in *Journey into Chaos,* he defined his project by mention of the trilogy of novels and also *How It Is* and asserted, "I believe that to gain a deeper understanding of these complex and abstract works it is essential to investigate the earlier fiction." He then treated *More Pricks Than Kicks,* along with *Murphy* and *Watt,* in a section of the book called "Social Reality" because these works represent "a forsaking of life not only as it is known in our modern society, but as it is depicted in traditional fiction. In other words, social reality is meant here in the sense of conventional realism" (viii). In other words, social reality is a literary style to slough off in quest of philosophical complexity and verbal ambiguity. However, common thought in Ireland or out of Ireland would question whether Dublin in the 1930s was an indubitably representative example of "modern society." Also, the literature of Dublin in the 1930s does not suggest that "traditional fiction" or "conventional realism" were there and then absolutely sine qua non. The local eccentricity from a hypothetical traditional realism was more general than the example of Joyce alone would suggest.

While examination of Beckett's later work on the basis of the early fiction can provide useful orientation and can produce helpful explication, such an approach also has the liability of reducing the early work to terms deduced from the later work. The elimination of dimensions specific to Beckett's early work may also help explain the general indifference to the specifically Irish social contexts of early texts, such as those collected in *More Pricks Than Kicks.* That, in turn may help explain the indifference to Beckett in Dublin until recent years. After all, what would be the local relevance of the early work if it is solely the anatomy of a species of traditional fiction that is not indigenous? *More Pricks Than Kicks,* apart from its aid to deeper understanding of Beckett's later works, apart from the interest of its opaque language and ironic self-referentiality or other subversion of conventional realism, is also a formidable anatomy of the social ideology of Ireland in the 1930s. In that regard, these stories may help explain why Beckett is unquestionably and incontestably an Irish writer.

One useful indication of the social milieu of Dublin in the 1930s — when Beckett wrote *More Pricks Than Kicks* and its earlier manuscript version, *Dream of Fair to Middling Women* — is Daniel Corkery's 1931 work, *Synge and Anglo-Irish Literature.* Corkery's book is less significant as criticism of Synge than as cultural polemic and more useful as cultural evidence for the debate it provoked than for the merits of its own argument. The Corkery formulation of cultural nationalism had sources in previous expositions on the potential of Irish culture, though none of those earlier sources coalesced with a current agenda for practical politics as neatly as Corkery's did in the 1930s. Nor did earlier arguments about "the Ireland that counts" ever pretend to factual legitimacy as stridently as did Corkery's.

A well-known, earlier, and compatible argument can be found in W. B. Yeats's "Celtic Element in Literature" of 1897. That essay opens with reference to Celtophiles outside Ireland: Ernest Renan and Matthew Arnold. Yeats was wary of accepting their endorsements of Celticism as a literary resource ripe for recovery or exploitation, and so in interesting fashion Yeats anticipated the current sense of colonial nationalism's susceptibility to the terms of colonialism. But Yeats did retain from those writers the claim that Celtic literature preserves imaginative capacities largely eradicated by modern, specifically Anglo-Saxon, culture: "the Celtic alone has been for centuries close to the main river of European literature" (*Essays and Introductions* 185). Yeats's revision, for "we must re-state a little Renan's and Arnold's arguments" (174), was that Ireland alone remained in vital contact with the virtually extinct Celtic element. Largely on the basis of previous and ongoing excavation by Samuel Ferguson, Standish O'Grady, and Douglas Hyde, Yeats could assert that "now a fountain of legends, and, as I think, a more abundant fountain than any in Europe, is being opened" (186). Yeats, of course, later shifted his most vocal allegiance to the Georgian and ascendancy "element," but his Celtic enthusiasm was among the strands that Corkery could gather up at a later date. Some of the grounds for Yeats's shift were also gathered up at the same time by Beckett in *More Pricks Than Kicks*.

Corkery's own argument was most timely because it meshed with the consolidation of political power by Eamon de Valera and Irish republicanism. In 1924, Corkery had published *The Hidden Ireland: A Study of Gaelic Munster in the Eighteenth Century*, an exercise in discovery of a refugee Gaelic-Irish culture that survived British colonialism. In large part an insistence on the continuing vitality of the Irish language, *The Hidden Ireland* and Corkery's later work defined Irish nationalism as a rejuvenation of this surviving culture, as a return of Ireland to that homogeneous though nearly eradicated culture. The argument of *The Hidden Ireland* was disputed then by many, including Sean O'Faolain, who characterized it as an "arrangement of facts, and of half-facts, and of pious beliefs, by a man with inadequate knowledge of Irish history" ("Daniel Corkery" 59). It has been disputed since, in particular by Louis M. Cullen in a "reassessment" published in 1969 and republished twenty years later as, the jacket copy says, a "classic of revisionism." "Corkery's concept of a Hidden Ireland," Cullen concluded, "seems to impoverish Irish nationality and the sense of identity, seeing it in the context of settlement and oppression, and not in the rich, complex and varied stream of identity and racial consciousness heightened in the course of centuries of Anglo-Irish relations" (37). Even these dissenters to the argument admit, however, that Corkery's "Irish Ireland" campaign occurred at an opportune time, when Irish nationalism needed revitalizing after qualified success in establishment of a Free State and discouraged diffusion in civil war. Though *More Pricks Than Kicks* would dissent, too, to a narrow view of Irish identity, it does not endorse Cullen's equation of complexity and richness. That is an early indication that incorporation by revisionism of Beckett into the national literary canon may require a reading as selective as the reading that once excluded Beckett from it.

Corkery's book on Synge in 1931 was especially opportune. As Peter Costello argues in *The Heart Grown Brutal: The Irish Revolution in Literature From Parnell to the Death of Yeats, 1891–1939*, "in the election of 1932 de Valera represented to the people an ideal which had lain behind the ideas of other leaders of his generation. When Daniel Corkery wrote the book which appeared in 1931 as *Synge and Anglo-Irish Literature,* he was writing a cultural polemic on behalf of that ideal. He was defending what his young protégés were by then abandoning, disillusioned as they were by the Civil War" (242–43). The principal polemic of the book is its first chapter, which hardly mentions Synge. Its fundamental ideal is a trinity of values that together constitute, in Corkery's incantatory phrase, "the Ireland that counts": "The three great forces which, working for long in the Irish national being, have made it so different from the English national being are: (1) The Religious Consciousness of the People; (2) Irish Nationalism; and (3) The Land" (19). In those terms, one finds the emphasis on Catholicism, exclusivism, and regression that together catalyze such developments as censorship legislation. The emphasis is also, as one might expect in matters of nationalism and polemic, on total unanimity. The form of qualification that galvanized Corkery most was expatriation: he lists thirty-six writers guilty of expatriation, including Joyce and MacGreevy but excepting Yeats because "it is not his habit to spend the whole of any year abroad" (4). Beckett, as yet, was of no note. For Corkery, the liability, especially after the urgency of nationalism waned, was that the expatriate "once again becomes a free agent; once again begins unduly to reflect movements and fashions in literature which do not take their rise in this country, which have nothing to do with the mental life of this country." This hypothesis of an absolutely homogeneous country is a conception that *More Pricks Than Kicks* helps examine. There is, of course, a revealing contradiction between the anti-intellectualism of Corkery's argument (or the policies adapted from it) and this ardent rhetoric in defense of "the mind of the country." Because of putative fashionable foreign movements, the work of expatriates (or all Anglo-Irish literature, of which Synge's work was for Corkery a provocative example) is, to Corkery, extraneous to "this country" and so colonial rather than "normal": Anglo-Irish literature "is therefore not normal, for a normal literature while welcoming the criticism of outsiders neither lives nor dies by such criticism. It abides the judgement of its own people, and by that judgement lives or dies. If this literature then be not a normal literature it is not a national literature, for normal and national are synonymous in literary criticism" (3).

The relevance of *Synge and Anglo-Irish Literature* to Beckett, and in particular to *More Pricks Than Kicks,* is not that Beckett refutes Corkery; it is, rather, that Corkery and his own formidable opponents together constitute a cultural impasse that is the social milieu of *More Pricks Than Kicks* and its case study of modern Irish indolence, Belacqua. Corkery's ideal seems absurd. As Costello observes, it suggests that "the only writer who could 'speak for Ireland' was, it would seem, a Gaelic writer who lived in one of the remoter parishes of Connaught where he devoted himself to celebrating the hardships of life and the beauties of nature" (245). But such an ideal had power, especially when bolstered by the de Valera government. Indeed, it may still have power. Thomas Kinsella, for example, speaking as a Dubliner, and in 1966, finds validity in Corkery's particular argument on the Irish language and the general position that follows from it: "For the Irish writer today — all but the very youngest, who may now be making the first moves toward dedication — the conditions described by Corkery still matter: we have come out of what he described" (61n). So too, Beckett, older than Kinsella and younger than Corkery's principal opponents, comes out of what Corkery described, though in less sympathy for it than Kinsella.

Corkery's opponents, most former protégés, responded to *Synge and Anglo-Irish Literature* with the argument for art as distinct from any ostensible normality. Frank O'Connor, for example, under the aegis of the 1938 Abbey Theatre Festival, attacked Corkery as a middle-class critic in a rebuttal that is, in terms of art, compatible with Beckett's own contemporary reviews and, in terms of nullity, suggestive of Beckett's later work: "if [the middle-class critic] once admits that an artist is representative of more things than one [i.e., nation] he surrenders his case, and admits by implication that the artist is representative of nothing: is only an individual soul, is in fact nothing but an artist" ("Synge" 33). Though Beckett could in reviews of works by MacGreevy or Jack B. Yeats compose similar formulations, his stories in *More Pricks Than Kicks,* with their ironic references and allusions to European art, address the clash between the Corkery ideology and the O'Connor alternative to it without endorsing either.

Another former protégé of Corkery, O'Faolain, published the revisionist position in the *Dublin Magazine* in 1936 as a critique of Corkery's historicism. "To us, Ireland is beginning, where to Corkery it is continuing. We have a sense of time, of background: we know the value of the Gaelic tongue to extend our vision of Irish life, to deepen it and enrich it: we know that an old cromlech in a field can dilate our imaginations with a sense of what was, what might have been, and *what is not* ("Daniel Corkery" 60–61, O'Faolain's emphasis). In *More Pricks Than Kicks*, Belacqua responds to comparable stimuli with neither Corkery's reverence for "what was" nor O'Faolain's liberation from it. Most of this debate is immediately concerned with literary culture, and *More Pricks Than Kicks* reflects that debate by making reference, with distinct irony, to Yeats, Synge, and Joyce (for Corkery, in 1931, a writer who "has gone astray" [*Synge* 20]). Its character, Belacqua, is neither "normal" nor expatriate. Also, *More Pricks Than Kicks* represents Protestantism with evident anxiety. That representation is neither assent to nor dissent from Corkery's promulgation of Catholicism as the literary and political destiny of Ireland; an immobilizing anxiety is here one 1930s Dublin representation of the Dantean archetype, Belacqua. These, then, are manifestations of the "social reality" to which *More Pricks Than Kicks* has specific reference, ones that place Beckett and these stories in Irish literature.

In the *Dublin Magazine* in 1934, Norah Hoult's review of *More Pricks Than Kicks* was more concerned with the stories' cosmopolitanism than with their abuse of "the Ireland that counts." Publication of such stories, "certainly not likely to achieve any wide circulation," she wrote, is evidence of the seduction of a "publisher who refuses to call himself a Philistine" (84). That publisher, Chatto and Windus, must desire, she continued, "to overawe all but the very plain man"; but that very plain man, in Hoult's view, "will close the book promptly, suspecting extreme cleverness" (85). The self-evident virtue of the very plain man was the standard for all things that Beckett adduced in "Censorship in the Saorstat" in the words of Deputy J. J. Byrne, who favored the phrase "the common sense man." It was a standard long-lived enough in Ireland to provide Brian O'Nolan/Flann O'Brien/Myles na Gopaleen with a mainstay for satire in his "The Plain People of Ireland" columns for the *Irish Times* after World War II. The Plain People of Ireland, of course, were also the constituency envisioned by Daniel Corkery. But their hypothetical suspicion of extreme cleverness would be an entirely inaccurate response to *More*

Pricks Than Kicks because its satire is directed more at erudite impos-
ture than at stolid common sense.

The stories, as is well known, were largely derived from the
manuscript novel *A Dream of Fair to Middling Women,* which was written
in Paris in 1932. As any examination of the manuscript shows, the
process of rewriting did, among other things, focus the text wholly on
Dublin. *Dream* opens with the character Belacqua peering out of Ireland from Carlyle Pier in Dun Laoghaire, where he departs for a journey across the Continent for an orgy of literary-philosophical chitchat,
including fragments of prose published separately by Beckett in *transition* and in *The New Review.* The later parts of *Dream* return to Dublin: the narrative includes materials adapted for *More Pricks Than
Kicks,* which is set throughout in Dublin and environs. In that reworking of the material, the character Belacqua is transformed from
expatriate to expatriate *manqué,* a change that permits satire of putative cosmopolitanism in terms not incompatible with Corkery's. The
Dublin setting of *More Pricks Than Kicks* provides opportunities for
satire of local manners, but the contrast between character and setting
also asserts the character's pretentious and facile affiliation with extra-
Irish fashions. Something of that shift in emphasis is evident from the
attribution in *More Pricks Than Kicks* of *Dream of Fair to Middling
Women* to one "Italianate Irishman," Walter Draffin, who "merely had
to close his eyes to be back in Pisa" (143), and who "drank just a little
in public for the sake of sociability, but made up for it in private"
(120). In Walter Draffin alone, the very plain man of Ireland should
not suspect extreme cleverness but should delight in chastisement for
such a vice: "Walter's book was a long time in coming out because he
refused to regard it as anything more than a mere dump for whatever
he could not get off his chest in the ordinary way" (133).

In the opening of *More Pricks Than Kicks,* Belacqua Shuah is ex-
ercising with comparable expertise just that capability of Walter
Draffin: with eyes closed to all but Dante, he is not in Dublin so much
as in the *Paradiso.* "It was morning and Belacqua was stuck in the first
of the canti in the moon. He was so bogged that he could move neither
backward nor forward. Blissful Beatrice was there, Dante also, and she
explained the spots on the moon to him. She shewed him in the first
place where he was at fault, then she put up her own explanation. She
had it from God, therefore he could rely on its being accurate in every

particular" (9). Not until the following paragraphs of "Dante and the Lobster" does the Dublin environment penetrate Belacqua's literary one. "He was running his brain against this impenetrable passage when he heard midday strike. At once he switched his mind off its task. . . . He leaned back in his chair to feel his mind subside and the itch of this mean quodlibet die down" (9–10). In a fashion, only when Belacqua "switched his mind off" did he enter Corkery's cherished "mental life of the country." Beckett's satire of Belacqua's literary environment and Dublin environment is predicated by reliance in both on received knowledge. In one, Belacqua relies on Beatrice "being accurate in every particular"; in the other, "he had it from his mother. . . . It had been good enough for his mother, it was good enough for him" (12), and "We live and learn, that was a true saying" (17). The representation of Dublin in the 1930s in *More Pricks Than Kicks* is of characters and cronies languishing in a plethora of literary and customary "true sayings."

Belacqua's own mental life is scarcely designed to overawe anyone. He is, as a later story states, "a dirty lowdown Low Church Protestant high-brow" (172). Throughout "Dante and the Lobster," his literary pretensions are patronized by his Italian instructor, and his social pretensions are tolerated by the more charitable Plain People of Ireland. Belacqua's tantrum concerning the first item on his "curriculum" (10), lunch, over the insufficiently full stench of his slab of gorgonzola, to which he is devoted because "he knew a man who came from Gorgonzola" (13–14), is borne with some grace by his grocer.

> The grocer, without closing his eyes or taking them off the receding figure, blew his nose in the skirt of his apron. Being a warm-hearted human man he felt sympathy and pity for this queer customer who always looked ill and dejected. But at the same time he was a small tradesman, don't forget that, with a small tradesman's sense of personal dignity and what was what. Thruppence, he cast it up, thruppence worth of cheese per day, one and a tanner per week. No, he would fawn on no man for that, no, not on the best in the land. He had his pride. (15)

Against that dignity, Belacqua can offer only condescension, as he does to his fishmonger in quest of the second item, the lobster. "Really a little bit of courtesy and good will went a long way in this world. A smile and a cheerful word from a common working-man and the face of the world was brightened" (17–18). Belacqua is also alienated from his own social class, and he seeks out a lowly pub because "the incontinent bosthoons of his own class, itching to pass on a big idea or inflict an appointment, were seldom at large in this shabby quarter of the city" (16). Belacqua's intellectual ambitions are no more than dilettantism: the third item, the lesson, is with the Signorina Adrianna Ottolenghi, whom Belacqua reveres "on a pedestal in his mind, apart from other women" (16), but whom the narrator establishes as "a lady of a certain age who had found being young and beautiful and pure more a bore than anything else" (18). She, too, bears with some grace Belacqua's relentless reduction of study of Dante to a matter of translation into English.

The opening story of *More Pricks Than Kicks* effectively deflates Belacqua's pretensions. Its erudition, literary allusion, and other "extreme clevernesses" function in character and narrative as just that "free agent" affectation so dreaded by Corkery. Here, the result of pretension is profound misinformation, especially in reference to God's pity, extracted from Dante; to the state's benevolence, taken from newspaper reports of a possible commutation of the Malahide Murderer's execution; and, most memorably, the "painless" death of a lobster, as Belacqua has it from his aunt.

> Belacqua looked at the old parchment of face, grey in the dim kitchen.
> "You make a fuss" she said angrily "and upset me and then lash into it for your dinner."
> She lifted the lobster clear of the table. It had about thirty seconds to live.
> Well, thought Belacqua, it's a quick death, God help us all.
> It is not. (22)

More Pricks Than Kicks is a study of Belacqua's eventual capitulation to social roles and norms, and these, too, are represented as forms extracted from doubtful sources.

Indolence, inertia, and, of course, waiting, are conditions central to all of Beckett's work. But the social context of *More Pricks Than*

Kicks provides a rather less metaphysical than usual origin and reference for those preoccupations. *More Pricks Than Kicks* counterpoises cosmopolitanism with the insular and exclusionist cultural nationalism of Dublin in the 1930s, and the stories qualify both forms of action with enough irony and satire to effect stasis and inaction. The opposition of cosmopolitanism and insularity is a fundamental dialectic in modern Irish culture, and Beckett's representation of the opposition as intractable is important evidence in that cultural history.

These stories are ambivalent about the prescriptions of both Corkery and those who rejected Corkery's positions. They also suggest corrections to other images of the time and place. Francis Stuart's *Things To Live For: Notes for an Autobiography* was published in the same year as *More Pricks Than Kicks;* and, like Beckett's stories, it takes up the topic of the politically significant class of Dublin shopkeepers. "I walk through those streets that I once fought to defend, feeling a little like a stranger," reported Stuart, a veteran of the civil war. "And it was this spirit of smugness and deadness that we fought against and were defeated by. The spirit of liberal democracy. We fought to stop Ireland falling into the hands of publicans and shop-keepers, and she has fallen into their hands" (253 – 54). Beckett's stories offer an image of the shopkeeper that is neither so denunciatory as Stuart's nor completely commendatory. Again, on the matter of expatriation, a feature of cosmopolitanism, the evidence of *More Pricks Than Kicks* can be put beside that of Francis MacManus's retrospective account. "Expatriates! The word roused voluble anger and years of resentment. To many writers of the time, it appeared to have offensive emotional associations, a suggestion of treachery or abandonment, as if expatriation were a different sort of emigration to that practised by farmers' sons' tradesmen, craftsmen and even priests. 'Expatriation' insisted Professor Corkery, 'is the badge of all the tribe of Anglo-Irish literary men; and in nearly all cases it is a life sentence'" (117 – 18). Beckett's stories offer instead images of the shopkeepers' boredom with the entire issue, a boredom only to a small extent attributable to the singular deficiencies of Belacqua.

Stuart's comments on the surrender of Dublin to shopkeepers were prefaced by comments on an earlier ideal ambience that included Sunday nights at George Russell's. Russell, or AE, who died in 1935, was a remarkable proponent both of cultural nationalism and of plurality in regard to internal representation and external relations. Earlier, like Yeats, Russell was a less complicated promulgator of exclusionist nationalism on the grounds of Ireland's crucial stage in development and its privileged contact with imaginative capabilities extinct elsewhere in Europe. For example, in 1899, in "Nationality and Cosmopolitanism in Literature," AE lamented a European trend toward a "cosmopolitan spirit" that, "whether for good or for evil, is hastily obliterating distinctions." "If nationality is to justify itself in the face of all this, it must be because the country which preserves its individuality does so with the profound conviction that its peculiar ideal is nobler than that which the cosmopolitan spirit suggests — that this ideal is so precious to it that its loss would be as the loss of the soul, and that it could not be realised without an aloofness from, if not an actual indifference to, the ideals which are spreading so rapidly over Europe" (82).

More than thirty years later, after Ireland's establishment of some degree of political autonomy, AE returned to the theme in "An Essay on the Character in Irish Literature," which appeared as the introduction to Frank O'Connor's English translations from Irish poems, *The Wild Bird's Nest*. In 1932, AE reiterated the thesis of Ireland's privileged contact with imaginative resources lost in prehistory elsewhere in Europe. But in 1932, he could no longer argue for Ireland's aloofness from and indifference to an external *Weltanschauung:* "The centuries have not brought us to the philosophic mind. I would like to speculate on the offsprings of a marriage of cultures, the Irish with the European, which cannot be kept apart forever. There are intimations in the later poetry and prose of Yeats that an exciting literature might be born from that union" (n.p.). Other than that brief reference to intimations in Yeats, however, Russell was unable to speculate on the marriage of cultures he thought, in the 1930s, inevitable. Elsewhere, Russell argues persuasively for the potential resource of an internal marriage of cultures — Gael, Dane, Norman, Saxon. This argument was, according to Terence Brown, "a doctrine of national synthesis in which no ethnic group is predominant" (*Ireland* 122). The doctrine survives in that fulfillment in complexity implied by Louis M. Cullen. Russell could not be expected to build on suggestions in *More*

Pricks Than Kicks, which was published the year before his death. But the ideas of both the marriage of internal cultures and the marriage with external cultures, which were to Russell valuable and inevitable, are central to Beckett's stories. Beckett's work is far less positivist than Russell's, however, and *More Pricks Than Kicks* represents the situation of Dublin in the 1930s as one of immobilizing cultural confusion rather than of imminent cultural resolution.

"Fingal," the second story in *More Pricks Than Kicks,* is a succinct representation of issues addressed by Russell in progressive terms and by Corkery in more reactionary ones. Beckett's own address is descriptive rather than prescriptive and politically inert rather than programmatic. As in "Dante and the Lobster," Belacqua affects cosmopolitanism, and the affectation is superficial enough a charade to confirm the worst fears of Corkery and Russell. In "Fingal" that superficiality is exposed by the presence of one of the Plain People of Ireland, Miss Winnie Coates, who was "pretty, hot and witty, in that order."

> She began to admire this and that, the ridge of Lambay Island rising out of the brown woods of the Castle, Ireland's Eye like a shark, and the ridiculous little hills far away to the north, what were they?
>
> "The Naul" said Belacqua. "Is it possible you didn't know the Naul?" This in the shocked tone of the travelled spinster: "You don't say you were in Milan (to rime with villain) and never saw the Cena?"
> "Can it be possible that you passed through Chambéry and never called on Mme de Warens?"
> "North Dublin" she said "I don't know at all. So flat and dull, all roads leading to Drogheda."
> "Fingal dull!" he said. "Winnie you astonish me."
> They considered Fingal for a time together in silence. Its coast eaten away with creeks and marshes, tesserae of small fields, patches of wood springing up like a weed, the line of hills too low to close the view.
> "When it's a magic land" he sighed "like Saône-et-Loire."
> "That means nothing to me" said Winnie.
> "Oh yes" he said, "bons vins et Lamartine, a champaign land for the sad and serious, not a bloody little toy Kindergarten like Wicklow."
> You make great play with your short stay abroad, thought Winnie.
> "You and your sad and serious" she said. "Will you never come off it?" (23–24)

Winnie's mental reproach and verbal taunt are relatively benevolent responses to the apprehension of Ireland in what Corkery called "alien considerations." Corkery condemned it with virulence, MacManus felt persecuted for it, and Winnie is bored with it. Such are the absurdities of Belacqua's effusions, however, that Winnie can be forced to verbal reproach: "This is all a dream," she says in response to another of Belacqua's theories of Fingal. "I see nothing but three acres and cows. You can't have Cincinnatus without a furrow" (25).

While the satire of cosmopolitanism in "Fingal" is compatible with the positions of Corkery and the early George Russell, the story is equally satirical of alternatives to cosmopolitanism and so is ultimately passive on the prospect of Ireland in the coming times. In "Fingal," Beckett also satirizes hypotheses on the innate nobility of the folk and of oral preservation of history and culture. Crossing a field, Belacqua and Winnie first encounter a man "scarifying the dry furrows with a fork," and they ask this man, no Cincinnatus, about the age of a local tower. "The man said it had been built for relief in the year of the Famine, so he had heard, by a Mrs Somebody whose name he misremembered in honour of her husband" (27–28). Corkery's assertion, of course, had been of preservation in oral culture of a prefamine Ireland. In Beckett's image, that orality cannot extend even to that event of cultural catastrophe. A second man attempts to resurrect a slightly more distant past but with no more success and from sources themselves alien to the hidden Ireland. This second representative of "the Ireland that counts" attempts to aid Winnie in her pursuit with Dr. Sholto, an acquaintance employed by the nearby Portrane Lunatic Asylum, of a fleeing Belacqua. As Sholto searches a church, the man begins to tell Winnie of his talent for capturing lunatic escapees.

> "I was born on Lambay" he said, by way of opening to an endless story of a recapture in which he had distinguished himself, "and I've worked here man and boy."
>
> "In that case" said Winnie "maybe you can tell me what the ruins are."
>
> "That's the church" he said, pointing to the near one, it had just absorbed Sholto, "and that" pointing to the far one "'s the tower."
>
> "Yes" said Winnie "but what tower, what was it?"

"The best I know" he said "is some Lady Something had it."

This was news indeed.

"Then before that again" it all came back to him with a rush "you might have heard tell of Dane Swift, he kep a"—he checked the word and then let it come regardless—"he kep a motte in it."

"A moth?" exclaimed Winnie.

"A motte" he said "of the name of Stella."

Winnie stared out across the grey field. No sign of Sholto, nor of Belacqua, only this puce mass up against her and a tale of a motte and a star. What was a motte?

"You mean" she said "that he lived there with a woman?"

"He kep her there" said the old man, he had read it in an old *Telegraph* and he would adhere to it, "and came down from Dublin." (33)

Swift did indeed know of the tower near Portrane, and Stella did indeed visit it, but the story is otherwise thoroughly inaccurate, no more or less useful than Belacqua's own assimilation of Fingal in reference to the Continent. Even as a local history alternative to Belacqua's associations, the inaccuracies of the Jonathan Swift story are scarcely communicable between urban and rural conversants and so are hardly the stuff of cultural unanimity. Further, the story is a mangled version of Anglo-Irish materials, ostensibly as accessible as Gaelic materials were obscured and, indeed, just the colonist veneer that was presumably hiding the hidden Ireland. The man's source, of course, is the press and not the cottage.

The reference to Swift is only a single element of the network of historical associations that rendered a haze of confusion in Beckett's story of Fingal, Mrs. Somebody, and Lady Something. Eoin O'Brien's *The Beckett Country* provides a useful annotation of landmarks in "Fingal" (227–40). These landmarks include relics of the presence of the Danes, the Normans, and the Augustans, a Victorian famine-relief project imitative of monastic Ireland, a modern Catholic church in Donabate, and a Taylor's Pub in Swords once burned by the Black and Tans. The story also mentions George Petrie (1790–1866), whose scientific enthusiasm for ancient Irish culture revised assumptions of pagan, prehistoric construction of round towers by proving them Christian in origin. Furthermore, Mary Power has annotated the story's obscure allusions to, besides Swift, James Macpherson's sham

Celtic epic poem *Fingal* (1762); the song "The Bridal of Malahide,"
slightly misremembered by Father Conmee in *Ulysses;* and the libel
action concerning Oscar Fingal O'Flahertie Wills Wilde by the Mar-
quess of Queensberry (John Sholto Douglas).

All of these references in "Fingal" construct an image of history
that is less nightmare than chaos: reference to histories that might be
favored by either Catholic or Protestant interpreters, misidentification
of vestiges of historical record, and conflation of the alternative positivisms of Corkery's sense of continuance from a residual hidden Ireland and in O'Faolain's sense of Ireland beginning afresh after virtual
obliteration. Such evidence indicates that the preoccupation with
chaos in all of Beckett's work is not purely linguistic or pholosophical
in origin or reference. *More Pricks Than Kicks,* as much as, say, *Godot,*
is elucidated by Beckett's much later, frequently quoted comment
that, in the modern world, there must be a form in art that "admits
the chaos and does not try to say that the chaos is really something
else. . . . That is why the form itself becomes a preoccupation, because
it exists as a problem separate from the material it accommodates. To
find a form that accommodates the mess, that is the task of the artist
now" (Driver 23). Form is also a preoccupation of most criticism of
Beckett's work. The material it accommodates, however separate, is
no less worthy a problem.

In *More Pricks Than Kicks,* the ineffectuality and indolence of Belacqua's cosmopolitanism is countered by the ineffectuality and bankruptcy of the available alternative in Dublin in the 1930s: the
mythology of the Celtic twilight sort and the literary models steeped
in it. Beckett was not alone among the Irish short story writers of the
1930s in decrying the models of the literary revival. But *More Pricks
Than Kicks* is the short story collection of that decade most integrally
centered on protest to the images of the revival. In "Ding Dong," Belacqua wanders through the inner city, noting that Pearse Street,
named for the hero of the Easter 1916 uprising, "was a most pleasant
street, despite its name" (40). He settles in a lowly pub, where "aes-
thetes and the impotent were far away" (41). There he serves as reification of Anglo-Irish literature that has been exhausted by extension
from the early romanticism to the predominant realism of the 1930s:
"he had come briskly all the way from Tommy Moore, and now he
suddenly found himself sitting paralysed and grieving in a pub of all

places, good for nothing but to stare at his spoiling porter, and wait for a sign" (43). The sign materializes from the Celtic twilight in the form of pastiche Cathleen Ni Houlihan. "Her speech was that of a woman of the people, but of a gentlewoman of the people. Her gown had served its time, but yet contrived to be respectable. He noticed with a pang that she sported about her neck the insidious little mock fur so prevalent in tony slumland. . . . But her face, ah her face, was what Belacqua had rather refer to as her countenance, it was so full of light. This she lifted up upon him and no error. Brimful of light and serene, serenissime, it bore no trace of suffering, and in this alone it might be said to be a notable face" (44). Then the noble-old-woman image of Ireland corners the cosmopolitan Belacqua, who squirms under the eyes of the characters of realism, "the dockers, railwaymen and, most terrible of all, the joxers" (45). The woman announces her scam—seats in heaven for alms—Belacqua capitulates to it, and "the woman went away and her countenance lighted her to her room" (46). Belacqua departs for Railway Street, the brothel district of Dublin, whose principal literary association is the Circe episode in *Ulysses*.

The literary models most associated with the Celtic twilight, fairly or unfairly, were Synge and Yeats, both of whom were also equivocal points of reference in *Ulysses*. Later in *More Pricks Than Kicks,* Synge's name helps restore Belacqua's determination to commit suicide with Ruby Tough in "Love and Lethe." After scanning the placid landscape south of Dublin and feeling himself swooning to the beauty of Wicklow, Belacqua "thought of Synge and recovered his spirits" (95). In "Walking Out," Belacqua admires the same landscape again, and then he turns to admire his latest, Lucy, who "was better than lovely, with its suggestion of the Nobel Yeats" (106). Both Synge and Yeats are treated with qualified admiration elsewhere in Beckett's work, including in his essay "Recent Irish Poetry" contemporary with *More Pricks Than Kicks*. On occasion, Beckett's later work by allusion suggests affinity with the work of Synge and Yeats; and on occasion, Beckett himself has made some effort to point this out to his explicators. But in *More Pricks Than Kicks,* both figures and the kind of literary work associated with them are matters of oppression to Belacqua and of indifference to other characters. Both reactions are of interest in regard to these stories and to their social record. Belacqua's revulsion with Yeats and Synge in conjunction with the sympathetic or allusive reference to their work elsewhere in Beckett's *oeuvre* indicates the extent to which the objects of criticism in *More Pricks Than Kicks* are the cultural manifestations of literary ideology, the social effects of the literary revival, and the limits of Belacqua's "bourgeoise poltroon" (161) reaction to them. The low level of interest in Yeats and Synge and the idealism they represent among the general cast of characters of *More Pricks Than Kicks* is among the stories' documentary evidence concerning Dublin in the 1930s. At the turn of the century, George Russell had urged Irish indifference to European culture; in the 1930s, Beckett suggested Irish indifference to Irish culture and, in particular, its Olympians.

Beckett's work is not alone in that suggestion. Terrence de Vere White recalls a similar status, however unfair, given the "Nobel Yeats" in the 1930s: "artistic taste in Dublin remained static. Jack Yeats found it hard to sell his later pictures and, if lip service was paid to W. B. Yeats, his later poems were not generally appreciated" (27). Corkery's book is an indication of the limited appreciation for Synge at the time, at least from one faction. Recovery of Synge from Corkery on the grounds of the sanctity of art, from another faction, could not expect to be any more generally appreciated than Yeats's later poems.

If the Yeats-Synge vision of Ireland was the single object of ridicule in *More Pricks Than Kicks*, Beckett's stories would, in effect, endorse the obvious alternative in local literary culture, that of the contemporary stories of O'Faolain, O'Connor, and others. That alternative to Celtic twilight centered on escape from restrictive affiliations and allegiances previously constructed as the means to cultural identity and autonomy. Abstract and implied liberation from them can be observed, for example, in the well-known title stories of Frank O'Connor's *Guests of the Nation* (1931) and Sean O'Faolain's *Midsummer Night Madness and Other Stories* (1932). The literary models for this view were Joycean, especially *Dubliners*, and Russian, especially Ivan Turgenev, summoned as extranational standards for the short story genre. The alternatives, individually associated with the Yeats of revival idealism or the Joyce of scandalous "realism," constituted an entrenched dilemma in Irish literary culture for some time. In 1976, Denis Donoghue defined its continuance in terms of cost: "The price we pay for Yeats and Joyce is that each in his way gave Irish experience a memorable but narrow definition; they established it not as the or-

dinary but as a special case of the ordinary. Synge and the minor writers of the Irish literary revival were not strong enough to counter Yeats'
incantatory rhetoric: no writer in Ireland has been strong enough to
modify Joyce's sense of Irish experience in fiction" ("State of Letters"
131). However one defines that "rhetoric" and that "sense of Irish experience in fiction," Beckett represented them in *More Pricks Than
Kicks* as equally suffocating, for the stories are equally ironic in reference to Joyce as to Yeats, Synge, and the Celtic twilight. In that regard, *More Pricks Than Kicks* is a salient record of Irish culture of the
1930s. Rather than endorse one alternative vision or the other, the
stories represent a literary and cultural impasse. *Godot* is a plausible
extension from such a base.

In the 1934 review of *More Pricks Than Kicks* in the *Dublin Magazine,* Norah Hoult, as part of her indictment of the stories as "a holiday for the highbrows," described Belacqua as a hybrid of Bloom and
Dedalus and the author as a "clever young man" who "knows his *Ulysses* as a Scotch Presbyterian knows his Bible" (85). In addition to Beckett's reputation as Joyce's secretary, or, later, most emphatically *not*
Joyce's secretary, there is ample internal evidence to support association of *More Pricks Than Kicks* with *Ulysses*. The inner-city Dublin geography of the stories refers to *Ulysses*'s landmarks too often to be
entirely coincidental, even in a small city. Some landmarks, such as
Thomas Moore's statue, appear in both books with similar associations: in this case, the urinal beneath the Moore statue and Moore's
authorship of "The Meeting of the Waters." Newspaper reports of the
imminent execution of Henry McCabe provide a chronology for *More
Pricks Than Kicks* in the same fashion as newspaper reports of the *General Slocum* disaster in *Ulysses*. In more cryptic fashion, *More Pricks
Than Kicks* updates Mina Purefoy's family, begun with a son in *Ulysses*
and including young adult triplets in "What a Misfortune." Beckett's
placement of Dante's Belacqua in Dublin is comparable to Joyce's
placement of Homer's Odysseus in Dublin, as is the effect of "giving
a shape and significance to the immense panorama of futility and anarchy which is contemporary history" attributed to "the mythic
method" by Eliot in *"Ulysses,* Order and Myth" in 1923 (483). Indeed, bringing Dante to Dublin effected a conception of Joyce's

method already described by Thomas MacGreevy in *transition* in 1932, two years before publication of the stories. Joyce's "Dublin is the eternal Dublin," MacGreevy wrote, "as Dante's Florence is the eternal Florence" (254). Beckett's stories roughly approximate that density of allusions integral to *Ulysses*. On a smaller scale, the stories incorporate the style of description by lists and congeries common in *Ulysses*, but, as may be inevitable, given the other designs of the stories and the epigonic status of such tropes, the lists and congeries create chaos in *More Pricks Than Kicks*, not the comprehensive detail found in *Ulysses*. Despite that minor adjustment, *More Pricks Than Kicks* does evince the knowledge of *Ulysses* attributed to it by Hoult. Beckett's stories in this collection seem so thoroughly conditioned by Joyce's memorable but narrow sense of Dublin in fiction that one might wonder of Belacqua what is asked of the eponymous character in *Watt:* "one wonders sometimes where Watt thought he was. In a culture-park?" (77).

However, as he used the occasion of invitation to discuss *Work in Progress* as an opportunity to discuss the early Joyce, so Beckett, the putative highbrow devotee of *Ulysses*, embedded in *More Pricks Than Kicks* more crucial references to the early Joyce, to *Dubliners*. The most deliberate and detailed allusion to *Dubliners* in *More Pricks Than Kicks* is the reworking of "The Dead" to chaotic effect in "A Wet Night." The famous concluding passage in Joyce's story describes the snow that Gabriel Conroy sees through a window of the Gresham Hotel. "It was falling on every part of the dark central plain, on the treeless hills, falling softly upon the Bog of Allen and, farther westward, softly falling into the dark mutinous Shannon waves" (223). As has been recognized before, a concluding passage in Beckett's story closely follows Joyce's: "the rain fell in a uniform untroubled manner. It fell upon the bay, the littoral, the mountains and the plains, and notably upon the Central Bog it fell with a rather desolate uniformity" (83). What is most notable here, of course, is Joyce's text and its Bog of Allen. The substitution of rain for snow deflates romanticism, just as the accompanying meteorological language diminishes Conroy's vision of insubstantial forms. "Now it began to rain again upon the earth beneath and greatly incommoded Christmas traffic of every kind by continuing to do so without remission for a matter of thirty-six hours" (82). Though Joyce may have inscribed a fairly permanent definition of Irish experience in fiction, that definition could be satirized. Conroy at least apprehends the possibility of identities other than his own; Belacqua's parallel apprehension satirizes the very notion of possibility. "What was that? He shook off his glasses and stooped his head to see. That was his hands. Now who would have thought that?" (83).

In *More Pricks Than Kicks,* Joyce's prognosis for Irish experience has not changed, but it certainly has worsened. In an increment to Joyce's representation of paralysis and limited possibilities in the post-Parnell era, Beckett's representation of indolence and futility in the Free State era pronounces cultural potential dead with greater finality than does "The Dead." Joyce's Christmas party is attended by a variety of Dubliners with modest Continental pretensions who are cognizant of and sensitive to the internal-external culture issue. Beckett's Christmas party is attended by a variety of caricatures of cosmopolitanism.

> Two banned novelists, a bibliomaniac and his mistress, a paleographer, a violist d'amore with his instrument in a bag, a popular parodist with his sister and six daughters, a still more popular Professor of Bullscrit and Comparative Ovoidology, the saprophile the better for drink, a communist painter and decorator fresh back from the Moscow reserves, a merchant prince, two grave Jews, a rising strumpet, three more poets with Lauras to match, a disaffected cicisbeo, a chorus of playwrights, the inevitable envoy of the Fourth Estate, a phalanx of Grafton Street Stürmers and Jemmy Higgins arrived now in a body. (65–66)

Gabriel Conroy's susceptibility to "West Briton" mannerisms is criticized to good effect in "The Dead" by the vital and vigorous nationalist and Gaelicist Miss Ivors. She asks him, "Haven't you your own language to keep in touch with — Irish?" (189). In "A Wet Night," the comparable characters are dictatorial, not interrogative, like the Frica and the boor out of touch with his affected language.

> "Mr Larry O'Murcahaodha" — the Frica pronounced it as though he were a connection of Hiawatha — "will now sing."
> Mr Larry O'Murcahaodha tore a greater quantity than seemed fair of his native speech material to flat tatters. (79–80)

The ridicule of antiquarianism in *More Pricks Than Kicks* is consistent with that of "Recent Irish Poetry" except that the stories include no suggestion of a living poetic in Ireland. Instead, Belacqua's and the Frica's barren pretensions — surely no nucleus of a living poetic in Ireland — stand as the single, equally barren alternative to Larry O'Murcahaodha or "the homespun Poet," who is accompanied by "a little saprophile of an anonymous politico-ploughboy" and who "gave the impression of having lost a harrow and found a figure of speech" (51).

The parodic connection between "The Dead" and "A Wet Night" indicates shared concern and marked difference between the writers, the texts, and the context suggested by dates of composition. To some extent, Beckett's early work is resolutely cynical, and the abuse of the Frica or Larry O'Murcahaodha in "A Wet Night," for example, could be taken as symptomatic of influence and belatedness. But evidence like the parodic element in "A Wet Night" must also at least suggest the issue of the relevance of a widely known literary model only two or three decades old in a new, immediate, local context. The issue of relevance may be a matter of textual poetics, as it has been pursued, for example, by Hugh Kenner, who, in his well-known *Reader's Guide to Samuel Beckett,* points to the "rejection of the unified polyphonic resolution" (55) at the end of "A Wet Night" and, more generally about *More Pricks Than Kicks,* to "centripetal cleverness" as "an unsatisfactory method, to be sure, presuming as it does the viability of the archetypes you are refuting, but it will do, if you are a young writer, while you work out a better one" (53). But an additional dimension of the issue is the matter of context: that is evident in the amount of social criticism in Beckett's stories and in the fact that Beckett's stories were not alone in making gestures toward *Dubliners* or in criticizing the social limitations and fragmentation of Ireland, most pointedly Dublin, in the 1930s. Joyce's work, especially *Dubliners,* represented social limitation with some remaining though diminishing potentiality. George J. Watson's assertion in *Irish Identity and the Literary Revival: Synge, Yeats, Joyce, and O'Casey* is that Joyce's "greatness was his ability to come to tolerant terms with a fractured culture" (21). That assertion is perhaps extraordinary, but the stories in *More Pricks Than Kicks* help validate it. Much has been made of the effect of Beckett's work in illuminating the most arbitrary and authoritarian dimensions of Yeats's work. Beckett's work may also be said to have an equivalent retroactive effect on Joyce's work, though with humanizing rather than alienating results.

Watson's assertion is persuasive given Beckett's and his contemporaries' stories and the retroactive shaping of tradition. The contemporary Irish short story writers were legion, and their often-noted interest in Russian models was not inconsistent with absorption in Irish ones, especially Joyce. In 1934, in the "Irish Number" of *The Bookman* that included Beckett's essay "Recent Irish Poetry," one Norreys Jephson O'Conor, writing on "The Trend of Anglo-Irish Literature," observed that "the search for realism [in] Russian and other Continental authors [was] an attitude strengthened by the experimentation and growing reputation of James Joyce" (234). The general attitude was also to update Joyce's example and to salvage what could be salvaged.

Sean O'Faolain, too, wrote a short story evocative of "The Dead": "A Broken World," published in 1936 and collected in *A Purse of Coppers* in 1937. At a later date, in the foreword to *The Finest Stories of Sean O'Faolain,* O'Faolain wrote, "A friend suggested to me that 'A Broken World' was my unconscious reply to Joyce's wonderful story, 'The Dead.' I certainly did not consciously mean any such thing; but I can agree that what with the snow over Dublin, and the suggestion that Ireland is not dead but sleeping, as against Joyce's feeling that Ireland is paralyzed by its past, one could, I suppose, say that the stories contrast the attitudes of two different generations. After all, Joyce grew up with a strong distaste for Ireland" (x). Here, after a disingenuous disclaimer of influence, O'Faolain indicates his program for salvaging something from Joyce's example in *Dubliners* and the positivism of latent possibility in his own stories. That program, of course, was compatible with and possibly consequential of the commendable social commitment that would lead O'Faolain to *The Bell.* Further, the passage suggests reasons why, apart from the later direction of his own *oeuvre,* Beckett's stories may have fallen out of Irish literary studies or general appreciation of modern Irish literature. Beckett's gesture toward "The Dead" in "A Wet Night" asserts, first, the rigidity of Joyce's example. To that effect, in "A Wet Night," the Frica reprimands Belacqua for his wet clothing with the warning, "You'll get your death," and then on rejoining her guests, she feels that "all this had happened to her before, by hearsay or in a dream" (76). It *had* happened to her before — in *Dream of Fair to Middling Women* — but the character is also suggesting the costs of a memorable and narrow sense of Irish experience in fiction. In *More Pricks Than Kicks,* the example of *Dubliners* appears unsalvageably rigid, incapable of the revisionism assumed by O'Faolain. Hence, Beckett's use of *Dubliners,* updating without positive revision, could not be assimilated productively by a literary culture committed to some social salvation, and so *More Pricks Than Kicks* would of course appear irrelevant. Recognition of that sort of selectivity is one result of considering Irish matters in Beckett's work and of adding Beckett's work to the Irish literary context. This slight alteration of the tradition — in Eliot's sense in "Tradition and the Individual Talent" — is an effect of admitting Beckett's texts into modern Irish literature. Some alteration is at work, surely, if Joyce's greatness, in light of Beckett, appears to be, as Watson has it, remarkable for tolerance. In reference to Beckett's thorough evisceration of local culture, Joyce's relation to it may indeed seem more genial.

Elsewhere in the 1934 "Irish Number" of *The Bookman,* along with contributions by Frank O'Connor and Sean O'Faolain, was Samuel Beckett's short story "A Case in a Thousand." Though not connected in any obvious way, other than date, with *More Pricks Than Kicks,* "A Case in a Thousand" is a corroborative example of how seriously at this point in his work Beckett took the poetics of *Dubliners.* The story, never collected or reprinted, concerns a Dr. Nye and his treatment of a tubercular boy whose condition worsens after surgery by another doctor. The case is complicated by the discovery that the boy's mother coincidently is Dr. Nye's former nanny, now named Mrs. Bray. After much deliberation, Dr. Nye orders a second operation, the boy dies, and Nye feels compelled to confront Mrs. Bray with a memory of infantile eroticism. Mrs. Bray clarifies the memory for him in a conversation denied the reader, and they part: "Mrs. Bray to go and pack up her things and the dead boy's things, Dr. Nye to carry out Wasserman's {sic} test on an old schoolfellow" (242).

As the title suggests, Beckett's story echoes in important instances Joyce's "A Painful Case" from *Dubliners.* Beckett's story opens with great economy and asserts in the opening of the second paragraph that "Dr. Nye belonged to the sad men, but not to the extent of accepting, in the blank way the most of them do, this condition as natural and proper. He looked upon it as a disorder" (241). Joyce's story opens with a more elaborate exposition of setting and scene and asserts in the opening of the second paragraph that "Mr. Duffy abhorred anything which betokened physical or metal disorder. A medieval doctor would have called him saturnine" (108). Both characters, intent on order, are troubled by women who threaten the males' assumed roles and assured selves. Mr. Duffy's relationship with Mrs. Sinico begins when "little by little he entangled his thoughts with hers" (110). Beckett's character resists his own thoughts and their entanglement with Mrs. Bray's but "little by little Dr. Nye reintegrated his pathological outlook" (242). The entanglements in both stories are confessional. "With almost maternal solicitude," Mrs. Sinico encourages Mr. Duffy "to let his nature open to the full; she became his confessor" (110). Mrs. Bray offers to Dr. Nye the opportunity to "disclose the trauma at the root of this attachment" (242). In Joyce's story, the relationship ends on a trivial indelicacy, and years later Mr. Duffy learns in reports about Mrs. Sinico's death that she had become one of "the hobbling wretches whom he had seen carrying cans and bottles to be filled by the barman" (115). In Beckett's story, the relationship ends in Dr. Nye's childhood; and years later, he is "troubled to find that of the woman whom as a baby and small boy he had adored, nothing remained but the strawberry mottle of the nose and the breath smelling heavily of clove and peppermint" (242). Near the end of "A Painful Case," Mr. Duffy is revolted by "the threadbare phrases, the inane expressions of sympathy, the cautious words of a reporter" (115) used in the newspaper report of Mrs. Sinico's death. At the end of "A Case in a Thousand," such words are elided: Mrs. Bray "related a matter connected with his earlier years, so trivial and intimate that it need not be enlarged on here, but from the elucidation of which Dr. Nye, that sad man, expected great things" (242). Both stories pivot on moments when the male characters recoil from their female confessors; when, in Beckett's words and in both cases, "he really could not bear another moment of her presence" (242). The consequence of Mr. Duffy's withdrawal is the eventual realization that he has sentenced himself, that his own "life would be lonely too until he, too, died" (116), and so, finally, that "no one wanted him; he was outcast from life's feast" (117). In "A Case in a Thousand," Dr. Nye has a comparable revelation, but at the beginning of the story and without context: "Without warning a proposition sprang up in his mind: Myself I cannot save" (241). Beckett's story most resembles those in *Dubliners* in the occurrence of such an epiphany, such a sudden perception of limitation. In the Beckett story, however, that epiphany is preliminary, not conclusive, and it is not explicitly connected with subsequent events. It is, rather, hearsay — propositional and probably misinformed, as is most hearsay in *More Pricks Than Kicks*. It is limitation without the cause-and-effect epistemology of *Dubliners*. It is, instead, inherited and irresistible limitation. "A Case in a Thousand," in its plot and in its literary parallel, dramatizes entrapment by culture, and *More Pricks Than Kicks* shares this emphasis on capitulation to antecedent frames of reference.

The stories in *More Pricks Than Kicks,* as well as that singular example, "A Case in a Thousand," contemporary with them, are as ironic in addressing the *Dubliners* poetics of paralysis as they are in addressing the Synge and "Nobel Yeats" images of nobility. In context, the stories repudiate both Corkery and the cultural politics of those seeking national vigor in terms relatively less authoritarian. Like "A Wet Night," "What a Misfortune" presents a cast of characters of varied class and implied religion, and it traces their peregrinations across Dublin locations of diverse associations. That anatomy accompanies the event of a marriage: Plain Person of Ireland Thelma bboggs' betrothal to Belacqua, and Belacqua's affiliation with a family whose business is selling off the furniture of countryside Big Houses in decline. The title is another allusion to a passage in Voltaire employed by Beckett before, but on this occasion it has the added relevance, coincidentally or not, of a prognosis on the much-bruited marriage of cultures.

Beckett's stories are not singular among Irish works of the 1930s in being disillusioned with prospects of Free State Ireland in general and intellectual Dublin in particular. Beckett may, though, be a rather extreme case of disillusionment for lack of any preliminary enthusiasm. In "Irish Poetry and Irish Nationalism," Seamus Deane suggests that the course of modern Irish poetry is one of idealism declining into disillusionment. Deane comments, "No one of these

writers (not Samuel Beckett either) escapes the disillusion which followed upon collapse of nationalism and poverty of the period between
1930 and 1955. Ireland ceased to be a mythological centre and became
a provincial backwater" (11). Presumably, Beckett's name is inserted
into the discussion of writers known principally for poetry owing to
the extremity of the disillusionment that is evident in his work. Re-
garding the Irish short story of the 1930s, Terence Brown has indicated the negative and positive elements of the critique of the Free
State by the majority of the writers: "The Irish short story of the 1930s
and forties registered a social reality that flew in the face of nationalistic self-congratulation. Instead of de Valera's Gaelic Eden and the
uncomplicated satisfactions of Ireland free, the writers revealed a mediocre, dishevelled, often neurotic and depressed petit-bourgeois society that atrophied for want of a liberating idea" (*Ireland* 159). For all
their strong terms of condemnation, these writers, typically O'Connor
and O'Faolain and O'Flaherty, did suggest liberating ideas, even if
only implied or abstract. *More Pricks Than Kicks*, however, is complete
in its negativism, comprehensive in its disparagement of local positivisms, and so is not detached from local literary culture but is an
extreme example of the disillusionment diagnosed as general by
Deane and Brown. Perhaps in keeping with its general representation
of Dantean purgatory, the only exceptions to the negative critique of
the Free State in *More Pricks Than Kicks* are the positive images of those
who remain silent, indifferent, and without theory, especially three of
Belacqua's women — Winnie, Ruby, and Thelma — and the "calm
and wistful" (191) gardener in the concluding passage of the volume.
That belies Norah Hoult's perception in the *Dublin Magazine* of the
book as a disappointment to the Plain People of Ireland. It is also politically problematic, as it suggests a post-nationality return to characteristics of pre-nationality.

    The comprehensiveness of Beckett's critique in *More Pricks Than
Kicks* extends to the most important marginal faction of a decade of
republicanism and Catholicism as official platform and ubiquitous
trend. It is the faction inherited by the Huguenot Foxrock author, and
it is not exempt from critique or privileged by nostalgia. The indictment is complete in the meeting in "Walking Out" of the "dirty lowdown Low Church Protestant high-brow" Belacqua with the sort of
dispossessed tinker ennobled in Celtic twilight politics and aesthetics.

Squatting under the cart a complete down-and-out was very busy with something or other. The sun beamed down on this as though it were a new-born lamb. Belacqua took in the whole outfit at a glance and felt, the wretched bourgeois, a paroxysm of shame for his capon belly. . . .

A smile proof against all adversity transformed the sad face of the man under the cart. He was most handsome with his thick, if unkempt, black hair and moustache.

"Game ball" he said.

After that further comment was impossible. The question of apology or compensation simply did not arise. The instinctive nobility of this splendid creature for whom private life, his joys and chagrins at evening under the cart, was not acquired, as Belacqua one day if he were lucky might acquire his, but antecedent, disarmed all the pot-hooks and hangers of civility. Belacqua made an inarticulate flourish with his stick and passed down the road out of the life of this tinker, this real man at last. (103 – 4)

The pot-beating tinker and the urination on him by Belacqua's dog satirize literary images of Catholic-peasant nobility. Belacqua's anxiety and condescension satirize the project of constructing such images as practiced by literary revival writers, such as Yeats, Synge, and Lady Gregory, who were themselves Protestant and in the range from middle to upper social class. The cultural fracture of particular interest to Corkery, to most of the Irish short story writers of the 1930s, and to the proponents of cultural exclusivism as a remedy, was the fracture of Gaelic-Catholic identity. But the syndrome was just as acute to the counterpart in a polarized society. "The exclusivist aggressiveness of native self-consciousness probably originates in the sense of a lost identity," George Watson argues, in regard first to the Gaelic-Catholic portion of the population. However, Watson continues, "similarly one detects again and again an underlying sense of insecurity behind Anglo-Irish confidence. Cut off by religion, by social class, history and their own tradition from the majority of their countrymen, the Anglo-Irish felt themselves isolated, even aliens, in their own land" (28 – 29). Though not Anglo-Irish in the strictest sense, Belacqua's shame and embarrassment at the sight of this putative "real man," one possessed of antecedent and not acquired integrity, is a demonstration of the Anglo-Irish isolation and insecurity described by Watson. For the best, or at least the most elaborate, defense of Anglo-Irish sensibility, one looks to Yeats, especially to Yeats during the 1930s. But in *More Pricks Than Kicks,* the Irish Protestant sensibility of the 1930s is represented as no more worthy of defense than its counterpart, the Irish Catholic sensibility. Vivian Mercier discusses Beckett and Protestantism in personal terms, including autobiographical recollections of Mercier's own and hypotheses about Beckett's biography. Mercier accounts for Beckett's difference from Synge and others, for Beckett's indifference to the possibility of repatriation, to unfamiliarity with daily consciousness of "minority or alien status" and to "lateness and foreignness of his intellectual awakening" (31–32). In addition, however, the evidence of *More Pricks Than Kicks* suggests some familiarity with a fractured Protestant culture but an unwillingness to substitute for it an equally fractured Catholic culture. Part of the social context and import of *More Pricks Than Kicks* is the absence of endorsement of one option, like Yeats's, or another, like Synge's.

Because of its equation of the sensibilities available in a polarized society, the capitulation to social expectations of its single protagonist, Belacqua, with one set of historical and circumstantial associations, "the grand old family Huguenot guts" (159), constitutes critique of capitulation to either. Belacqua, as Dante's indolent procrastinator and as Beckett's symptomatic Dubliner, fails to preserve identity against affiliations and historical entanglements. His moment of failure occurs in the story "Yellow" just before death in surgery from medical incompetence. At that moment, Belacqua may adhere to the resolution "I am what I am" (160), which he misremembers from Iago, or he may "efface himself altogether and do the little soldier" (163). He follows the latter course, which here constitutes failure. "He was an indolent bourgeois poltroon, very talented up to a point, but not fitted for private life in the best and brightest sense, in the sense to which he referred when he bragged of how he furnished his mind and lived there, because it was the last ditch when all was said and done" (161).

Like many in *More Pricks Than Kicks,* the passage is allusive. But a particular allusion here helps illuminate Beckett's commentary on gallantry and Belacqua's surrender of "private life in the best and brightest sense" to the forms of his class, religion, and family. In "Young Beckett's Irish Roots," James Mays recounts an occasion on which Beckett responded to a question about the reasons for plethora of notable writers in a very brief period of time from a very small country known for its Catholic puritanism and for its lost language. "When you are in the last ditch, there is nothing left but to sing," Beckett is said to have responded. "It's the English Government and the Catholic Church — they have buggered us into existence." As Mays points out, *the last ditch* is a phrase attributed to William of Orange and used in recent memory in a book on Northern Ireland, *The Last Ditch* by Roy Bradford. It may be worth recalling that the phrase has also been attributed to Gilbert Burnet, opponent of the Stuarts, Bishop of Salisbury under William, and author of tracts on the Reformation in England and on the Thirty-nine Articles. "Whether or not the other allusion [William's] was present at any level of Beckett's mind is an open question," Mays observes, "it gives a curious extra twist to the predicament [Beckett] describes" (20 – 21). Further, it gives a twist to Belacqua's reference in "Yellow" to his mind as "the last ditch when all was said and done." The phrase, whether an intentional allusion or a revealing colloquialism, also appears earlier in *More Pricks Than Kicks,* in "Fingal," when Winnie recalls Belacqua's effusion on the landscape and the legendary meeting place of Swift and Stella: "A land of sanctuary, he had said, where much had been suffered secretly. Yes, the last ditch" (33). The *last ditch* phrase is a Protestant motif, and by that very origin it is not an ordinary feature of modern Irish literature as defined by the revival and institutionalized subsequently. It is also a motif of imminent failure, used in "Yellow" as the preliminary to demonstrable failure, and so the phrase cannot be taken as evocative of an alternative to the Gaelic-Catholic ethos understandably and justifiably subject to backlash ridicule in Dublin during the 1930s. It is, rather, a wholly appropriate literary motif for *More Pricks Than Kicks:* the last ditch as a condition without remedial options; a phrase often suggestive of certainty and gallantry given connotations of failure and resignation. Ditches, though not specifically last ditches, proliferate in *Molloy, Godot, All That Fall,* and other later works.

In *More Pricks Than Kicks,* Belacqua, representing one class, falls under the same indictment as the other class, Irish Catholic, in the setting of a polarized society. The charge is capitulation to forms of social behavior inherited as hearsay and slavish devotion to assumptions defined by either of the opposed literary-cultural factions. All of this is consistent with the other formulations of the stories and the suggestion of the title of the volume. It is, though, of some interest that this closure on failure may have been a matter of accident. There is an additional story, "Echo's Bones," which remains unpublished but was described by Beckett to MacGreevy as the "recessional story" of *More Pricks Than Kicks* (Bair 172). Its addition would have upset the image of social acquiescence as passive and offset the balance of antagonisms to both Catholic and Protestant forms of surrender of "private life in the best and brightest sense." For in "Echo's Bones," Belacqua's Dantean fate includes serving as stud for one barren Lord Gall's wife. Such a postscript would surely contribute something to the sense of "social reality" in Beckett's book. But its exclusion, by the author's tardiness or by the editor's impatience, preserves the passivity of the end of Belacqua and the general sense of inertia and futility that stands as the book's social commentary. In *More Pricks Than Kicks*, the lack of a liberating idea is not specific to either alternative social vision. That unpleasant analysis of the social condition of Ireland in the 1930s gives the narrator of *More Pricks Than Kicks* the opportunity to attribute to Belacqua in "Yellow" Beckett's favorite Bruno paradox and to give it new local relevance: "It is true that he did not care for these black and white alternatives as such. Indeed he even went so far as to hazard a little paradox on his own account, to the effect that between contraries no alternation was possible" (162–63).

The "little paradox," and the representation of it in these stories, helps situate *More Pricks Than Kicks* and Samuel Beckett in a specifically Irish context. The paradox is fundamental to the collection, especially without "Echo's Bones," and it is at the center of the stories' critique of a middle-class reality. The representation of the specifically Irish middle-class reality of Dublin in the 1930s in these stories centers on the futility of the available and alternative social visions. The first is the vision of the revival maintained in "the homespun Poet": "But seldom one without two and scarecely had Chas been shed than lo from out the Grosvenor sprang the homespun Poet wiping his mouth and a little saprophile of an anonymous politico-ploughboy setting him off. The Poet sucked his teeth over this unexpected pleasure. The golden eastern lay of his bullet head was muted by no cov-

ering. Beneath the Wally Whitmaneen of his Donegal tweeds a body
was to be presumed" (51). The passage contexualizes one available alternative, a caricature of Corkery's hypothetical poet of Catholicism,
exclusivism, and regression, with its opposite, the cosmopolitanism
of Chas, a character resurrected from Beckett's earlier spoof on acade-
micism, "Le Concentrisme." In a symmetrical later passage, the alternative vision, Protestant, international, and progressive, is
caricatured in Hairy, Belacqua's best man and then mourner, and con-
textualized so that excoriation of one form of babble demonstrates
another.

> "Now in Gaelic" said Hairy on the way home "they could not say
> that."
> "What could they not say?" said the parson. He would not rest un-
> til he knew.
> "O Death where is thy sting?" replied Hairy. They have no words
> for these big ideas." . . .
> By the mercy of God the good canon was slow to wrath.
> "And so on" said Hairy "and so forth. They can't say it once and for
> all. A spalpeen's babble." (186–87)

Beckett is an Irish writer, so far as *More Pricks Than Kicks* is concerned, because of the detail of this social critique. In *More Pricks Than
Kicks,* Belacqua capitulates to one of these available alternatives, the
latter, the Protestant option; and so Belacqua is not merely a precursor
of the better-known (or at least more influential in criticism) exiles of
the later works. Nor can the "social reality" of these stories simply be
equated with "conventional realism." Thus, as these stories become
better known, a process already begun, Beckett becomes an Irish
writer in ways not previously visible.

The act of equating alternative social formulations in their futility, of Belacqua's little paradox applied to Irish cultural positivisms,
was the tenor of Beckett's work recognized — at an early moment in
the emphatically *not*-Irish phase of Beckett's works—by another problematic Irish writer: Patrick Kavanagh. In 1956, in the *Irish Times,*
Kavanagh published "Some Reflections on *Waiting for Godot*" that
questioned, like Beckett twenty years before in "Recent Irish Poetry,"
Irish writers' awareness of a new thing. Like Beckett, Kavanagh pro-

posed self-awareness as the new thing. For both, self-awareness was contrary to what Kavanagh defined as "national literature, being based on convention, not born of the unpredictable individual and his problem, [that] is a vulnerable racket and is protected by fierce wild men." Kavanagh saw in *Godot* relief from that racket in a carnival-esque purgation of convention, especially the conventional attribution of the sorrows of Ireland to forces outside Ireland and alien to its peo-ple. "It is because of its awareness of the peculiar sickness of society and a possible remedy suggested that I like Beckett's play," Kavanagh wrote. "The remedy is that Beckett has put futility and despair on the stage for us to laugh at them" (297). Like most writing about Beckett then, Kavanagh followed the *oeuvre* forward from *Godot* and not back from it. In the poem "Mermaid Tavern," Kavanagh pursued a similar argument in reference to *Endgame*.

> No System, no Plan,
> Yeatsian invention
> No all-over
> Organizational prover.
> Let words laugh
> And people be stimulated by our stuff.
>
> Michelangelo's Moses
> Is one of the poses
> Of Hemingway
> Jungle-crashing after prey
> Beckett's garbage-can
> Contains all our man
> Who without fright on his face
> Dominates the place
> And makes all feel
> That all is well.
>
> (*Collected Poems* 173)

As Declan Kiberd has written of this poem in a comparison of Beckett and Kavanagh, "The plan is a Yeatsian invention, parodied by System with a capital S, Plan with a capital P, but against this false prophet Kavanagh puts his own hero Beckett, author of *Endgame*" (47). Ka-vanagh could have found a more specific diagnosis of "the peculiar sickness of society" (as he called it in the piece on *Godot*) in *More Pricks Than Kicks*. Even on the basis of *Endgame*, however, he makes the interesting dismissal of Michelangelo's Moses and of Hemingway in favor of Beckett, who "Contains all our man / . . . And makes all feel / That all is well." That poem is an unusual but provocative exposition of the preference for indigenous over alien writers, like Corkery's formulations in 1931, but resulting in endorsement of a "free agent" known for expatriation and pessimism.

In "Some Reflections on *Waiting for Godot*," Kavanagh referred to "the 'Irish' writers" as no longer being "Corkery and O'Connor and the others" (297). O'Connor, of course, thought of himself as an opponent of Corkery. But Kavanagh's equation of the two is a confirmation of the equation of alternative social visions in *More Pricks Than Kicks*. It is a suggestion of the obsolescence of the formulations promulgated by Corkery in 1931, the futility of O'Connor's symmetrical counterargument, and the pertinence of Beckett's stories. In the first-chapter manifesto of *Synge and Anglo-Irish Literature*, Corkery presented a series of questions that, while all rhetorical for him, in application to *More Pricks Than Kicks* can be answered—surprisingly—in generally positive fashion.

> A national literature is written primarily for its own people: every new book in it—no matter what its theme, foreign or native—is referable to their life, and its literary traits to the traits already established in the literature. The nation's own critical opinion of it is the warrant of life or death for it. Can Anglo-Irish, then, be a distinctive literature if it is not a national literature? And if it has not primarily been written for Ireland, if it be impossible to refer it to Irish life for its elucidation, if its continued existence or non-existence be independent of Irish opinion—can it be a national literature? (2)

More Pricks Than Kicks is referable to the life of the people, though that life is construed rather differently than Corkery assumed. *More Pricks Than Kicks* has disappeared and then reappeared owing, at least to some extent, to "the nation's own critical opinion of it," however unexamined that opinion may be. Can it be a national literature? In this chapter, I have established that *More Pricks Than Kicks* can be elucidated in reference to Ireland, especially in reference to Dublin at the time of its composition. But it would be reductive to assert that *More Pricks Than Kicks* is referable only to Ireland. The obsolescence of Corkery's formulations is not the terms but the priorities: his insistence that an Irish national literature must be *"primarily* written for Ireland." Dissent to positivistic priorities is the commentary of *More Pricks Than Kicks* on the didacticism and definition by exclusion of Corkery's argument and the related cultural agendas at the time and the place represented in the stories. That dissent, however, does not dismiss those priorities from Beckett's work. The mixed blessings of antecedence and the problems of dissent without recourse remain central to all of Beckett's work. In Ireland, the rediscovery of and sympathy with such dissent and the capacity to question priorities are factors in the re-creation and reestablishment of Beckett as an Irish writer.

3

MURPHY AND THE
GAELIC PROSODOTURFY

THOUGH BECKETT'S "IRISHNESS" is not a biographical problem,
Beckett's biography does offer interesting examples of personal entanglements in Irish culture during and after establishing primary resi-
dence in France. A particularly instructive example of this sort
occurred in 1937, when Beckett, having published stories on the local
social culture, *More Pricks Than Kicks,* and about to publish a novel on
the local literary culture, *Murphy,* appeared on the stand during a
fairly newsworthy trial at the Four Courts in Dublin. The case, as is
well known, was a libel action brought by Henry Sinclair, Beckett's
uncle by marriage, against Oliver St. John Gogarty on grounds of de-
famatory passages in Gogarty's autobiographical work *As I Was Going
Down Sackville Street.* The two-day trial was given substantial space in
the Dublin newspapers (though not the front-page splash often suggested) because it brought forward a number of local celebrities. Beckett, in 1937, was not a bona fide member of that group. Sinclair and
Gogarty were both represented by solicitors capable of sustained
courtroom drama and persuasive fits of absolute astonishment at the
moral character of the opposition's witnesses. After Beckett became
an object of attention in his own right, this action, which ended in a
decision for Sinclair but a limited damages award, has been memo-
rialized as the crucial alienation of a rebellious and idealistic artist
from a laughably provincial and disgracefully repressive Ireland.

Beckett was indeed pilloried on the stand. His appearance followed his submission of an affidavit on behalf of Sinclair that stated

that Beckett recognized Sinclair, who was not named, in two abusive and anti-Semitic passages in Gogarty's book. In court, J. M. Fitzgerald, attorney for Gogarty, took the understandable course in a jury trial of character assassination. He established that Beckett had removed himself from Foxrock to Paris and had written a book about an author of works devoted to the psychology of sex. By all accounts, Fitzgerald, an educated man, baited Beckett by calling the author Marcel *Prowst*. Newspaper accounts do not verify the widespread rumor that the bait was taken and that the witness thus inadvertently confirmed suspicious sophistication. As the cross-examination continued, Fitzgerald, by intention or by insufficient research, confused Beckett's *Proust* with *More Pricks Than Kicks*, a matter Beckett certainly did not correct. As reported in the *Irish Press* story "Dr. Gogarty's Book," the exchange continued as follows:

> But you have written about him [Proust]. How long did it take before your book was banned by the Censorship Board of Ireland? — About six months.
>
> I suggest that it was banned because it was a blasphemous and obscene book? — I never discovered why it was banned.
>
> Mr. Fitzgerald then read an extract from the book, describing a conversation in a 'bus between "The Polar Bear" and a member of the Jesuit Order, and asked the witness if that conversation was not a blasphemous caricature of Our Redeemer.
>
> Mr. Beckett replied that the characters were fictitious and that he could put words into the mouths of characters which he did not share.
>
> Mr. Fitzgerald — Do you call yourself a Christian, Jew, or Atheist? — None of the three. (6)

In the second and final day of the trial, Fitzgerald returned to the point in his summation. As recorded in the *Irish Press* story "Book Libel Suit," Beckett, Fitzgerald argued, "might well have stayed in Paris because they [the jury] would like to know why, of all the respectable people he knew, Mr. Sinclair should select that bawd and blasphemer from Paris to make an affidavit in the case to lead to the belief that an ordinary reasonable man reading the book would have identified Mr. Sinclair?" (2). In his final instructions to the jury, Mr. Justice O'Byrne helped them along in this ordinary, reasonable direction of the Plain People of Ireland.

> You saw the witness in the witness box and I have no doubt that you
> will be able to appraise very accurately the amount of weight which
> you ought to attach to his testimony.
> He did not strike me as a particularly satisfactory witness. He did
> not strike me as a witness on whose work I, personally, would place a
> great deal of reliance.
> But when it comes to a question of weighing up the evidence and
> dealing with the weight to be attached to the testimony of different
> individuals — that is a matter entirely for you and not for me. (12)

Entirely up to them indeed. In under two hours, the jury found for
Sinclair — in effect affirming the testimony of the bawd and blasphemer of Paris — and made a stupendous award of nine hundred
pounds. All O'Byrne could do in the ordinary, reasonable way was re-
duce the award.

There are reasons in addition to the verdict to see Beckett in the
trial as other than a victim of social exclusionism or anti-intellectualism. Fitzgerald's *Prowst* certainly was a well-staged boorish taunt to
an alleged sophisticate, but Beckett had himself affected the same sarcasm when he castigated the studious in his review in *Dublin Magazine* in 1936 of Jack Yeats' *Amaranthers*. There, in "An Imaginative
Work," Beckett wrote that Yeats' fiction constituted an act of imagination "of the same order if not so intense as the 'ideal real' of Prowst,
so obnoxious to the continuity girls" (*Disjecta* 89). Beckett's appearance against Gogarty might seem to be dissent to a prevailing literary
hierarchy and support for a kind of cosmopolitanism in the person of
Sinclair, who had earlier left Dublin for Kassel and entertained a
younger Beckett there. But Gogarty was himself an opponent of entrenched Gaelic-Catholic provincialism in literature and in life-style.
In fact, Beckett's assistance to the case against Gogarty abetted Free
State provincialism and the ethos of its principal ideologue. J. B.
Lyons, in his biography of Gogarty, reports that an anonymous member of the jury explained the verdict with the comment, "Whatever
about the jewman [Sinclair] he [Gogarty] must be made to pay for
what he said about de Valera" (194). Moreover, the attorney for whom
Beckett appeared was no more restrained in courtroom rhetoric than
was Fitzgerald. The case for Sinclair, as articulated by Albert Wood,
was that "Dr. Gogarty has villified the living and the dead in a pen

dipped in the scourgings of a putrid and amoral mind. He has pursued the plaintiff with savagery and ghoulishness which could only fit in with the aberrations of an amoral mind in a pot-boiling scurrility run for the private gain of the author" (Ulick O'Connor 279). Also, Gogarty's defense, which Beckett helped shatter, was Beckett's own for *More Pricks Than Kicks:* that an author puts into the mouths of fictitious characters ideas the author may not endorse.

The trial was a lamentable but symptomatic resurrection of old Dublin business, and Beckett's role was not as a passive victim profoundly alienated from Ireland by it but as a new player in a long-running local game. The specific libelous passages, always reprinted in journalistic and literary-critical accounts of the case, were not the only matters under contention. Also at issue were the affairs of Morris Harris, adoptive father of Sinclair; the local assumption, famously reiterated by Mr. Deasy in *Ulysses,* that Ireland had never persecuted the Jews; and a verse ditty recorded by Gogarty but composed by George Redding and rehearsed years before the publication of *As I Was Going Down Sackville Street* in a hotel gathering of Sinclair, Gogarty, F. R. Higgins (whose name appears in *Murphy* as that of a mental patient) and Norah Hoult (*Dublin Magazine*'s reviewer of *More Pricks Than Kicks*). The immediate upshot in literary circles was that Gogarty, afterwards understandably vindictive, sued Patrick Kavanagh for libel in *The Green Fool* and won. Gogarty also urged Austin Clarke to sue Beckett for libel because of the character of the pot poet Austin Ticklepenny in *Murphy*. Beckett's libel of Clarke exceeded Gogarty's libel of Sinclair, but Clarke, for one, waived the opportunity for litigation. He did not, apparently, pass the opportunity to write the *Dublin Magazine*'s very late notice on *Murphy* (Bair 292). That brief, unpleasant review, no doubt in part a retaliation for Beckett's comments about Clarke in "Recent Irish Poetry," as well as the trial and the caricature in *Murphy,* avoided the question of a pot poet in the novel but concluded that "the whole thing is a bizarre fantasy, with a nasty twist about it that its self-evident cleverness and scholarship cannot redeem" ("Murphy" 98). Alleged cleverness, of course, had already compromised *More Pricks Than Kicks* for the *Dublin Magazine*.

In the same issue of the *Dublin Magazine* in which the *Murphy* review appeared, Clarke initialed his very equivocal review of Gogarty's next exercise in autobiography, *Tumbling in the Hay*. There Clarke confirmed familiarity with *As I Was Going Down Sackville Street*. He passed over the possibility, much later argued by Sighle Kennedy, that in *Sackville Street*, besides the passages probably pointed out by Sinclair, Beckett likely had found material in Gogarty's character Endymion that was incorporated into his own *Murphy*. Moreover, in *Murphy's Bed: A Study of Real Sources and Surreal Associations in Samuel Beckett's First Novel*, Kennedy thickens the plot by pointing to Beckett's likely borrowing of the scenario of Murphy's will from a Gogarty story later published as "George Moore's Ultimate Joke" (Kennedy 226–28, 270–71). The plot could be thickened further, but the significance would be the same. The episode does not suggest vindictive abuse of an idealistic artist by a provincial and repressive society. Rather, on the brink of publication of *Murphy*, it indicates Beckett's involvement in, even complicity with, a local literary culture at a formative stage in his work. Indeed, all of this suggests the likelihood that directions in later stages of his work may not be wholly irrelevant to an unusually spiteful local cultural code to which Beckett was an initiate and into which he was initiated.

The Sinclair case is in retrospect an amusing indication of Beckett's personal, public, and textual involvement in Dublin's parochial conflicts at an early stage of the composition of literary works that he often identifies as a coherent "series" (Bair 364, 372, 379, 639). The case, its context, and the rather large cast of major and minor characters is also a useful indicator of the ambience of Free State Dublin in the late 1930s. Of particular interest is its example of Dublin's noted proclivity for litigation among writers whom one might think ought to preoccupy themselves with forming a unified bloc against forces contrary to the usual platform of an intelligentsia. To be alienated from the pragmatic ideology of Ireland in its Free State stage was not to be rendered solitary and marginal; to be alienated there and then, rather, was to be part of one contentious and generally ineffectual faction in a national debate over cultural priorities. In *The Dynamics of Cultural Nationalism: The Gaelic Revival and the Creation of the Irish Nation State*, John Hutchinson, who among modern analysts of nationalism is unusually sympathetic to the effort of cultural self-definition in emerging states, offers as epilogue an attentive description of post-independence retrenchment in the Irish and in comparable situations. Hutchinson argues that a newly autonomous state is inevitably compromised by success.

> For the attempt to impose from above a homogeneous identity, defined in legal-rational terms, has alienating effects, particularly in countries with few civic traditions and imbued with a deep suspicion of the political centre. In the first place, the expansion of the state tends to stimulate group conflicts about which norms and practices should form the official culture of the nation, and about the allocation of resources. In the second place, the new state, by defining nationality increasingly in terms of an allegiance to sets of routinized practices rather than as a living faith that inspires individuals in all that they do, fails to realize the initial revivalist dreams of an inner transformation. The heroic impulse has been subordinated to the task of constructing a stable order of citizens. (314)

In Beckett's work, like that of his contemporaries, one finds expression of these "alienating effects," which are distinct from the complete alienation commonly ascribed to Beckett. The critique of modern Ireland in *Murphy* directly addresses the subordination of the heroic impulse formulated in the literary revival era and inevitably deflated by the realities of the Free State. That deflation is the principal cultural criticism of the novel. Beckett's dissent to antiquarianism centers on conventionalism, not on those fictive qualities of the myths of the revival stressed by other scholars of nationalism and by recent revisionists of Irish culture history. Beckett's earlier and contemporary criticism demonstrated his participation in the "group conflicts" of which Hutchinson speaks. His periodical publications document shared sympathies with the more influential journalistic contributions by better-established Irish writers, such as O'Faolain and O'Connor, who evince similar "alienating effects." *More Pricks Than Kicks,* from the same period in Beckett's work, documents his entry into specifically Irish public debate over alternative social visions and representation of that debate as intractable impasse. *Murphy,* published in 1938, extends Beckett's critique to the revival terms of cultural self-definition, especially in literary ambitions and W. B. Yeats's conception of antinomies empowering inspired resolution. *Murphy* is not intent on deflating the ambitions of revival terms, it is focused instead on the deflating effect of those idealisms on less ambitious inheritors of them. Because *Murphy* represents that deflation as a paradigm of failure, the novel provides a base in social and cultural issues for those more aloof expositions on failure that follow *Murphy* in the "series" of Beckett's work.

Concentration on this particular cultural situation is, of course, a singular reading of Beckett's first published novel. But it is a reading that is neither contradictory nor incompatible with other, well-known readings of *Murphy*. The novel invites explication in terms of several Continental philosophers, as perhaps Beckett by association invited explication as "the bawd and basphemer of Paris." As has already been discussed in relation to *More Pricks Than Kicks,* a formalist criticism can find a consistent level of metaphysical imagery in Beckett's early fiction that may appear to be as hermetically sealed to particular social issues as Murphy's mind hopes to be to its own context. The principal imagery in *Murphy* is of antinomies, and the principal commentary in the novel is the futility of attempted resolution of antinomies. This formalist quality of the novel has been addressed most influentially by Raymond Federman in his commentary on the novel's thematic "dualism of mind and body, projected into the duality of form and content" (59). That reading of the novel invites reference to Descartes and Arnold Geulincx, especially, and emphasis on the sixth chapter, a brief disquisition on Murphy's mind. But the narrative context for Murphy's mind elsewhere in the novel makes reference to AE, Father Prout, "Cathleen na Hennessey" (46), Austin Ticklepenny the card-carrying "Pot Poet From the County of Dublin" (84), the statue of Cuchulain in the Dublin General Post Office, the Abbey Theatre as distinct from the Gate Theatre, and a host of other of quite specific Irish references that collectively constitute far more than passing sarcasm or "conventional" mimesis not yet eradicated by the young apprentice to postmodernism.

Murphy's escape from frustrating antinomies is a trance "studied under a man in Cork" and reserved for "situations irksome beyond endurance, as when he wanted a drink and could not get one, or fell among Gaels and could not escape" (3). In another reading, then, *Murphy* can plausibly be examined for the dualisms, or antinomies, that Andrew Belis had already proclaimed particularly acute in Ireland. In more specific categories than dualism of body and mind,

Murphy anatomizes antinomies of reality and illusion, of personal identity and social expectations, of contemporary Ireland and its mythological associations. These are, notably, the antinomies of Yeats, the opposition of "the filthy modern tide" and the Irish mandate to "climb to our proper dark" (*Collected Poems* 323). Curiously, these are terms frequently elided from discussion of *Murphy* by Irish critics then and now. In the *Dublin Magazine*'s review, Clarke, himself then negotiating a difficult transition from revivalism to modernism, out of either personal pique or literary-cultural prospectus, asserted that "as it is not a novel, neither is it, as the title would indicate, Irish" ("Murphy" 98). About sixty years later, in his 1988 study *Transitions: Narratives in Modern Irish Culture,* Richard Kearney focuses on the sixth chapter, "Murphy's Leibnizean ideal of splendid self-adequacy," and also, despite his subtitle, reads it neither as a novel nor as Irish. "Beckett introduces the chapter with the heading, *Amor intellectualis quo Murphy se ipsum amat,* an explicit reference to the metaphysical definition of god, in common currency since Augustine, as that Love which is sufficient unto itself (*Amor quo Deus se Ipsum amat*). This definition is modelled, in turn, on the Aristotelian ideal of an incorporeal self-thinking thought (*noesis tes noeseos*), an ideal which the author of *Murphy* never ceases to satirically undermine" (66–67). These representative readings make meanings of *Murphy* that, however plausible in themselves, are curiously inattentive to the local context established throughout the text as the consistent framework of its narrative.

Beckett's work has the interesting quality of appearing throughout most of the first six decades or so of the autonomous Irish state. The historic moment of *Murphy* is now recognized as a propitious one for a rehash of Irish national identity and the literary preoccupations of that time's loosely collegial group of Irish writers. F. S. L. Lyons, for example, chose the date 1939 as a suitable closing point for his Ford lectures delivered at Oxford in 1978 and published a year later under the title *Culture and Anarchy in Ireland 1870–1939.* For Lyons, 1939 is a watershed for the effective end of Anglo-Irish influence, an end marked by the death of Yeats, and also for the effective beginning of a major social transformation in Northern Ireland with the initiation of wartime economy. That transformation, of course, is relevant to the continuing conflict in Northern Ireland that entered its most recent violent period in 1969. Francis MacManus, for another, chose a shorter span but the same end point for the Thomas Davis lectures aired on Radio Erin in 1962 and published in 1967. For MacManus, 1939 significantly marks the end of the social and literary adjustments attendant on the shift from the Cosgrave to the de Valera administration and from the Free State to the Republican constitution.

Literary historians also choose 1939 as a significant crux for Irish writers, though they may identify the significant writers differently. For W. J. McCormack, in *The Battle of the Books*, the writers are Beckett, Louis MacNeice, Flann O'Brien, Elizabeth Bowen, and Francis Stuart. These are "the Group of '39" brought together because behind "their interrogation of the idea of the self lies a broader involvement in the issue of Ireland's identity and integrity *vis-à-vis* Europe at war" (66). For James Mays, writing on "Mythologized Presences: *Murphy* in Its Time," the Group of '39 is Beckett, Mervyn Wall, Niall Montgomery, Denis Devlin, and Thomas MacGreevy: "Beckett is very much of his generation in his understanding of the situation in more than national terms, in feeling the alternative to Yeats lies not in realism but, following the example of Joyce, in European writers of a quite different ambiance" (203). Of course, 1939 was also the year *Finnegans Wake* was published. It was, too, the year of Yeats's *Death of Cuchulain*, in which the old man on the stage, proxy for the author, says, "I have been selected [to stage this play] because I am out of fashion and out of date like the antiquated stuff the thing is made of" (*Collected Plays* 138).

The London setting of the opening of *Murphy* might seem to indicate, especially in light of Beckett's later work, one writer's defection from the Group of '39. But England was, as a matter of fact, a nearby outlet for emigration from Ireland, legal and illegal, predicated by economic needs more ordinary than the literary aspirations that motivated Beckett's own preference for Paris. In addition, at that moment emigration stood as a matter of some embarrassment to a Fianna Fail administration proudly articulating its independence from the former British colonialist overtaker. The opening of *Murphy*, then, is a strident example of that identity thinking vis-à-vis Europe at war suggested by McCormack. *Murphy* is virtually unique in Beckett's fiction for its partial setting in a particular identifiable place outside Ireland. As if to underscore connections with issues peculiar to Ireland, other portions of *Murphy* are set in Cork and in Dublin. Even when the setting is in London, the cast of Irish characters and the matter of narrative interpolations consistently ground the action in Irish contexts. Miss Counihan, who loves Murphy, is described as "just like any other beautiful Irish girl, except, as noted, more markedly anthropoid" (118). Wylie, who loves Miss Counihan, remarks on departure for London, "It is always pleasant to leave this country" (129). When in London and spurned by Miss Counihan,

> Wylie protested bitterly against this cruel treatment, which suited him down to the muck. For Miss Counihan was not one of those delights peculiar to London, with which he proposed to indulge himself up to the hilt and the utmost limit of her liberality. It was only in Dublin, where the profession had gone to the dogs, that Miss Counihan could stand out as the object of desire of a man of taste. If Neary had not been cured of her by London, he was less than a man, or more than a saint. Turf is compulsory in the Saorstat, but one need not bring a private supply to Newcastle. (196–97)

The London setting of *Murphy*, then, is an opportunity for commentary on Ireland by contrast and by caricature of Irish types and manners removed from natural and habitual habitat. Use of this extra-Irish setting is less an extrication from local context than a resurrection and reiteration of "alienating effects" demonstrated by Irish writers before and in the midst of the Group of '39. Shaw, in a 1921 autobiographical preface to the novel *Immaturity*, recalled moving to London in 1876 because "there was no Gaelic League in those days, nor any sense that Ireland had in herself the seed of culture. Every Irishman who felt that his business in life was on the higher planes of the cultural professions felt that he must have a metropolitan domicile and an international culture: that is, he felt that his first business was to get out of Ireland" (*The Matter With Ireland* 10). The success of the Gaelic League and the political and cultural ramifications of that success, however, did little to alleviate this syndrome.

In *The Green Fool*, published in the same year as *Murphy*, Patrick Kavanagh, who surely belongs in the Group of '39, attributed his move to London to the Irish culture that filled the vacuum described by Shaw. For Kavanagh, the motivation for movement to London in *The Green Fool* was economic and was a reaction to the political heirs of the Gaelic League: "I got to know Dublin much better later on. It is a city overrun by patrons of poetry and art who praise the poets and secure the jobs for their own relations. A Government — since — to whom poet, prophet, and imbecile are fellows with votes. . . . Irish writers leave Ireland because sentimental praise, or hysterical pietarian dispraise, is no use in the mouth of a hungry man" (231). In such chronological shifts of motivation, continuing down to the present, the antinomies of cultural action or reaction resemble the antinomies of Miss Counihan's affections in *Murphy:* regular in alternation.

In *Murphy,* given the most common Irish surname, Beckett represents these antinomies of action and reaction, of desire and repulsion, of cultural limitations and the limitations of culture. The plot, presented in fractured chronology, entails Dubliner Murphy's flight from Cork to London, which offers the combined attractions of employment in support of Murphy's engagement to Miss Counihan and relief from Irish acquaintances, including Miss Counihan. Once in London, Murphy meets Celia Kelly, an Irish girl practicing prostitution to support her invalid grandfather. When Murphy fails to write home, he is pursued for clarification of romantic commitments by Miss Counihan, Neary, Wylie, and Cooper, a private investigator employed by the others. They present themselves at Murphy's rooming house ("'We have come all the way from Cork,' said Neary, 'we have torn ourselves away from the groves of Blarney, for the sole purpose of cajoling him in private'") only to discover that Murphy, "the ruins of the ruins of the broth of a boy" (226), has taken a live-in position as a menial at a mental asylum. When the pursuers arrive there, they discover that Murphy has died in an accidental explosion of a gas contraption rigged by the pot poet Austin Ticklepenny. Trusting Murphy's ashes to Cooper, who loses them in a London pub, the Irish contingent depart. "Oh, hand in hand let us return to the dear land of our birth, the bays, the bogs, the moors, the glens, the lakes, the rivers, the streams, the brooks, the mists, the — er — fens, the — er — glens, by to-night's mail-train" (272). The novel closes with a sentimental vignette in which Celia takes her grandfather to a London park to fly his kite and meditates on "that unction of the soft sunless light in her eyes that was all she remembered of Ireland" (280).

The cast of characters, then, collectively offers an almost operatic chorus of desire to exist outside Ireland and inability to do so. This is one level of the antinomies on which the novel is constructed. Wylie's formulation is: "the syndrome known as life is too diffuse to admit of palliation. For every symptom that is eased, another is made worse. The horse leech's daughter is a closed system. Her quantum of wantum cannot vary" (57). That formulation of desire is universal, but Beckett's application of it in *Murphy* is quite local. The local context is on occasion apparent in matters of fact. The "novel is a *roman à clef*, which satirizes and says farewell to the Dublin literary scene," Mays argues in "Young Beckett's Irish Roots." "Miss Counihan in the novel is Ireland's Kathleen Ni Houlihan, whom the novel's characters chase round in circles at a distance from anything central. Neary is a Trinity philosopher named H. S. Macran, a great Hegelian and eccentric, who was often to be found in Neary's pub. Austin Ticklepenny is Austin Clarke. Mr. Endon has touches of Beckett's friend, Thomas MacGreevy, and Mr. Willoughby Kelly of Joyce" (23). The satire is indeed quite specific, but *Murphy* and Beckett's later work make doubtful any suggestion of farewell to the Dublin literary scene. The local context is also more figurative and on occasion more provocative in regard to Beckett's own later work and the representation of the national ethos in modern Irish literature. When Murphy's body is identified before cremation, "Neary saw Clonmachnois on the slab, the castle of the O'Melaghlins, meadow, eskers, thatch on white, something red, the wide bright water, Connaught" (267).

The framework of literary references in *Murphy* is one adjunct to this personification in character of dissatisfaction in Ireland and disorientation outside Ireland. On the level of literary reference, *Murphy* exercises equivalent dissatisfaction with national literary formulations and dependence on such orientation as they provide. The principal navigational guide on the sustenance and frustration of literary nationalism is, and in this *Murphy* is scarcely alone, W. B. Yeats. The "Nobel Yeats" of *More Pricks Than Kicks* is present in *Murphy* in the evocation of the associations of the Abbey Theatre. However, in *Murphy*, as he had in "Recent Irish Poetry," Beckett sorts through the Yeats work and, by allusion, finds much that is positively, as well as negatively, applicable to his needs, which is in itself a further paradigm of desire and repulsion, of literary history and tradition. The Yeatsian conception of greatest relevance to *Murphy* is just that sort of paradigm of conflict, opposition, and resolvable or unresolvable antinomies. This is a dimension of Yeats already central to criticism of his work, as, for example, in Denis Donoghue's description of Yeats's "consciousness as conflict" (*William Butler Yeats* 42–43), or in Peter Ure's emphasis on "conflict, choice, disorder" in Yeats's poetry and prose (96). A pertinent text from the poetry, of course, is "Vacillation," the meditation on life and work, which opens,

> Between extremities
> Man runs his course;
> A brand, or flaming breath,
> Comes to destroy
> All those antinomies
> Of day and night;
> The body calls it death
> The heart remorse.
> But if these be right
> What is Joy?
>
> (*Collected Poems* 245)

The poem-long exploration of mind-body antitheses adopts dramatic dialogue in its seventh section.

> *The Soul:* Seek out reality, leave things that seem.
> *The Heart:* What, be a singer and lack a theme?
>
> (247)

This is the question misleadingly cited in "Recent Irish Poetry" as "the exclamation of Mr. Yeats's 'fanatic heart'" (*Disjecta* 71). But it is a Yeats dialogue admitting a likelihood of disorder, and so a Yeats compatible with Beckett's own characteristic discovery of disorder in apparent order. In "Vacillation," Yeats only implies resolution of fundamental antinomies, only implies resolution in the interrogative mode, and even in conclusion entertains qualification and equivocation.

The narrative metacommentary in *Murphy* observes, "all the puppets in this book whinge sooner or later, except Murphy, who is not a puppet" (122), and that observation survives in *The Unnamable,* where the narrator notes, "I think Murphy spoke now and then, the others too perhaps, I don't remember, but it was clumsily done, you could see the ventriloquist" (*Three Novels* 348). One justification for that irony is the mechanism of antinomies governing most of the characters in *Murphy*. Celia is forced to choose between a sexual liaison with Murphy and a platonic one with her grandfather. Neary vacillates between his lust for Miss Counihan and Pythagorean idealism. Miss Counihan's affection is active only in the "regularity of its alternation" (55), as already noted. Cooper serves two opposed employers "with the beautiful indifference of a shuttle" (198). Unreconcilable oppositions also affect the patients in the Magdalen Mental Mercyseat. There Murphy assumes Ticklepenny's position in a parody of the anthropological and folkloric exploration of Connaught Celticism undertaken by Synge and many others: "Murphy was only too anxious to test his striking impression that here was the race of people he had long dispaired of finding" (169). There he finds patients "'cut off' from reality" and isolated in undiscoverable dreams. "The function of treatment was to bridge the gulf, translate the sufferer from his own pernicious little private dungheap to the glorious world of discrete particles, where it would be his inestimable prerogative once again to wonder, love, hate, desire, rejoice and howl in a reasonable balanced manner, and comfort himself with the society of others in the same predicament" (177). The treatment has no success in the novel, which opposes the patients in their dreams to the other characters in their dungheaps. The patients fail in respect to Yeats's imperative to "seek out reality, leave things that seem," and the other characters fail in their converse effort to leave reality and discover a theme.

The most detailed specimen of patently Yeatsian antinomies is Murphy, the "ethical yo-yo" (108). Murphy's vacillation is between his desire for Celia and his desire for serene isolation. "The part of him that he hated craved for Celia, the part of him that he loved shrivelled up at the thought of her" (8). It is this syndrome of being "split in two, a body and a mind" (109) that brings him to Neary, author of *The Doctrine of the Limit,* but "Neary could not blend the opposites of Murphy's heart" (4). The sixth chapter's anatomy of Murphy's mind follows as much from the verbal constructions of Yeats as it does from Gottfried Leibniz. In *Per Amica Silentia Lunae,* where Yeats worked out theories of "anti-mask" and antinomies, he wrote, "There are two realities, the terrestrial and the condition of fire. All power is from the terrestrial condition, for there all opposites meet and there only is the extreme of choice possible, full freedom. And there the heterogeneous is, and evil, for evil is the strain one upon another of opposites; but in the condition of fire is all music and rest" (*Mythologies* 356–57). Neary's advice to Murphy includes the hypothesis that love is a "compact blotch in the tumult of heterogeneous stimulation" (6), and music is Murphy's euphemism for sexual satisfaction, a euphemism ascribed in a narrative aside to the vigilance of censors. The absorption in mind Murphy seeks is just that Yeatsian "full freedom": in the deepest regions of his mind "there was nothing but commotion and the pure forms of commotion. Here he was not free, but a mote in the dark of absolute freedom" (112).

Murphy's end in the condition of fire is engineered by the pot poet Austin Ticklepenny in a parodic reification of Yeats's most visionary antinomies. The character seems indeed a rather petty libel of Austin Clarke, who later would quite powerfully describe his own episode of institutionalization in the poem "Mnemosyne Lay in the Dust." But the less petty and less personal emphasis in Beckett's character is on the rigid literary convention as practiced by "a distinguished indigent drunken Irish bard" (88). Ticklepenny's syndrome is diagnosed as "due less to the pints than to the pentameters. . . . This view of the matter will not seem strange to anyone familiar with the class of pentameter that Ticklepenny felt it his duty to Erin to compose, as free as a canary in the fifth foot (a cruel sacrifice, for Ticklepenny hiccuped in end rimes) and at the caesura as hard and fast as his own divine flatus and otherwise bulging with as many minor beauties from the gaelic prosodoturfy as could be sucked out of a mug of Beamish's porter" (88–89). In the late 1930s, there was some case for typifying Austin Clarke as bound by antiquarian prosody. But the real brunt of Beckett's caricature is the failure of apparent heirs to Yeats. In the portion of *The Autobiography of William Butler Yeats* called "The Trembling of the Veil," published in 1922, Yeats had warned that Douglas Hyde was plagued by the pot poetry syndrome: "The Harps and Pepperpots got him and the Harps and Pepperpots kept him till he wrote in our common English" (132–33). Had Andrew Belis been permitted a later view of Austin Clarke, he might have generalized in a similar fashion. The pot poetry syndrome in *Murphy* is directed not at Yeats's work but at derivatives of it.

Ticklepenny's mechanized support for Murphy's pursuit of pure freedom is a makeshift radiator arrangement that "had developed, step by step, typically, from the furthest-fetched of visions to a reality that would not function" (171). "The extremes having thus been established, nothing remained but to make them meet. This was a difficulty whose fascinations were familiar to him from the days when as a pot poet he had laboured so long and so lovingly to join the ends of his pentameters. He solved it in less than two hours by means of a series of discarded feed tubes eked out with caesurae of glass, thanks to which gas was now being poured into the radiator" (172). This entire episode in *Murphy* is quite explicit in its reference to Yeats's conception in "Vacillation" of life between extremities ending when a "flaming breath, / Comes to destroy / All those antinomies." In the larger context, the predicament of extremities and hope for resolution is useful as an analogy for Irish poetry. The extremes are the antiquarians and the "others," and the commentary offered in that analogy or dialectical model for literary tradition in *Murphy* is the impossibility of productive meeting, the impossibility of synthesis.

Murphy, like *More Pricks Than Kicks,* is dense in reference and allusion, including many not immediately relevant to Yeats or to Ireland: Blake, Malraux, Wordsworth, Rabelais, Homer, Tintoretto, and D. W. Griffith. One may, for example, object to another's reading of *Murphy* for insufficient attention to allusions to William James and Edgar Rubin (Acheson 188). The novel is a network of allusion, and that quality of it is part of its internal poetics, its place in Beckett's *oeuvre,* and Beckett's place in modernism and postmodernism. However, no Blake or Wordsworth allusion is as fundamental or developed in *Murphy* as the paradigm of Yeatsian antinomies, and no extranational framework of iconology is proportionate to the attention to Irish iconology in *Murphy*. The extraneous references and allusions are the kind of extracircumferential phenomena that Beckett adumbrated in *Proust*. The center is, instead, local and specific, the material of the "microcosmopolitans" (240).

A result of attention to the consistently Irish and consistently Yeatsian framework of allusions in *Murphy* is that one may extract a profoundly pessimistic commentary on the initiatives of cultural nationalism in the early years of postcolonialism. That pessimism can be analyzed on other grounds, particularly in reference to forms exercised elsewhere in Beckett's work. The matter can be referred to the aesthetic of suffering, experimentation, and failure articulated in *Proust;* or to the "art of impotence" dramatized in the poetics of the later fiction and typically cast in contrast to the poetics of Joyce, as in Richard Kearney's *Transitions* (61 – 63); or to a more general literary-philosophical position, as in Stephen J. Rosen's *Samuel Beckett and the Pessimistic Tradition*. But pessimism in *Murphy* is also in reference to operative symbols of Irish cultural nationalism. Two symbols directly addressed in *Murphy,* both of them associated with Yeats, had specific value in Dublin in the 1930s and have continuing value in Irish national identity.

Murphy's last will and testament, of course, is quite specific about the disposal of his remains: "With regard to the disposal of these my body, mind and soul, I desire that they be burnt and placed in a paper bag and brought to the Abbey Theatre, Lr. Abbey Street, Dublin, and without pause into what the great and good Lord Chesterfield calls the necessary house, where their happiest hours have been spent, on the right as one goes down into the pit, and I desire that the chain be there pulled upon them, if possible during the performance of a piece, the whole to be executed without ceremony or show of grief" (269). It is convenient to gloss this passage with great neatness of identifications as a cynical derogation of Yeats's national theater by the future pioneer of the Theater of the Absurd. However, the passage itself, with its reference to a colonialist euphemism and the context it appropriates, is, like most of Beckett's references to Yeats, less derision of the ludicrous than lament for the failed initiatives. The initial declaration of the Irish National Theatre stated one such initiative, as recorded by Lady Gregory in *Our Irish Theatre: A Chapter of Autobiography:*

> We propose to have performed in Dublin in the opening of every year certain Celtic and Irish plays, which whatever their degree of excellence will be written with a high ambition, and so to build up a Celtic and Irish school of dramatic literature. We hope to find in Ireland an uncorrupted and imaginative audience trained to listen by its passion for oratory, and believe that our desire to bring upon the stage the deeper thoughts and emotions of Ireland will ensure for us a tolerant

welcome, and that freedom to experiment which is not found in the theatres of England, and without which no new movement in art or literature can succeed. We will show that Ireland is not the home of buffoonery and of easy sentiment, as it has been represented, but the home of an ancient idealism. We are confident of the support of all Irish people, who are weary of misrepresentation, in carrying out a work that is outside all the political questions that divide us. (20)

Murphy doubts the "uncorrupted and imaginative audience" presumed to reside in Ireland. Yeats, also, had once planned an Irish theater in London but moved the project to Dublin at the urging of Lady Gregory. *Murphy* represents Ireland as just that "home of buffoonery and of easy sentiment" the writers of the declaration admit as the prevalent view. But there is no suggestion in *Murphy* of skepticism about "high ambition." *Murphy,* indeed any of Beckett's work, can never be construed as suggesting a skepticism of experimentation. Beckett's work offers as addendum to this declaration predetermination of failure, a factor that even the coaxing rhetoric of the declaration suggests was a possibility foreseen by the founders of the Irish theater. But Beckett offers no critique of high ambition. In the immediate context of *Murphy,* the factor of failure can be located in the distance between the founders' intentions and the local audience's expectations. That distance took shape in the 1930s in the diversion of Yeats's intentions for "an Irish school of dramatic literature" into a socially efficacious entrenchment of a rural Gaelic-Catholic identity that appeared on the Abbey stage as PQ (peasant quality). Yeats was vocal on the topic, though cognizant of his responsibilities as a public figure. Beckett's letter to MacGreevy in 1938, on the occasion of the latter's work on Jack Yeats, offers something of W. B. Yeats's known sentiments on the topic in unvarnished form. In the letter, Beckett described his "chronic inability to understand . . . a phrase like 'The Irish People' or to imagine that it ever gave a fart in its corduroys for any form of art whatsoever, whether before the union or after, or that it was ever capable of any thought or act other than rudimentary thoughts and acts delved into by the priests and demagogues in service of the priests" (Bair 281–83). Murphy seeks refuge from this frustration in dreaming, in "the downright dreaming of an infant, from the spermarium to the crematorium" (78). The repose of dreaming is the state Murphy plans for his remains in the lavatory at the Abbey The-atre. Beckett himself had no reservations about Abbey productions that approached the intentions of Yeats for the national theater. Asked in 1956 by the Gaiety Theatre for a tribute to Shaw, Beckett replied, "I wouldn't suggest that G.B.S. is not a great playwright, whatever that is when it's at home. What I would do is give the whole unup-settable applecart for a sup of the Hawk's Well, or the Saints', or a whiff of Juno, to go no further" (Knowlson 14). The demonstration of buffoonery and easy sentiment in the characters of *Murphy* is a rebuke for failure to meet Yeats's expectations for an imaginative audience weary of misrepresentation. It is not a rebuke to the Abbey or to the suggestive list of three plays by Yeats, Synge, and O'Casey that Beck-ett thought more interesting than the one by Shaw.

High ambition and predetermined failure is also the core of the direct address in *Murphy* to the Cuchulain myth and its symbolic rep-resentation in Oliver Sheppard's newly erected statue in the Dublin General Post Office (GPO). The statue commemorates the act of re-bellion and the death of many participants in the Easter Rising of 1916 launched in the GPO. This, too, appropriates the text of a public dec-laration, the 1916 Proclamation of the Republic. Like the Abbey The-atre declaration, this one, whose principal authors were Padraig Pearse and James Connolly, was a call for independence, political rather than artistic, based on an ancient idealism and insistent on the obligations of the Irish people.

Irishmen and Irishwomen: In the name of God and of the dead gen-erations from which she receives her old tradition and nationhood, Ire-land, through us, summons her children to her flag and strikes for her freedom. . . . The Irish Republic is entitled to, and hereby claims, the allegiance of every Irishman and Irishwoman. . . . We place the cause of the Irish Republic under the protection of the Most High God, Whose blessing we invoke upon our arms, and we pray that no one who serves that cause will dishonour it by cowardice, inhumanity, or rap-ine. In this supreme hour the Irish nation must, by its valour and dis-cipline and by the readiness of its children to sacrifice themselves for the common good, prove itself worthy of the august destiny to which it is called. (Dangerfield 179–80)

There is a great deal of interest in this document, especially its coau-
thors' conjunction of socialist and Roman Catholic ideologies. But the
principal relevance of the proclamation to the Yeats-Beckett texts is
the summons to the Irish people. Yeats was writing his last poems as
Beckett was writing his first novel, and their focus on the Sheppard
statue is a result of the statue's importance rather than any direct influence. Yeats's poem "The Statues" and his play *The Death of Cuchulain* both use Sheppard's statue as symbol of potential national order.
The poem first joins the antinomies of Pythagorean abstraction and
youthful passion in Greek sculpture.

> Pythagoras planned it. Why did people stare?
> His numbers, though they moved or seemed to
>   move
> In marble or in bronze, lacked character.
> But boys and girls, pale from the imagined love
> Of solitary beds, knew what they were,
> That passion could bring character enough,
> And pressed at midnight in some public place
> Live lips upon a plummet-measured face.
>
> (*Collected Poems* 322)

The poem proceeds through progressively more localized references to
the imperative extricated from antinomies that the Irish people
"Climb to our proper dark, that we may trace/The lineaments of a
plummet-measured face" (323). In *The Death of Cuchulain*, the passion of Pearse and Connolly is linked even more specifically to Sheppard's statue:

> What stood in the Post Office
> With Pearse and Connolly?
> What comes out of the mountain
> Where men first shed their blood?
> Who thought Cuchulain till it seemed
> He stood where they had stood?
>
> No body like his body
> Has modern woman borne,
> But an old man looking on life

Imagines it in scorn.
A statue's there to mark the place,
By Oliver Sheppard done.
So ends the tale that the harlot
Sang to the beggar-man.

(*Collected Plays* 446)

Beckett, contemplating the same statue at the same time, cites this very sort of imperative; but in *Murphy's* own tale of a harlot and a "beggar-man," the modern swamps the ancient. In *Murphy,* Neary is drawn to the Sheppard statue and is discovered "in the General Post Office contemplating from behind the statue of Cuchulain. Neary had bared his head, as though the holy ground meant something to him. Suddenly he flung aside his hat, sprang forward, seized the dying hero by the thighs and began to dash his head against his buttocks, such as they are" (42).

Like any memorial sculpture in service of national ideology, Sheppard's statue joins a heroism of the past with the present and summons the present to imperative heroism. For Yeats, the summons is a bulwark against "the filthy modern tide." For Beckett, the summons is an affront. Neary recognizes the call of the Red Branch tales: "that deathless rump was trying to stare me down" (57). He recognizes it, however, as an obstruction rather than as an inspiration: "'The limit of Cork endurance had been reached,' said Neary. 'That Red Branch bum was the camel's back'" (46). In the Yeats and Beckett contemporary texts an equivalent power is ascribed to a single symbol. The consequence of that power is contrary, as is the converse anatomical focus on "the lineaments of a plummet-measured face" or a "deathless rump." In that ascription of equivalent power, Beckett and Yeats are equally enmeshed in the national ideology. In description of a symptomatic Irish cyclicism in *States of Mind: A Study of Anglo-Irish Conflict, 1780 – 1980,* Oliver MacDonagh isolates "the *locus classicus*" in the 1916 Proclamation of the Republic and argues, "that the characteristic Irish time-frame inclines Irishmen to a repetitive view of history and that such a view inclines them—perhaps in defensive wariness and from fear of failure—to prize the moral as against the actual, and the bearing of witness as against success" (13). In both the intended lavatory resting place in the Abbey Theatre and in the flailings of Neary against the Sheppard statue, Beckett represents acts of witness as repetitive demonstrations of failure.

Murphy is in many ways symptomatic of its time and place. When Arland Ussher addressed the topic of "The Contemporary Thought of Ireland" in 1947, he chose *Murphy* as one indication of a syndrome he lamented. Ussher's argument, devoted to domestic matters rather than to the worldwide events of the early 1940s, concentrated on contemplative and escapist tendencies in Irish culture and "the lack of a synthesising philosophy of life" (26). The antinomies Ussher identifies are those of Yeats: dream and reality. Against these, he locates *Murphy* for its protagonist's affiliation with the mental institution. "The novel *Murphy,* by an expatriate Dubliner, Samuel Beckett, expresses this contradiction in a bitterly farcical form; its hero determines to become an attendant in a lunatic-asylum. He prefers the mad to the sane *because* they are mad — not because he loves madness, but because he hates the sensibly ordered world more" (27). This predicament, which Ussher finds represented also in Synge's *Well of the Saints,* is by the 1940s a matter of some disappointment to Ussher. Looking back to Shaw, Yeats, and Joyce, and to a subsequent Irish literary culture of inert contemplation of local contradictions, Ussher asserted that "it is hard to believe that Ireland has become a No-Man's-Land of the mind, or that she has grown provincial at the moment when she is, for the first time after centuries, a nation" (28). He *did* believe it, despite the difficulty of confronting such stasis in a phase of national autonomy that might be expected in any context to be one of initiation. Ussher is particularly helpful for his emphasis on the excruciating reality of the moment as a local problem, not a cosmopolitan or metaphysical construction of reality. This is the emphasis, too, of the closing vignette in *Murphy,* when Mr. Kelly lofts his kite, hoping that "he could measure the distance from the unseen to the seen, now that he was in a position to determine the point at which seen and unseen met," and Celia localizes the problem in contemplation of "all she remembered of Ireland" (280). Kelly's kite string breaks, of course, and *Murphy* offers no positive speculation on the unseen, future possibilities of Ireland.

Ussher's point about unhappy provincialism relies on particular local connotations of the term. These connotations have been unpacked by F. S. L. Lyons in *Culture and Anarchy* without reference to Beckett or to *Murphy* but in reference to other works of the Group of '39 that bear comparison with *Murphy*. Lyons, too, casts the entire problem in Yeatsian antinomies, in "an anarchy in the mind and in the heart" (177). The antitheses in local literary culture are, for Lyons, Kavanagh, "who sought refuge in passionate attachment to the place — what Patrick Kavanagh called 'parochialism'" (172), and Flann O'Brien, who "took refuge in satirical comment on the Ireland of his day" (171). In the case of these and others, Lyons argues, "it would not only be trite to say that what these writers were reacting against was Irish provincialism, it would also be inadequate." The same warning is pertinent to the case of Beckett, whose reaction to the literary revival is not simply dismissal of claptrap and whose subsequent work shifts in primary topic only between identifiable Ireland and more generalized representations of it. For Lyons, the static, unresolved antinomies are all bound up in the local versions of provincialism: the abasement before external culture, the effect of Flann O'Brien's satire, and the passionate attachment to a place within the place, the tenor of Kavanagh's parochialism. Just as it was for Ussher, this is difficult for Lyons to believe because "the whole Anglo-Irish drive towards fusion had been intended to create a culture which would avoid equally the extremes of abject servility to alien modes and complacent contemplation of native modes" (172). *Murphy* asserts the failure of that drive and the whole idea of fusion.

What emerged instead of fusion can be seen in works by Kavanagh and Flann O'Brien published at the same time as *Murphy*. *The Green Fool* is as abusive and even as libelous as *Murphy* of Dublin's literary coterie in competitive manufacture of pot poetry. *The Green Fool*, like *Murphy*, leaves Dublin for London as a matter of passive withdrawal. "To Ireland I bade no patriotic emigrant's farewell; towards London I did not turn hope-wide eyes in vision. I did not care, I was going half against my will. I was a fatalist drifting inconsequently on the winds of Chance, and I did not care whither they blew me" (253). But unlike the unresolved dilemma of relation to Ireland in *Murphy*, *The Green Fool* concludes with endorsement in virtually biblical style of a further withdrawal into a place within the place. "I returned to

Ireland. Ireland green and chaste and foolish. And when I wandered over my own hills and talked again to my own people I looked into the heart of this life and I saw that it was good" (264). The matter of goodness of that life later proved more problematic in Kavanagh's subsequent exposition on the local pertinence of *Godot*.

There is another provincialism apparent in Flann O'Brien's *At Swim-Two-Birds*, which shares with *Murphy* a parodic deflation of the contemporary power of Celtic myth—for O'Brien the Finn legend of the Leinster cycle as for Beckett the Cuchulain legend of the Ulster cycle. It is of some interest that the two novels have been consistently paired by Irish writers. Joyce recommended them together to Adrienne Monnier in 1940. Vivian Mercier recalls writing about them together in the *Dublin Magazine* in 1943. Aidan Higgins described them together as early "great discoveries in my own literature" (59) after *A Portrait* and *Ulysses*. Beckett and O'Brien met once and discussed Joyce: Beckett reported to Anne Clissmann that the occasion "is better forgotten" (310). Joyce yoked the two novels together for Monnier as Irish examples of a new theory of composition (Monnier 123), and they have since been joined together repeatedly for their formal modernism. But there are many comparisons of local import as well. Among the possible crises for Murphy at the beginning of the novel is his fear that he might "fall among Gaels." After he finished *At Swim-Two-Birds*, O'Brien wrote to Sean O'Casey about "a certain type of 'Gael,' which I find the most nauseating phenomenon in Europe" (Clissmann 238).

A half century after publication of these three works, the dilemma they represent has scarcely changed. But from the present historical moment, Kavanagh and Flann O'Brien are likely passed over as casualties of it while Beckett is enjoying a local revival. The entry of Beckett into Irish studies is a product of factors already discussed in relation to *More Pricks Than Kicks* and also of a debate over revisionism of local cultural history. The debate dominates several fields, notably history and literary history, and dominates periodicals, notably the last issue in 1985 of *Crane Bag*, which was devoted entirely to "Irish Ideologies." In 1988, *Irish Review* offered in printed version an overview of the debate itself as "Nationalist Perspectives on the Past: A Symposium," which was based on a seminar on revisionism at UCD in 1987. In it, Ronan Fanning and Desmond Fennell contributed powerful arguments for and against revisionism. For Fennell, in "Against Revisionism," the issue is "a *new moral interpretation* of the known major facts . . . a new allocation, with regard to the known major facts and the general course of events, of *rightness* and *wrongness*, as between the ideas and actions of the Irish and the intentions and actions of the British (or Ulster British)." The moral shift, he argues, is not attributable to new evidence or even to persuasive new interpretation of it, but to "British, American and German capital providing the wealth which Sinn Fein economics had failed to provide, and the rise to power in Dublin of a new elite of businessmen, bureaucrats, media people and politicians who adopted swinging London as their cultural and moral lodestar" (22, 23). For Fanning, on "The Meaning of Revisionism," opposition to the trend, "the sound and the fury obfuscating the revisionist debate stems from a national loss of innocence. For national innocence could not survive what has happened in Northern Ireland since 1969. . . . That the debate coincided with the examination of the national conscience triggered by the Northern crisis has accentuated the sense of an affront to the traditional nationalist certainties" (17, 18). The most recent and most succinct overview of the debate in terms of literary history is provided in the introduction to Richard Kearney's *Transitions:* "Some narrative reinterpretations seek to revive the past; others choose to rewrite or repudiate it altogether. Apropos of Irish culture in this century, we call the former option *revivalism* and the latter *modernism*" (x). Revivalism, for Kearney and other revisionists, is associated with Yeats, with the immediate pragmatics of movement from colonialism to political autonomy, and with the extension of a secure local identity from past to present on the basis of traditional certainties and exclusion of outside influences. Modernism, for Kearney, "affirms a radical break with tradition and endorses a practice of cultural self-reflection where inherited concepts of identity are subjected to question" (12). Here modernist Joyce is counterpart to revivalist Yeats. In pursuit of this modernism, Beckett is summoned frequently. For Kearney, "Beckett too [like Joyce] rejected the myths of the Irish literary Revival concentrating instead on the modernist problematic of language itself" (13). Hence, in a later chapter of *Transitions* devoted entirely to Beckett, the matter of local import hardly appears.

In this debate over adherence to tradition in relation to rejection of it, Beckett is not summoned by revisionists as symptomatic of the limits of revivalism (like Flann O'Brien or Kavanagh) but as exemplary modernist for protracted interrogation of the idea of identity and unequivocal rejection of inherited certainties. In this last, however, Beckett's work does not wholly support the program of revisionism. In an earlier essay, "Beckett: The Demythologising Intellect," Kearney argued that *Murphy* is "exposure of the Irish Revival pretensions and particularly its claim to a fixed national identity" (269). But as closer attention to *Murphy* shows, Beckett's address to symbols of national identity, such as Sheppard's statue or the Abbey Theatre, is much more qualified and ambivalent. Nor can *Murphy* be considered an unequivocal rejection of Yeats and his revivalist associations; rather, *Murphy* assumes Yeatsian terms of antinomies as virtually axiomatic and reworks them for its own pessimistic purposes. The very presence of Beckett in an Irish Group of '39 indicates ties between *Murphy* and contemporary works delinquent in modernism. Even the episode of the Sinclair libel trial cannot be reduced to simple and complete alienation of Beckett from Ireland. It is, rather, an indication of alienating *effects* (Hutchinson's term) that are predictable among intellectuals and other groups in an immediately postcolonial stage of national status. Alienating effects are a factor, though not a whole condition, of the production of a literary work in such circumstances. *Murphy* is an illustration of alienating effects in its dissatisfaction with national terms of identity and collateral inability or unwillingness to depart from them or to reject them absolutely. *Murphy,* as read here, is not a text indicative of rejection of the myths of the revival and replacement of them with something else.

A passing image in *Murphy* addresses this predicament quite memorably. In a fire, "the turf was truly Irish in its eleutheromania, it would not burn behind bars" (131). In the novel, burning, specifically in the death of Murphy, is exhaustion in the indifference he seeks: "The freedom of indifference, the indifference of freedom, the will dust in the dust of its object, the act a handful of sand let fall—these were some of the shapes he had sighted, sunset landfall after many days" (105). Though desired, such freedom is never realized by Murphy, by Beckett's other protagonists, or even by Murphy redivivus in

Fizzles: "as destitute of history as on that first day, on this same path, which is his beginning, on days of great recall" (12). The problematics of language, certainly an object of concentration in Beckett's late prose, does not eliminate the problematics of history. Like the turf in *Murphy,* Irish eleutheromania is contained by bars in the form of terms of debate. In a Field Day Theatre Company pamphlet called *Heroic Styles: The Tradition of an Idea,* Seamus Deane, though he too in service of revisionism is reductive on Beckett, touches on just this predicament of polarized terms of debate: tradition and rejection of it. "Between these hot and cold rhetorics there is little room for choice. Yet the polarization they identify is an inescapable and understandable feature of the social and political realities we inhabit. These are by no means extravagant examples of Irish linguistic energy exercised in a world foreign to every onlooker. They inhabit the highly recognisable world of modern colonialism" (18). In counterargument to that same formulation, Denis Donoghue responded, "the man to beat is Yeats" ("Afterword" 120). Just so; though Deane in turn could respond that he had. For Irish revisionism, the man to beat is Yeats; for Irish revivalism, the man to beat is Joyce. At the present moment in Irish cultural studies, because those hot and cold rhetorics are in place, and because he put the argument into definitive form, the man to beat is Beckett.

4

 WATT AND KNOTT'S BIG HOUSE

BECKETT'S WORK IS SIGNIFICANT in modern Irish literature for its excavation from specifically Irish, local cultural paradigms one of the more influential representations in literary modernism of a general, cosmopolitan intractability. Beckett first set the schema in 1930 in reference to "Proust's treasury of nutshell phrases" (*Proust* 17); and at this later point, the schema can be set in reference to Beckett's own treasury of nutshell phrases in *Proust*. There "the pendulum oscillates" between the terms of suffering and boredom, and the action of oscillation is "perpetual adjustment and readjustment of our organic sensibility to the conditions of its worlds." In all of Beckett's work, those extremities of imagination and antecedence remain intractable, and the dialectic permits only an "endless series of renovations." The renovations of intractable terms are progressive not in synthesis but only in comprehensive delineation, centripetal focus, and deeper excavation: "if I may add this nox vomica to an aperitif of metaphors—the heart of the cauliflower or the ideal core of the onion would represent a more appropriate tribute to the labours of poetical excavation than the crown of bay" (16–17).

Watt is a crucial demonstration of this problem and of adjustment and readjustment of it in all of Beckett's work. As Arsene, Watt's predecessor in Knott's house, says of Watt, "having oscillated all his life between the torments of a superficial loitering and the horrors of disinterested endeavour, he finds himself at last in a situation where to do nothing exclusively would be an act of the highest value, and significance" (*Watt* 41). Inertia, in the face of contrary possibilities, is the outcome in *Watt* of the problem of those extremities of antecedence and imagination. The problem and the result are consistent in all of Beckett's work, but *Watt* is singular for representation of it in both the recognizable Ireland of Beckett's previous work and the analogical setting of his later, more influential works. In *Watt*, that distinction of setting is very explicit: the specifically Irish setting of the first and last of the four parts of the novel frame two middle parts of vaguer reference. *Watt* is instructive for this manner of doing nothing exclusively.

The great relevance of *Watt* to the Irish Beckett and to Irish literature is all the more striking because the novel's place in Beckett's literary production, the circumstances of its composition, and its rhetoric of decontextualized exposition might suggest irrelevance to local context. The time of composition was 1942 to 1945: the crux between the earlier exercises in local satire of the sort Dylan Thomas glossed as "Sodom and Begorrah" (291) and the subsequent exercises in French of the sort mined for diverse purposes of their own adaptable treasury of nutshell phrases by a variety of commentators on Euro-American modernism and postmodernism. The place of composition was mostly France. Beckett perhaps said, "I preferred France in war to Ireland in peace" (Shenker 1), and he certainly reported to Gottfried Büttner, "*Watt* was begun in Paris in 1942, then continued evenings mostly in Roussillon and finished 1945 in Dublin and Paris" (Büttner 5). The novel was largely composed in hiding during the German occupation, when Beckett's credentials as an associate of the French Resistance outweighed his credentials as a citizen of neutral Ireland. Beckett wrote to Büttner that *Watt* "was written as it came, without preestablished plan" (6). Of what "came," the most striking to the majority of critics were passages of "great formal brilliance and indeterminable purport" (*Watt* 74). To wit,

> Watt began to invert, no longer the order of the letters in the word together with that of the sentences in the period, but that of the letters in the word together with that of the words in the sentence together with that of the sentences in the period.
>
> For example:
>
> *Dis yb dis, nem owt. Yad la, tin fo trap. Skin, skin, skin. Od su did ned taw? On. Taw ot klat tonk? On. Tonk ot klat taw? On. Tonk ta kool taw?*

On. *Taw ta kool tonk? Nilb, mun, mud. Tin fo trap, yad la. Nem owt, dis yb dis.*

It took me some time to get used to this. (167–68)

As *Watt* was not published until the 1950s, most commentators on *Watt* came to it from *Molloy, Malone Dies, The Unnamable,* and *Godot.* From that perspective, it took less time "to get used to this." John J. Mood, in a formidable explication in 1971 of "the personal system" in *Watt,* was succinct in his summary of symbol hunting, hortatory existentialist phenomenology, and logical positivism as glosses on *Watt,* all of which served as a preface to his own identification of *Watt* as Beckett's "most devastating depiction of the cul-de-sac of modern Western rationalistic philosophy" (255).

For all its adaptability, however, *Watt* is also significant as extension of the critique of alternative social visions in *More Pricks Than Kicks* and of comparable literary visions in *Murphy. Watt* is indeed a "missing link," as Büttner asserts (7). But the link is not only as it may seem when working backward from *Godot.* It is also the link as it seems when working forward from *More Pricks Than Kicks:* accommodating general modernist concerns without eradicating the fundamental local context or replacing the Irish frame of reference with another. As Beckett wrote to George Reavey in 1947, *Watt* "is an unsatisfactory book, written in dribs and drabs, first on the run, then of an evening after the clod-hopping, during the occupation, but it has its place in the series, as will perhaps appear in time" (Bair 364); the series, that is, of Beckett's *oeuvre,* and *Watt*'s place is a position in a series of renovated forms of consistent problems.

Watt as missing link indicates that the forces predicating Beckett's series of works are not only those most decontextualized epistemologies deduced from that small part of the large *oeuvre* that was most commonly associated with Beckett's name at the time he received the Nobel Prize. *Watt* also verifies the sentiment noted in the addenda to *Watt,* that "for all the good that frequent departures out of Ireland had done him, he might just as well have stayed there" (248). *More Pricks Than Kicks* and *Murphy* centered on the maladies of the Irish Free State; *Watt* extracts equivalent intellectual and political impasse from conventions common over a period of Irish social and literary culture. The difference between *Murphy* and *Molloy* effected in *Watt* is this significantly broader historical frame of local reference, with attendant increment in generalized and archetypal evocations of setting and scene. The effect is no diminishment of "poetical excavation" in search of "the ideal core of the onion." It is, rather, just that sort of penetration through the most visible and proportionately superficial manifestations of culture.

A focus of *Murphy* is Oliver Sheppard's statue of Cuchulain in the Dublin GPO; a focus in *Molloy* is the Turdy Madonna: the difference is relinquishment of identifiable cultural icons for vaguer but distinctly Irish ones having reference to more than immediate (in the sense of short-term) history. That conception is observable in *Watt*, where the fictional narrator, named Sam, dismisses Watt's wistful illusion that he existed in a "culture-park" (77). As that dismissal is recorded, the illusion is not absent, and that sort of equivocal relation to specifically Irish culture is established clearly in *Watt*. The equivocation appears in many characteristic *Watt* passages, such as "that nothing had happened, that a thing that was nothing had happened, with the utmost formal distinctness" (76).

Representations in *Watt* of contrary perceptions and possibilities include the contrasting worldviews of Watt and the narrator, Sam. Watt is as passive and nostalgic as Sam is relentless and rational; the first is as thwarted in his search for relief in "a pillow of old words" (117) as the second is thwarted in his search for a formulation without "cracks" (148). The rhetoric of the narrative generated by Sam — as opposed to the content generated by Watt — dominates the critical conceptions of the originality of *Watt*. The text (lacerated by omissions, annotated with footnotes, supplemented with addenda) and the style (typically mired in legalistic qualifications and quasi-philosophical terminologies) of some of *Watt* suggest the discourse of nonfiction more than that of the discursive novel. Hence, *Watt* has been placed by many critics in the tradition of *A Tale of a Tub* by Jonathan Swift, *Tristram Shandy* by Laurence Sterne, and *Ulysses* by James Joyce, all joined by a penchant for extending rhetorical conceits to absurd extremes. Relevant readings of *Watt* typically relate it to a tradition called the *anti-novel* for lack of a better term. For example, Christine Brooke-Rose, in an essay called "Samuel Beckett and the Anti-Novel," notable for its insistence that *Watt* is not "a mere preamble to

Beckett's trilogy and plays" (42), makes the equation of her title on the grounds that *Watt's* "effects are carefully built up and depend, not on adornment but on pattern, a pattern made of rhythm, repetition, antithesis, and lucid but long intricate periods" (39–40). The Irish context of *Watt* is generally located in Sterne and Swift, as in John Chalker's observation that the "narrative devices that link *Tristram Shandy, A Tale of a Tub,* and *Watt* are clear in the very typography and layout of the book" (24), including footnotes, lacunae, and addenda as back matter. Sam's narrative is indeed, in John Mood's phrase, "a highly successful comedy of *apparently* exhaustive enumeration" (262).

These narrative elements in *Watt* have been treated most often solely in formalistic terms, but these precedents alone also suggest the specifically Irish context. The issue of rhetorical detachment from "material" for fiction, just the detachment that may make *Watt* appear irrelevant to Ireland, is a consistent problem in Beckett's work and in Irish literature over a historical period longer than the modern Irish literary revival and its immediate aftermath. In Beckett's work, the problem as presented in *Watt* is renovation of the subject-object rupture argued in general terms in *Proust* in 1930 and in Irish contexts in "Recent Irish Poetry" in 1934. In "Recent Irish Poetry," the rupture had an aura of positivistic imperatives, as it seemed to suggest "the nucleus of a living poetic in Ireland" (*Disjecta* 76). However, the rupture, even as defined then, was in essence the formulation of an aesthetic impasse. "The artist who is aware of this [rupture] may state the space that intervenes between him and the world of objects" (70). This particular item from Beckett's treasury of nutshell phrases appears to license application of *Watt* to a number of objects. For example, W. J. McCormack, in the essay "Seeing Darkly: Notes on T. W. Adorno and Samuel Beckett," summons the novel in reference to Adorno's identification of Beckett's work as crucially post–World War II and then identifies *Watt* with World War II because of its space, or distance, from that object and because of Beckett's notable resistance to the postwar culture industry as defined by Adorno.

But the idea of distance between writer and material was already treated as a matter of Irish literary history at the time of the war. In January 1942, Cyril Connolly assembled a special issue of *Horizon* on wartime, neutral Ireland. The most interesting contribution he solicited was Frank O'Connor's essay, "The Future of Irish Literature," a future O'Connor thought bleak because local repression (i.e., censorship) was inimical to local art and consequently the reason for Irish writers' adaptation of English literary preoccupations. In condemnation of doctrinaire "peasant quality" (PQ), O'Connor quoted a letter from W. B. Yeats to Florence Farr. "I have noticed, by the way, that the writers of this country who come from the mass of the people—or no, I should say, who come from Catholic Ireland, have more reason than fantasy. It is the other way with those who come from the leisured classes. They stand above the subject and play with it, and their writing is, as it were, a victory as well as a creation." O'Connor largely concurred with that assessment, stating that "writers who come from Catholic Ireland . . . [are] more identified with their material; they tend to sentimentalize or brutalize it, and rarely does one find a Catholic Irish writer playing with his material as Synge played with his" (58). These generalizations by religion and social class are problematic, even though O'Connor made qualifications. But the interest of his argument is that this whole idea of space, distance, and play is not a recent critical discovery or a derivative of postwar culture. O'Connor portrayed it as a matter of literary history and not, as Yeats appeared to think, an inescapable fate. For O'Connor, these terms of identification and distance, of material and play, of object and subject, are the terms of modern Irish literature: "it is true that the literature of Catholic Ireland (and one needn't go beyond Joyce to prove it) is dominated by its material in a way in which the work of Synge and Yeats rarely was" (59).

In 1942, O'Connor could hardly be expected to bring Beckett into his thesis, and not surprisingly, he later proved indifferent to elements of play in *Godot*. However, the subsequent availability of Beckett's work as data does serve to extend the notion of distance and detachment as a principal factor in Beckett's work and in Irish literature extending back before Yeats and Synge. At a more recent date, James Mays, defining the dilemma in "Young Beckett's Irish Roots," stated, "dependence and renunciation link Beckett with a tradition of Anglo-Irish writing which extends centuries beyond the Revival and earlier writers like Mangan and Ferguson and their predecessors, to the beginning of the Irish contribution to writing in English. Beckett's isolation, exposure, and sense of distance from his materials are not unusual in this larger context" (29). The names Beckett brings forth, for Mays, include Yeats and Joyce but also William Congreve, Richard Brinsley Sheridan, Oscar Wilde, and George Bernard Shaw, all of whom demonstrate, as Mays argues, varying degress of independence from and dependence on patently Irish literary material. The extension of the argument provoked by Beckett essentially reiterates O'Connor's premise and leaves his Catholic-Protestant polarization unrevised.

Watt is as fundamentally concerned with Irish literary precedents as was *Murphy*. Individual episodes in the most abstracted, analogical portions in the middle sections of the novel explicitly evoke a cultural history in the forms of the piano tuners the Galls, the prolific Catholic Lynch family, and the pseudo-anthropologist Ernest Louit's presentation of a pure Celt captured in the wild to a board of Anglo-Irish academic examiners. All of these characters appear only as related by Sam's systematic and analytical narration. The contrary epistemology of Watt, however, also brings to *Watt* elements of Irish literary precedents that are an alternative to the Swift, Sterne, Joyce modernism. The narrative of the novel concerns the journey of Watt from and back to Dublin and environs. Watt's destination, by design or accident, is Mr. Knott's house, an eccentric but rather grand affair with servants and gardeners. The text certainly supports the "What?/Not?" line of questioning now customary. But it just as certainly supports analysis in terms of that distinctly Irish subspecies of the novel, the "Big House" novel. The Big House novel is as passive, nostalgic, and traditionalist as Watt; and in the assemblage of Irish literary precedents in *Watt,* those precedents are the essential counterpart to the obsessive, rhetorical innovations of textual practice associated with Swift, Sterne, and Joyce. Therefore, *Watt* offers a dialectic of literary precedents that are all Irish.

Beckett's work has this effect of provoking conception of Irish literature in terms broader than the literary revival. Though Beckett has been read reductively to indicate an utter separation from local precedents, his works, and *Watt* in particular, demonstrate what Mays calls a "measure of detachment" (30): that is, distance without complete separation. Though *Watt* may be apprehended as inevitably an allegory for World War II or the bankruptcy of Western rationalism, the text itself can be read with equal plausibility as fulfillment in unforeseen ways of Yeats's dictum, in "Ireland and the Arts" of 1901, "I would have our writers and craftsmen of many kinds master this history and these legends, and fix upon their memory the appearance of mountains and rivers and make it all visible again in their arts, so that Irishmen, even though they had gone thousands of miles away, would still be in their own country" (*Essays and Introduction* 205–6).

Preferring France in war to Ireland in peace, Beckett wrote in Roussillon a novel that opens and closes in detailed representation of places and manners of Dublin and of its southern suburb, Foxrock, Beckett's own home. The first part of the novel describes Watt's departure from Dublin via the Foxrock train, and the last part describes Watt's return from Knott's house to the Foxrock station. In these episodes, the setting is "throttled" into Ireland, as Beckett wrote in reference to Jack Yeats, though not precisely into the best-known literary Dublin of the geography of Joyce's *Ulysses*. Lest the scheme seem too consequential, the narrator, Sam, qualifies it without altering the distinction between middle and opening and closing parts: "Two, one, four, three, that was the order in which Watt told his story" (215).

Watt opens with a Mr. Hackett, of "the Glencullen Hacketts" (15), in conversation of a wholly conventional literary sort with the Nixons when Watt appears before them. Nixon recognizes Watt as one to whom he has loaned money, and Hackett inquires about Watt's past.

> I really know nothing, said Mr Nixon.
> But you must know something, said Mr Hackett. One does not part with five shillings to a shadow. Nationality, family, birthplace, confession, occupation, means of existence, distinctive signs, you cannot be in ignorance of all this.
> Utter ignorance, said Mr Nixon. (21)

This whole issue of "antecedents" (22) is raised in the opening of *Watt*. The issue, of course, appears memorably in *A Portrait of the Artist as a Young Man,* where Stephen Dedalus says, "When the soul of a man is born in this country there are nets flung at it to hold it back from flight. You talk to me of nationality, language, religion. I shall try to fly by those nets" (203). Joyce's expression of the issue is ambiguous. Against Stephen's intention stand his formulation of flight as evasion, his *Young Man* syndrome, and his reappearance, crestfallen, in *Ulysses*. Watt's intention, rather, is to find the support of those nets, however arbitrary that support may be. His difficulty is discovery that self-defining nets may be largely a matter of coincidence. "Haw!" Arsene says on greeting him, "All the old ways led to this" (40). Entrapment by these nets is also the effect in *Watt* of the failures of Sam's rationalism and of the allusiveness of language beyond a narrator's control.

Antecedence is a pervasive focus in *Watt*, though its counterpart, the enumerations of possibilities by the narrator, disproportionately dominate explication of the novel. In the opening chapter, the conversation between Hackett and the Nixons is retrospective. After a short train ride in the chapter, Watt is confronted by Lady McCann, "thanks to her traditions, catholic and military" (31), who, "faithful to the spirit of her cavalier ascendants" (32), hits him with a stone. The landmarks of the chapter, such as the Harcourt Street and Foxrock stations and Prince William's Seat, are those of Beckett's own past, as has been generally observed and identified in detail by Eoin O'Brien in *The Beckett Country*. It would have interested Beckett to know that Noelle Ryan, writing a brief booklet *Samuel Beckett: Early Days in Foxrock* for the Foxrock Local History Club in 1982, was certain about the setting of *Watt* around Leopardstown and Stillorgan but uncertain in other matters, such as reference to *Watt* as Beckett's first novel written in English.

In the opening of *Watt*, anagrams offer another model of antecedent allowing limited latitude for revision. On the train, Watt meets Mr. Spiro who edits a journal bent on renewing in anagrams unalterable matters of inherited dogma.

> I edit *Crux*, said Mr Spiro, the popular catholic monthly. We do not pay our contributors, but they benefit in other ways. Our advertisements are extraordinary. We keep our tonsure above water. Our prize competitions are very nice. Times are hard, water in every wine. Of a devout twist, they do more good than harm. For example: *Rearrange the fifteen letters of the Holy Family to form a question and answer.* Winning Entry: *Has J. Jurms a po? Yes.* (27)

Together, the autobiographical Foxrock setting and the representation of the demographically predominant religious affiliation that is not Beckett's own make the setting of *Watt* specifically Irish in ways both personal and social.

In addition to these specific details of setting, the first chapter of *Watt* also includes allusions to the literature of the revival and its immediate aftermath. Like specifications of place, these allusions in *Watt* are briefer and more obscure than functionally similar ones in *More Pricks Than Kicks* and *Murphy*. The allusions in *Watt*, however, are all the more suggestive for balanced reference to the two figures, Yeats and Joyce, now taken in Ireland as representative of revivalism and revisionism of it, respectively. The Watt character is governed mainly by a desire for precedence and "the old ways." The narrative in *Watt* qualifies that desire in a narrator governed principally by alternative desires. In passing but complex allusions to Yeats and Joyce, *Watt* suggests similar qualification of desire — the allusions are to Yeats and Joyce, but they are ironic allusions.

As Sighle Kennedy first pointed out ("Spirals of Need"), during Watt's journey from Foxrock Station toward Knott's house, he has an incidental experience that closely parallels "The Legend of Knockgrafton" in Yeats's collection *Fairy and Folk Tales of the Irish Peasantry* (1888). Yeats takes the story from T. Crofton Croker, an early nineteenth-century folklorist from Cork, but he also cites the recording of essentially the same story in Connaught by Douglas Hyde. Indeed, the folklore tale is a common enough type: Robert Darnton described a parallel tale in French folklore in his "Peasants Tell Tales" essay in *The Great Cat Massacre: And Other Episodes in French Cultural History* (53–54). But the tale as incorporated into *Watt* is close enough in specific language to constitute allusion, direct or indirect, to the volume by Yeats. The Irish story concerns a hunchback, like Mr. Hackett, who on the opening pages of *Watt* is associated by Mr. Nixon with Watt. Like Watt and like Hackett, the hunchback in the tale is so peculiar "that he scarcely appeared to be a human creature," and so, as for Watt and Hackett, "some ill-minded persons had set strange stories about him afloat" (43). Watt enters the parallel episode with the curse of an irritable porter: "The Devil raise a hump on you" (24). Like Watt, the hunchback in the tale also has a peculiar hat, and his name, Lushmore, is the Irish word for the foxglove sprig in it. Lushmore, "tired and weary," rests beside the "moat" of the road, which Yeats is helpful enough to define in a note as not "a place with water, but a tumulus or barrow" (288). In the parallel episode, Watt, "feeling weak," "left the crown of the road and sat down on the path, which was high, and edged with thick neglected grass" (32). Resting, Lushmore hears "many voices, each mingling and blending with the other so strangely that they seemed to be one, though all singing different strains" (44). Resting, Watt, "half buried in the wild long grass, the foxgloves," hears "the voices, indifferent in quality, of a mixed choir" (33), which Beckett is helpful enough to define in a note as a threne. The round in "The Legend of Knockgrafton" evokes time with the words *"Da Luan, Da Mort, Da Luan, Da Mort, Da Luan, Da Mort"* (44), or "Monday, Tuesday," and so on. Attentive to its music, Lushmore adds *"angus Da Dardeen"* (40), or "and Wednesday too." For this addition, he is rewarded by the singers with removal of his hump. When another less attentive hunchback attempts the same, he is punished by the singers with a second hump. The threne in *Watt* evokes time with the irrational number obtained when calibrating the number of weeks in a leap year: 52.285714285714. Watt mulls the threne, without joining in, and leaves in the ditch not a hump but "his evening meal of goat's milk and insufficiently cooked cod" before proceeding to Knott's house "with confidence" (36). As an endnote to *Fairy and Folk Tales of the Irish Peasantry,* Yeats attached music for the round heard by the hunchback. As a final addendum to *Watt,* Beckett attached substantially more music for the threne heard by Watt. Beckett's score, Susan Field Senneff has shown, consists of "rhythmic variations [that] are random and end not with variation but with invention" (141). Beckett's introduction of a folkloric element from Yeats into *Watt,* then, extracts random coincidence from a preceding cautionary tale. Watt appears in Lushmore's setting and scene without purpose or result.

Watt's allusion to Joyce exercises equal irony. First identified by David Hayman, the parallel is between a brief digression in Arsene's long speech on receiving Watt at Knott's house and HCE's encounter with the cad early in *Finnegans Wake.* In Joyce's text, HCE enters Phoenix Park, "the wind billowing across the wide expanse," clad in layers of antiquated and vaguely military gear. There he meets "the cad with a pipe," who inquires the time. Producing from "his gun-pocket his Jurgensen's shrapnel waterbury" (35), HCE gives the time as noon, just after a nearby church bell has rung ten o'clock. In Beckett's text, Arsene recalls meeting a Mr. Ash on Westminster Bridge on a day when "it was blowing heavily." Mr. Ash loosens layers of heavy-weather gear, consults his "gunmetal half-hunter," and offers without being asked the time of "seventeen minutes past five exactly, as God is my witness" (45–46) instants before Big Ben strikes six o'clock.

Joyce's passage suggests intrigue, especially in suggestions of Richard Piggott, betrayer of Parnell. Beckett's passage concludes with random coincidence. Arsene says, "This is in my opinion the type of all information whatsoever. . . . This Ash was what I believe is still called an Admiralty Clerk of the Second class and with that a sterling fellow. Such vermin pullulate. He died of premature exhaustion, the following week, oiled and houselled, leaving his half-hunter to his house-plumber" (46). For Hayman, "since the *Wake* in 1945 was a closed universe to all but a tiny elite, we may read this passage as an oblique and probably reflexive homage" (381). He also reports in an interesting endnote of his own that he discussed the passages with Beckett in 1969, that Beckett denied intention, and that Beckett showed a "lively interest in the parallel." "In fact, during my relatively brief visit, he returned frequently to the subject, asking first to see the passage, then to hear it, and finally to have the page reference" (384). In all likelihood, Beckett's reaction to the parallel to the Yeats text would be the same. Both of these passages in *Watt* are brief and inconsequential episodes. If these parallels were intended as deconstruction of obscure precedents, the presence of the precedents qualifies independence of them. If these parallels were unintentional, they contribute to the representation in *Watt* of inevitable entrapment in culture, in, as Arsene says, "all the old ways." Even in construction of coincidence, then, *Watt* offers only a measure of detachment from antecedents.

The second part of *Watt* opens with equivocation: "Mr Knott was a good master, in a way" (67). The second and third parts of the novel contain a disproportionate amount of the prolonged lists and series that link *Watt* to *A Tale of a Tub*, *Tristram Shandy*, and parts of *Ulysses*. These passages of "*apparently* exhaustive enumeration," as Mood documented in his own enumeration of them, are the most manifest extremity of the narrator, Sam's, modernism. It is, as Brooke-Rose asserts, the rhetorical extreme of addressing "something utterly pointless and unimportant as if it were important, using the language we use of our big ideas and great passions" (43). Lists and series constitute the dimension of the novel that has preoccupied most American criticism of it. In *Flaubert, Joyce, and Beckett: The Stoic Comedians*, Hugh Kenner distinguishes inventories in *Watt* from inventories in *Ulysses*. "[*Watt's*] technique of inventory, very like Joyce's, is handling less and less real material . . . what Beckett is doing is subtracting from the methods of *Ulysses* all the irreducible realities of Joyce's Dublin, and so transposing the novel to a plane of empty but oddly gripping construction" (81). That transposition is the effect of the journey form of the novel, though the setting of the middle parts, certainly distant from Joyce's Dublin, brings with it irreducible realities of longer literary tenure.

After his journey from the city and before his return to it, Watt seeks "semantic succour" (83) at Mr. Knott's house and Sam the narrator offers critique in his record of that search. Watt is uninterested in reality, "For since when were Watt's concerns with what things were, in reality?" (227), and he hopes to make "a pillow of old words" (117). While Watt is sensitive to "what was acceptable to the ear, and the aesthetic judgement," Sam is "desirous above all of information" (165). Sam treats Watt's aesthetic conventionalism as a pathology and an item in evidence of that diagnosis as "a very interesting excercise" (126) or "a fascinating study" (136). The most sustained or "fascinating" of these studies are the permutations of syntax and semantics in Watt's speech, as quoted at the opening of this chapter. Sam's efforts to record them are as inconclusive as his other formulations. He acknowledges failure to record the final permutation of Watt's speech, "I recall no example of this manner," because "these were sounds that at first, though we walked glued together, were so much Irish to me." Having reached that barrier, Sam concludes, "Thus I missed I suppose much I presume of great interest touching I suspect the eighth or final stage of the second or closing period of Watt's stay in Mr Knott's house" (169).

The most protracted exercises of enumeration in *Watt* are narrative manipulations of the material of Watt's conventional, traditional, and comforting fictions. Sam's modernist version of Watt's preoccupations obscures their distinctly local elements. As a joining of the elements of Watt's desires with Sam's narrative deconstructions of them, *Watt* is an exemplary text of that measure of detachment sought by Frank O'Connor during World War II and offered as extended Irish tradition by Irish critics since. *Watt* is, of course, no wholly traditionalist work in form, style, or commentary; but its critique of rationalist epistemology is countered by a roughly proportionate critique of entrenched traditionalism. Hence, *Watt* shares that quality recognized in Knott by Watt and reported by Sam: "Here is one who seems on the one hand reluctant to change his state, and one the other impatient to do so" (86). That the converse may be equally plausible is compatible with the paralyzing equivocation fundamental to the prose of *Watt* and many of the Beckett texts that follow it in order of composition.

Watt's destination in the middle parts of the novel materializes when he sights, "with awe," "the chimneys of Mr Knott's house . . . visible at last, in the light, of the moon" (36). Such a Big House, so-called for associations more than size, is the most durable icon in Irish fiction. By various hands and at various times, the Big House serves in fiction as a provocative symbol of Irish culture, its past and its possibilites. Big House fiction is a minor local genre of continuing pertinence, from the virtual beginning of the Irish novel in Maria Edgeworth's *Castle Rackrent* (1800); through Joseph Sheridan Le Fanu's *Uncle Silas* (1864); through several novels signed E. Œ. Somerville and Martin Ross, including *The Real Charlotte* (1894) and *The Big House of Inver* (1925); as well as a number of contemporary novels, such as Aidan Higgins's *Langrishe, Go Down* (1966) and John Banville's *Birchwood* (1973). The greatest relevance of *Watt* to this local tradition is the relation of Mr. Knott's house to the various isolated and enigmatic houses that stand as the central symbols in each of these novels. Beckett was not alone in considering the Big House at the time of World War II and at some physical remove from Ireland. In 1942, Elizabeth Bowen, who maintained a degree of physical distance from Ireland comparable to Beckett's, published an essay called "The Big House" in the Irish journal *The Bell*. Bowen, of course, was a practitioner of Big House literature, especially in the novel *The Last September* (1929) and the history-autobiography *Bowen's Court* (1942). But "The Big House" essay is useful as a succinct summation of some of the emblematic qualities of the Irish Big House, one written at roughly the same time as *Watt,* and one whose fomulations are consistent with the associations of Mr. Knott's house.

The Irish Big Houses, which remain common in the countryside, in varying stages of repair, generally originated with the Anglo-Irish class in the eighteenth century, though estates and original structures may predate that. They are occasionally, but not invariably, large in scale, and sometimes in past and present they function as secondary residences or summer or country homes. The principal association of Big Houses, especially in historical retrospect, is nobility of intention. As Bowen has it, "after an era of greed, roughness and panic, after an era of camping in charred or desolate ruins (as my Cromwellian ancestors did certainly) the new settlers who had been imposed on Ireland began to wish to add something to life. The security that they had, by the eighteenth century, however ignobly gained, they did not use ignobly. They began to feel, and exert, the European idea — to seek what was humanistic, classic, and disciplined" (197). Most relevant novels embed this sort of idealism in comedy, perhaps as ingratiation with the book market and perhaps as studied modesty. The effort at comedy, however, scarcely conceals the rigidity of class boundaries in a stratified society. Somerville and Ross's *Big House of Inver* is characteristic of the genre in its cheery opening-page description of the Norman Prendeville family's establishment of an estate with a tower of improbable design erected as protection against those they "called, with soldierly arrogance, The Wild Irish — and who, in later days, should say The Gorillas" (7).

Some of the bitterness of the class humor in Big House novels is both historically inevitable and to some degree politically neutralized because the novels began to appear with the decline of the Anglo-Irish class. Big House novels generally chronicle that decline in internal profligacy and external interference, and they chart the misfortunes of the Anglo-Irish class in terms of mismanagement and usurpation by local "Gorillas" by means of liberal tax legislation, bourgeois finance, or political insurrection. But Bowen's very positive estimation of the intention of the Big House was not eccentric apologism in the twentieth century. At the height of the literary revival, John M. Synge wrote a sketch called "A Landlord's Garden in County Wicklow," after he made a visit to a demesne in the possession of relatives. "Everyone is used in Ireland to the tragedy that is bound up with the lives of farmers and fishing people; but in this garden one seemed to feel the tragedy of the landlord class also, and of the innumerable old families that are quickly dwindling away. . . . The broken greenhouses and mouse-eaten libraries, that were designed and collected by men who voted with Grattan, are perhaps as mournful in the end as the four mud walls that are so often left in Wicklow as the only remnants of a farmhouse. The desolation of this life is often of a peculiarly local kind" (230–31). As did so many people, Bowen also found the garden to be a particularly poignant and significant aspect of the decline of the Big House. So, the garden at Mr. Knott's house is introduced by Beckett as the opening of the second part of *Watt*.

> Watt had instructions to empty these slops, not in the way that slops are usually emptied, no, but in the garden, before sunrise, or after sunset, on the violet bed in violet time, and on the pansy bed in pansy time, and on the rose bed in rose time, and on the celery banks in celery time, and on the seakale pits in seakale time, and in the tomato house in tomato time, and so on, always in the garden, in the flower garden, and in the vegetable garden, and in the fruit garden, on some growing thirsty thing at the moment of its most need. (67 – 68)

The final phrase of this passage offers something of the implied idealism in the midst of comedy common to Big House novels. The passage, especially in connection with Synge and Bowen, is an indication that the "interesting exercises" in *Watt* do not always totally obscure the materials of antecedence and tradition, that the text itself refers to a presence-absence dynamic of significance for its cultural suggestions, and that the text has interest apart from its narrative and self-reflexive poetics as well.

The decline of Big Houses during the nineteenth century and especially in the early twentieth century is inarguable fact, but the import, "of a peculiarly local kind" as Synge wrote, is subject to alternative perspectives and arguments. The decline may be attributed to the fragility of a chain of isolated pockets of civilization or, alternatively, to the inevitable collapse of a fabricated and inherently contradictory culture. For Bowen, the idealism of the Big Houses is very much of the soldier, scholar, horseman sort of thing familiar from Yeats; for Bowen, "a sort of order, a reason for living, to every minute and hour. This is the order, the form of life, the tradition to which big house people still sacrifice much." To attack that order is to "impoverish life all round. . . . Well, why not *be* polite — are not humane manners the crown of being human at all? Politeness is not constriction; it is grace" ("The Big House" 199 – 200). A similar sentiment in this vein of *sprezzatura* was made by T. R. Henn in direct address to Yeats's Anglo-Irish enthusiasms. For Henn, the Big House was "beauty and stability in the midst of poverty and defeat. . . . everywhere the Big House, with its estates surrounding it, was a centre of hospitality, of country life and society, apt to heed a passionate attachment, so that the attempt to save it from burning and bankruptcy became an obsession (in the nineteen twenties and onwards) when that civilization was passing" (5, 7). Something of this position can be found in Watt's sensibility: the representation of this position in *Watt* is not entirely satirical.

The alternative critique of big house culture, one more parallel to Sam's sensibility, requires a notably more material sense of poverty and a significantly more disapproving view of nostalgia. In direct response to Henn, W. J. McCormack, in *Ascendancy and Tradition*, replies that "this is a recurrent Anglo-Irish complaint — the Golden Age always existed *before* some movable disaster, before the Union, before the Famine, before the Encumbered Estates Court, the Land War, Parnell, the Rising, the Troubles, an accelerating succession of unfortunate falls each one briefly inaugurating some (retrospectively acknowledged) idyll which is itself soon dissolved by the next disaster. Ascendancy is the principal medium by which this fleeting vision of a stable, pre-lapsarian order is imposed on the insolence of fact and circumstance" (13).

Both of these alternative conceptions of Big House culture are incorporated into *Watt*. Watt's fleeting visions of stability whet his "longing for a voice . . . to speak of the little world of Mr Knott's establishment, with the old words, the old credentials" (85), and they baffle Sam the narrator who is intent on insolent fact and circumstance. *Watt*'s representation of the issue lacks the conclusion of either Henn or McCormack. The Big House element of *Watt* has this useful quality of evoking local literary credentials of significant durability and also of comprehending the factors by which those credentials may be defined and revised.

Bowen's comments about the Irish Big House during the war years also approximate Beckett's wartime literary representation of Mr. Knott's home in *Watt*. "When I visit other big houses [other than Bowen's Court]," she wrote in "The Big House," "I *am* struck by some quality that they all have—not so much isolation as mystery" (195). Mr. Knott's house is an isolated and mysterious scene of a continuing series of phenomenological enigmas. Bowen proposes that when one approaches a Big House one "meets the faded, dark-windowed and somehow hypnotic stare of the big house" and that "their size, like their loneliness, is an effect rather than a reality" (196). Just so, Watt is baffled by Knott's house and drawn to it; he attempts entry by different locked doors, ultimately enters by the inexplicably open back-door, and remains unable to satisfy himself about how he entered, though he and Sam the narrator offer multiple possible explanations for access to a house that is indeed consistently more effect than reality. Watt's tenure in Knott's establishment is a series of such episodes, all recorded in a dialectic of Watt's satisfaction with fabricated meanings and Sam's insistence on insolent and contrary fact. "Watt could not accept them for what they perhaps were, the simple games that time plays with space, now with these toys, and now with those, but was obliged, because of his peculiar character, to enquire into what they meant, oh not into what they really meant, his character was not so peculiar as all that, but into what they might be induced to mean, with the help of a little patience, a little ingenuity" (75).

In *Bowen's Court*, written at about the same time as "The Big House," Bowen observed that "each of these houses, with its intense, centripetal life, is isolated by something very much more lasting than the physical fact of space: isolation is innate; it is an affair of origin" (14). *Watt* offers an equivalent affair of antecedence culminating in impasse, qualification, and equivocation. In that equivocation, one may by inclination find a degree of detachment linking Beckett's work with a number of prerevival Anglo-Irish precedents, or one may find a degree of political and cultural inertia contrary to the interests of any revisionism of doctrinaire revival ideology.

One of the first incidents in the second part of the novel—the appearance of the Galls, father and son—is typical of most incidents at Mr. Knott's house for inconclusive epistemological treatment and also typical of *Watt* for local subtext. The name *Gall* occurs in Beckett's earlier work: Lord Gall of Wormwood, the hale, hearty, and sterile golfer in search of a stud and an heir in the unpublished story "Echo's Bones" intended for *More Pricks Than Kicks;* and another Lord Gall, wooer with gifts of Rosie Dew in *Murphy*. In *Mercier and Camier,* Mercier calls an unfamiliar pub owner Mr. Gall, though his name is, or as part of the comic confusion of the novel appears to be, Mr. Gast. In *Watt,* the Galls come from town to Knott's country house to tune the piano. They give every indication of having fallen in economic class, a common motif in Big House fiction. They find Knott's piano, with which they are familiar, in disrepair, and they depart after offering bleak suppositions on the significance of that:

> The strings are in flitters, said the younger.
> The elder had nothing to say to this either.
> The piano is doomed, in my opinion, said the younger.
> The piano-tuner also, said the elder.
> The pianist also, said the younger.
> This was perhaps the principal incident of Watt's early days in Mr Knott's house. (72)

The following pages offer exhaustive consideration of what the Galls might have meant, of what the episode of the piano tuning might have meant, and of what changes of meaning may have occurred in the course of consideration.

In 1962, in one of the first important books on Beckett's work, *Samuel Beckett: The Comic Gamut,* Ruby Cohn, attending to formalist study of irony, offers only the connotation of bile in regard to the Galls: "could such an incident be other than bitter as gall?" (73). But *Gall* also has the local connotation of foreigner and colonist, as distinct from native and Gael, and that connotation is intact in the various reappearances of Gall as a name in Beckett's works. The whole matter of that distinction is as old as English colonization. The Gael-Gall polarity is the useful organizing principle of the first chapter of D. George Boyce's *Nationalism in Ireland*. Concerned with premodern history in that first chapter, Boyce offers a paradigm of general significance in Irish cultural history: "Ireland emerged from the middle

ages without a central unifying myth, and with the distinction between native and colonist, Gael and Gall, still strong and thriving:
cultural exchange intermarriage, temporary alliances for political convenience, modified, but could not destroy, this distinction" (43).

The conception of stranger is central to the episode of the Galls
in *Watt,* and the matter of entrenched distinctions that can be modified but never obliterated is central to all of Beckett's work. The episode of the Galls begins with the note that, "on only one occasion,
during Watt's period of service on the ground floor, was the threshold
crossed by a stranger, by other feet that is than Mr Knott's, or Er-
skine's, or Watt's, for all were strangers to Mr Knott's establishment,
as far as Watt could see, with the exception of Mr Knott himself, and
his personnel at any given moment" (70). The idea of consistent waves
of variable strangers can also be found, for example, in *The Big House
of Inver* by Somerville and Ross; and Terence Brown offers it as the core
of Bowen's commentary on the Big House: "she reflected on the isolation which she felt was a central feature of Anglo-Ireland's experience, made the more severe by the development of the Irish Free State
and the depredations of war-time, but a constant in its history" (*Ireland* 111). In *Watt,* too, this episode of "fugitive penetration" (70),
which "in a sense resembled all the incidents of note proposed to Watt
during his stay in Mr Knott's house" (72), is a constant condition subject more to various interpretations than to differing circumstances.
The local connotations of the name Gall give historicity to the episode, and the historicism offered is regularly alternating hypotheses
on a constant condition. "When one of the series of hypotheses, with
which Watt laboured to preserve his peace of mind, lost its virtue, and
had to be laid aside, and another set up in its place, then it sometimes
happened that the hypothesis in question, after a sufficient period of
rest, recovered its virtue and could be made to serve again, in the place
of another, whose usefulness had come to an end, for the time being
at least" (78). The formulation in *Watt* of alternative hypotheses in
regular alternation is one indication of a historical passivity consequent on a measured but never complete degree of detachment from
material.

In *Watt,* specifically Irish materials, including the conventions of
Big House fiction, are not always matters of local connotation or obscure allusion. In the second part of the novel, after the visit of the

Galls, an extended digression on the miserable Lynch family places the Gaels in a parallel historicism of constant conditions only interpreted, never affected, by alternative hypotheses. The entire digression is an exercise in explanation — predictably, of qualified success — rather than a record of any action in the narrative of Watt's journey. The premise is quite simple: "Watt's instructions were to give what Mr Knott left of this dish, on the days that he did not eat it all, to the dog" (91). As Mr. Knott does not wish to keep a dog, bringing together the scraps and a dog requires selection of a suitable middle party from the "immense impoverished families [who] abounded for miles around in every conceivable direction, and must have always done so" (100). The result is an elaborate construction less concerned with poverty than with obsessive detail. The ingenuity of the scheme to dispose of Knott's scraps, of the role of the Lynches, and of Watt's effort to understand a mechanism of unknown origin, all fills time at this Big House as the passing amusements of Didi and Gogo fill time in *Godot*. Filling time is not an overlay of modernism or an innovative fiction of the conventions of the Big House novel but a common motif of the genre. In her essay, "The Big House," Elizabeth Bowen gives emphasis to the tendency in Big House ambience to ennui and gratitude for preoccupations: "Ennui, that threat to life in Ireland, is kept at bay by the constant exigencies, some of them unexpected, of the house and the place" (198).

The treatment of "this fortunate family" (100), the Lynches, is further evidence that Beckett is an Irish writer—but not in the revival mode. It is a paradigm of the local, centered on "an unmistakeable specimen of local indigent proliferation" (100), and it is an exercise in a hypothesis contrary to the idealization of the Gael so fundamental to the Irish literary revival. The Lynches are Catholic, they include twins with names from Celtic mythology, Art and Con, and they attribute foul play to the "stranger from without" (109). The Lynch twins are also mentioned in *All That Fall,* an exercise of distinctly local dimensions written after *Endgame.* One ideological hypothesis on such a family, the hypothesis of the revival, was of limitless potential. One widely cited suggestion of that potential is young Padraig Pearse's declaration to a university debating society, "The Gael is not like other men; the spade, and the loom, and the sword are not for him. But a destiny more glorious than that of Rome, more glorious than that of

Britain awaits him: to become the saviour of idealism in modern intellectual and social life, the regenerator and rejuvenator of the literature of the world, the instructor of nations, the preacher of the.gospel
of nature-worship, God-worship — such, Mr. Chairman, is the destiny of the Gael" (221). Such declarations help account, of course, for
the observation in *More Pricks Than Kicks* that Pearse Street is pleasant
despite its name. Of these Gaels, for Pearse awaiting almost unimaginably glorious destiny, Beckett offers a rather different account.

> There was Tom Lynch, widower, aged eighty-five years, confined to
> his bed with constant undiagnosed pains in the caecum, and his three
> surviving boys Joe, aged sixty-five years, a rheumatic cripple, and
> Jim, aged sixty-four years, a hunchbacked inebriate, and Bill, wid
> ower, aged sixty-three years, greatly hampered in his movements by
> the loss of both legs as the result of a slip, followed by a fall, and his
> only surviving daughter May Sharpe, widow, aged sixty-two years, in
> full possession of all her faculties with the exception of that of vision.
> Then there was Joe's wife née Doyly-Byrne, aged sixty-five years, a suf
> ferer from Parkinson's palsy but otherwise very fit and well, and Jim's
> wife Kate née Sharpe aged sixty-four years, covered all over with run
> ning sores of an unidentified nature but otherwise fit and well. (101)

And so on through "five generations, twenty-eight souls, nine
hundred and eighty years" (103) of a family less interested in their destiny than in having the sum of their ages equal precisely one thousand.
Beckett neutralizes suggestions of abject misery and class poverty
with the irony of footnotes, including that oft-cited note, "Haemophilia is, like enlargement of the prostate, an exclusively male disorder. But not in this work" (102). In a similar fashion, Big House
novels, particularly in the nineteenth century, neutralized the element
of exploitation with the begosh-and begorra humor of stage Irishman
caricature. Such neutralization of political import is one likely effect
of that distance from material linking Beckett to prerevival Irish
writers.

The paradigm extracted from local sources in this digression on
the Lynches is one of inert conditions brightened only by the play with
preoccupations familiar in less local representation in *Godot* and in the
works that followed it. In *Watt,* "this little matter of the food and the
dog, Watt pieced it together from the remarks let fall, every now and

then, in the evening, by the twin dwarfs Art and Con. For it was they who led the famished dog, every evening, to the door. They had done this since the age of twelve, that is to say for the past quarter of a century. . . . it was still Art and Con who led the dog, every evening, at nine o'clock, to Mr Knott's backdoor, even when Watt was no longer there to witness it, for they were sturdy little fellows, and wrapped up in their work" (111). They continue to do so through the lives of six dogs, and the entire condition remains one consistent from "that far distant past, when Mr Knott set up his establishment" (93). The condition could be construed in the terms of potential like those of Pearse or others utterly devoted to the needs of the revival, or it could be construed in terms of nostalgia for a rather more rigid, or "polite," social structure like that endemic to nineteenth-century Big House fiction.

Comprehending at a later date both historical constructions, *Watt,* as it had in the Galls episode, offers as outcome of dilemma only an aesthetic arrangement of light and shape. Having understood the "mechanism of this arrangement," and having secured "a comparative peace of mind," Watt loses interest in the entire problem. "Kate [the dog] eating from her dish, for example, with the dwarfs standing by, how he [Watt] had laboured to know what that was, to know which the doer, and what the doer, and what the doing, and which the sufferer, and what the sufferer, and what the suffering, and what those shapes, that were not rooted to the ground, like veronica, but melted away, into the dark, after a while" (117). Such is Watt's desire, however qualified by Sam's narration of it. Watt yearns for a satisfactorily ordered retrospect, and Sam dismantles the hypotheses of such a construction. Fully cognizant of the difference between these methodologies, and fundamentally focused on the matter of history and ideology, on phenomena "not rooted to the ground," *Watt* offers as synthesis a passive aesthetic formalism that is itself relative, "a *comparative* peace of mind."

Having indicated the conditions of the Galls and of the Gaels, *Watt* must as a matter of comprehensiveness indicate the condition of that hypenated intermediary group central to Big House fiction, the Anglo-Irish. In the second part of *Watt,* the digression on the Lynch family satirized Gaelicism and the anticolonialist ideology; in the third part of *Watt,* the digression on Ernest Louit and his specimen, Nackybal, satirizes the Anglo-Irish and colonialism. The digression stems from the discussion by Mr. Graves, the gardener, of Bando, the sexual aid banned by the State. To clarify the significance of that embargo, Mr. Graves offers the tale of Louit, faithful school friend who is unappreciated in Ireland and is presumably free of a papal embargo on sex-related goods. So, Louit is both forced and able to support himself by running Bando. All of this suggests the feelings of undeserved antagonism and displacement likely among the Anglo-Irish citizenry of an Irish Free State enacting distinctly Catholic and Gaelic legislation, such as bans on contraceptives. Modern Ireland may be best-known for Gaelic enthusiasm, particularly in revival drama, but there has been a consistent alternative fatigue and digust with Gaelicism. In his social and cultural history of Ireland, Terence Brown notes this anti-Gaelicism in a chapter devoted to "The Fate of Minorities" and cites as instance John Pentland Mahaffy's sentiments in 1929.

> The Gael was a rung on the ladder, a rung which has long been over-stepped. The modern movement in the new political entity—the Irish Free State—the modern movement backward towards this Gaelic Hey-Day is pathetic; or if you wish it is comic; certainly it is useless. . . . any such retrograde movement as an attempt at the compulsory revival of a dead language only becomes a local racial injury. . . . There is not a thought in me that does not want well-being for the land of my birth; yet there is no room today in their own land for thousands of Irishmen of similar views. (Brown 117)

The episode of Ernest Louit in *Watt* is satire of the Gaelic heyday and the overstepping of a useful rung while establishing a cultural identity. It might be read in itself as an instance of local racial injury, but that reading would require ignorance of the preceding satires of other parties to the Free State on its way to becoming a Republic. It differs from Mahaffy's sentiment in that it represents the Anglo-Irish as the instigators of the Gaelic heyday rather than the victims of it, a possibility common in reflection on the literary idealization of a mostly fictional "Kiltartan" peasantry by, in particular, Yeats, Lady Gregory, and Synge. At its moment, after the death of the last of those figures and the end of the literary revival they represented, *Watt* specifically and quite plausibly satirizes idealization of the peasantry as a matter of pragmatics by TCD academics with limited enthusiasm or comprehension of their job. Brown also notes that TCD was, especially in the 1930s, dilapidated, lethargic, generally ignored, and wholly congruent with that other decaying institution in *Watt:* the Big House. "Indeed, the college in the centre of Dublin wore in its isolation and decline a striking resemblance in social terms to the Big Houses of the countryside — each symbolizing a ruling caste in the aftermath of its power" (116). As much as power may be manifested in terms other than the current legislative hegemony, *Watt* would have us see the situation in terms of inadequately compelling fictions, or, as Boyce has it, lack of central unifying myths.

A further example of those fictions in *Watt* is the story of Louit in the isolated and declining college. The episode is framed by reference to Mr. Knott's house. As Arthur, a domestic like Watt, tells the story to Mr. Graves, the gardener, "the great mass of the empty house was hard by" (169). The premise is that Ernest Louit, in research for a dissertation called *The Mathematical Intuitions of the Visicelts,* obtains from the college a small travel grant for transportation, supplies, colored beads, and gratuities required for an expedition with his dog, O'Connor, into the Burren in County Clare. On return, having lost his manuscript in a railway station, like Wilde's Miss Prism, he instead offers to the board members who are responsible for examining his use of the grant a pure peasant Celt, Thomas Nackybal, innocence intact, untouched by the modern world. "That, replied Louit, is the bold claim I make for my friend, in whose mind, save for the pale music of the innocence you mention, and, in some corner of the cerebellum, where all agricultural ideation has its seat, dumbly flickering, the knowledge of how to extract, from the ancestral half-acre of moraine, the maximum of nourishment, for himself and his pig, with the minimum of labour, all, I am convinced, is an ecstasy of darkness, and of silence" (174 – 75). The specimen, though dressed in the well-known fraudulent "invented tradition," the Irish kilt, delights the intellectually barren and fastidiously bureaucratic examiners named O'Meldon, Magershon, Fitzwein, de Baker, and MacStern. With their mad logic, the text of the Louit digression digresses even further in apparently exhaustive exercises in enumeration, including committee table maneuvers, punctilious pleasantries, and artithmetic operations. This last, of course, because here the genius of Thomas Nackybal, protected by profound ignorance, West Clare's isolation, and the Celt's vaunted impermeability, is intuitive calibration in seconds of the cube roots of numbers of six figures. Though receptive to the premise of *The Mathematical Intutition of the Visicelts,* the board proceeds to examine Nackybal apart from Louit, or, in a local version of the Clever Hans syndrome of performing animals, the pure Celt apart from his handler. "The precautions recommended by Louit were adopted, except that Louit was not sent out of the room, but posted with his back to it before the open window, and that Mr Nackybal was permitted to retain many of his underclothes. From this severe trial Mr Nackybal emerged with distinction, having in his cubing made only twenty-five slight mistakes out of the forty-six cubes demanded, and in his rooting, out of the fifty-three extractions propounded, committed a mere matter of four trifling errors!" (189–90).

The matter of mathematics and the cube root of 389,057 ("Sivinty-thray" [186]) is a convenient problem, treated with arithmetic proof by some Beckett commentators. But in *Watt,* the Louit digression is also a satirical superstructure on a problematical cultural base. *Watt* represents the Anglo-Irish interest in Celticism as a passing amusement bereft of the element of social reform at least ostensible in idealization of the peasantry. Further, it represents the Anglo-Irish and Gaelic-Catholic classes in the Irish Free State as comparable in their vacuous preoccupations — the mathematics of the academic board and the mathematics of the Lynch family's sum total age. Last, it represents the state of things in what Mahaffy called "the new political entity" as a matter of uninterrupted and irreversible decline. In the epilogue, it is revealed that Louit could succeed in the Irish Free State only by running Bando and that the true Celt Nackybal was a fraud: "his real name was Tisler and he lived in a room on the canal" (198). The digression is suspended rather than concluded. "Arthur seemed to tire, of his story, for he left Mr Graves, and went back, into the house" (197). Before he does so, the story adverts to the matter of light commenting bodies. The board of examiners, Louit, and Nackybal, in a room suggestive of TCD, all "to those shimmering windows turned them round, to the sky dark grey below, and lighter grey above. For the night seemed less to fall, than to rise, from below, like another day" (195). As in the episodes of the Galls and of the Lynches, the tale of Louit ends with Watt's withdrawal to a reassuring nostalgia, in this case specifically the Big House: "to Mr Knott's house, to its mysteries, to its fixity" (199).

Watt's attraction to the house is compatible with Elizabeth Bowen's emphasis on the utility of the mystery, the spell, and the tradition of the Irish Big House. *Watt's* confidence in certainties is qualified only by the miscellaneous and problematic addenda attached to the end of the novel as back matter. The last part of *Watt* concludes with middle-class Irish characters in the recognizable setting of the Foxrock Station, all secure in their preestablished hypotheses, in antecedence, just as the first part of *Watt* opened with equivalent certainties of Hackett and the Nixons at the other end of the rail line, Harcourt Street Station. The parallel is made complete by the reappearance at the end of the novel of Lady McCann: "a lady who daily left the neighbourhood by the first train in the morning, and returned to it by the last at night. Her reasons for doing this were not known. On Sundays she remained in bed, receiving there the mass, and other meals and visitors" (240). Through the middle parts of the novel exposed the problematic dimensions of assured certainties, the conclusion of the novel, minus the addenda, leaves unexamined the satisfying assumptions of Lady McCann and the railroad station hands. Significant among these is Mr. Case's attachment to AE. "To while away the time, and at the same time to improve his mind, Mr Case was reading a book: *Songs by the Way,* by George Russell (A.E.). Mr Case, his head flung back, held this book out at arm's length. Mr Case had a very superior taste in books, for a signal-man" (228).

Homeward: Songs by the Way, though largely theosophical, was an early (1894) contribution by AE to a burgeoning literary revival bent on defining and establishing a unity of local culture. That optimism is a final hypothesis layered over a novel whose local contexts focus on the decay of the Galls, the Gaelic Lynches, and the Anglo-Irish examiners of Louit, all without imminent heirs. AE's reader, Mr. Case, like Miss Carridge the reader of AE's *Candle of Vision* in *Murphy,* cannot be supposed to adopt AE's sentiments as any more than a convenience. His "very superior" fashioning of identity in reference to AE suits his immediate circumstances for its suggestion of compelling fiction in easily domesticated import, all circumstances established in *Watt* as likely to change in detail and so necessitating a refashioning and revision of identity. The conclusion of the novel proper, including the allusion to AE's affirmation and the hopeful orderly management of the station, is ironic in the context of earlier protracted examinations of Watt's variously improvised moments of "comparative peace of mind." The final episode at the station is an exercise in filling time and maintaining useful certainties. It might be called Waiting for the Train. Its final passage is, like the final assertion of *Waiting for Godot,* ironic because of all that came before. "And so they stayed a little while, Mr Case and Mr Nolan looking at Mr Gorman, and Mr Gorman looking straight before him, at nothing in particular, though the sky falling to the hills, and the hills falling to the plain, made as pretty a picture, in the early morning light, as a man could hope to meet with, in a day's march" (246).

The first part of *Watt* also ends with a sunrise, with "the unspoiled light of the new day, of the new day at last, the day without precedent at last" (64). The novel contradicts without ever entirely dismissing possibilities of hope and originality in its exhaustive, though inconclusive, examination of the flaws, contexts, and revisions inherent in any hypothesis. The novel is capable of dismantling the axioms, literary and social, of conventional Big House fiction, but its critique remains about Big House fiction and not about any unprecedented possibility. The operative paradigm in *Watt,* in immediate reference to the succession of Knott's servants but of broader relevance, is that "in this long chain of consistence, a chain stretching from the long dead to the far unborn, the notion of the arbitrary could only survive as the notion of a pre-established arbitrary" (134). *Watt* is a particularly strong demonstration of that characteristic common to all of Beckett's work, first noted by Beckett in *Proust* and cited at the opening of this chapter: the paradigm of "perpetual adjustment and readjustment of our organic sensibility to the condition of its worlds" and of an "endless series of renovations."

This reading of the novel is a matter of significant interst not only in regard to *Watt* but also in regard to Beckett's later works and to the current placement of those works in Irish culture. *Watt,* which has as its final line the signature "Paris, 1945," was followed by a time Beckett is known to have described as "the siege in the room" (Bair 346). It included composition of the stories, poems, and plays through the early 1950s that had the most formative influence on the perception of the Beckett *oeuvre.* The room was in Paris, though the notion of enclosed siege and the writer's contemplation of a Foxrock signalman's reading of AE while in Roussillon during World War II suggest how insulated an endless renovation may be from immediate physical location. Beckett's best-known works are adjustments and renovations of terms already in place in *Watt*.

However, the demonstration in *Watt* of intractability cast in specifically Irish terms also indicates the problems of incorporating Beckett into the Irish literary canon as deviser of new discourses without precedent and corrector of inherited provincialisms. The existence of that ongoing incorporation has already been described in reference to *More Pricks Than Kicks*. But it may be worth observing here that the process extends beyond academic bounds to such items as the official 1988 Dublin Millennium commemorative hot-cast bronze triple-headed bust of Yeats, Joyce, and Beckett joined at the mahogany base and advertised as a symbol of a "magnificent tradition," as well as a "magnificent corporate or personal presentation." The Yeats-Joyce-Beckett linkage is at least somewhat more complicated for those writing about Irish literature and its implications in the advanced state of sectarian violence contemporary with that resolutely jolly Dublin Millennium celebration of the departure of the Vikings. The matter is taken up by Richard Kearney, for example, in *Transitions,* as Yeats constructing a dialectic, Joyce deconstructing that dialectic by exposing superseding complexities of language, and Beckett in linear progress replacing the bankrupt "self-sufficient author of a single discourse with the self-differentiating author of a plurality of discourses" (65).

Even granting that Beckett's work may offer a plurality of discourses, my reading of Beckett's work (*Watt* in particular) differs from that of Kearney in finding instead an intractable dialectic and an endless renovation of the same problem of precedence and liberation from it. The matter is also taken up by Seamus Deane in the Field Day Theatre Company pamphlet *Heroic Styles,* mentioned briefly before in reference to *Murphy*. There Deane organizes the three as the Yeats of essential Irishness and mystique of nationalist stereotypes, the Joyce of modernism at play revising an ample supply of anachronisms, and the Beckett in lockstep march with that part of Joyce that makes a "fetish of exile, alienation, and dislocation." The end that Deane imagines is liberation by obsolescence, that is, "Everything, including our politics and our literature, has to be rewritten—i.e. re-read. That will enable new writing, new politics, unblemished by Irishness, but securely Irish" (18). In my study, examination of Beckett's work suggests instead a persistence of antecedents rather than a blush of newness. As already noted, Denis Donoghue had his "Afterword" to Deane in the British edition of a collection of Field Day pamphlets. Thomas Flanagan has his "Afterword" to Deane in the American edition of the collection. Like Donoghue, Flanagan found the crux of disagreement with all Field Day writers in Deane's *Heroic Styles*. Flanagan is resigned to an "old-fashioned, unregenerate suspicion that essentialism is a permanent mode of mental being" (116), though he allows that there is reason to read Field Day writers, including Deane, because they "are Irish writers debating, without provincialism, the condition and the future of their culture and their country. It is our good fortune that we can overhear what they say, because the debate extends, by implication, well beyond Ireland. They are talking, ultimately, about the place of the imagination in a world like ours" (117).

One of the most interesting, though potentially discouraging, dimensions of this debate is that Samuel Beckett entered it in 1945, when the pertinent issues, on examination, prove roughly congruent with those we may overhear nearly fifty years later. In 1945, Beckett, who was leaving Ireland, reviewed a polemical monograph by Thomas MacGreevy, who was returning to Ireland, about Jack Yeats, who was a fixture at home. On 4 August 1945, upon completion of *Watt* and the end of that war known in neutral Ireland as "the emergency," Beckett's review of MacGreevy's *Jack B. Yeats: An Appreciation and an Interpretation* appeared in the *Irish Times* under the title "MacGreevy on Yeats." MacGreevy was repatriating himself, settling in Dublin after years as expatriate poet and factotum to Joyce, entertaining Dubliners with stories of his salad days in cosmopolis, and currying the connections that would bring him the directorship of the National Gallery in 1950. Jack Yeats had joined the Victor Waddington Galleries in Dublin in 1940, and the publication of MacGreevy's book by Waddington coincided with Yeats' National Loan Exhibit at the National College of Art (McHugh 108).

That moment in some respects resembles the present. *Field Day, Crane Bag,* and *The Irish Review* have been arguing for a relinquishment of essentialist national identity and stereotypical Irish mystique — Deane's is just a single example of that argument. Around 1945, as Brian O'Doherty has observed in direct reference to Jack Yeats,

Irish republicanism was devitalized, resulting in disillusionment with the inherited mythologies of essentialism and Irish mystique: "Part of the disillusionment of the forties and fifties was that the bougeoise discovered that they weren't witty and poetic and marvellous at all. Nationhood proved that national image superfluous, and thus, in the rigorous law of Irish assimilation, it was made essential, but on a very different basis" (86). Part of that difference was an attempt to accommodate the obvious dislocation between proud, hair-in-the-wind Sons of Usna and the realities of middle-class culture in place in Dublin and evident in the provinces. Part of that different basis, also, was the attempt to supersede a restrictive local dialectic. That attempt is as central to MacGreevy's book as it is to the criticism of Kearney and Deane.

MacGreevy's monograph was written in circumstances very like those of *Watt:* composition outside Ireland and delayed publication. As MacGreevy explains in an introductory note, and Beckett reiterates in his review, *Jack B. Yeats* was "undertaken in the first instance as an act of hommage to a great artist and a great Irishman. . . . however, not at home where I think best, but in London." Beckett, of course, in 1954 would use the title *"Hommage à Jack B. Yeats"* for his own appreciation of the artist. MacGreevy drew an opening distinction between the "English mind," which he termed "secularist," and the "Irish mind," which he characterized only as "not secularist" (3). It is of some interest that Richard Kearney used the title *The Irish Mind* for an influential collection published in 1985. MacGreevy's distinction, even though it was offered as an explanation of London publishers' lack of interest in the monograph, is consistent with the cultural nationalism defined during the Irish literary revival. Further, MacGreevy argues that Jack Yeats paints "the Ireland that matters" (5, 33) with the same incantatory insistence that Daniel Corkery deployed the phrase "the Ireland that counts" in *Synge and Anglo-Irish Literature.* Like Corkery, MacGreevy spun what matters out of historical evidence. He offers a thumbnail sketch of nationalistic coercion in the 1880s, the fall of Parnell, and the loss of political romanticism as fundamental influences on Yeats. These influences had the effect, in MacGreevy's words, that Yeats "so identified himself with the people of Ireland as to be able to give good and beautiful and artistic expression to the life they lived, and to that sense of themselves as the Irish nation" (10).

Beckett's review disapproves of that sort of thing, yet neither does it approve of the idea of liberating pluralities. His gesture toward personal friendship took the form of praise of MacGreevy's work as an "affirmation of capital importance, not only for those who feel in this way about Mr Yeats, or for those who as yet feel little or nothing about Mr Yeats, but also for those, such as myself, who feel in quite a different way about Mr Yeats" (*Disjecta* 96). Of all possible citations from MacGreevy, Beckett chose for single, extended quotation just that passage about the people of Ireland, the life they lived, and their sense of themselves as the Irish nation. In demurral, Beckett states, "the national aspects of Mr Yeats's genius have, I think, been over-stated, and for motives not always remarkable for their aesthetic purity" (96). Instead, Beckett plumps for Yeats the painter of "the issueless predicament of existence . . . these [Yeats's] are characteristic notations having reference, I imagine, to processes less simple, and less delicious, than those to which the plastic *vis* is commonly reduced, and to a world where Tir-na-nOgue makes no more sense than Bachelor's Walk, nor Helen than the apple-woman, nor asses than men, nor Abel's blood than Useful's, nor morning than night, nor inward than the outward search" (97). This is a reiteration of the aesthetic outcome of *Watt:* representation of intractable hypotheses in regular adjustment and endless renovation. The continuity of argument from Corkery to MacGreevy to Kearney and Deane lends some credibility to that representation. Cast in terms immediately referable to Yeats's paintings, that formulation by Beckett also reconstitutes the larger antinomies of the literary revival: Celticism and realism; the power of compelling myth like Tir-na-nOgue and of political exigency like the shooting of patriots on Bachelor's Walk in 1914; the collateral literary representations of Ireland by W. B. Yeats and Joyce. The formulation may appear to be synthesis extracted from dialectic, but like *Watt,* it is, rather, evidence of both dissatisfaction with restrictive orders and inability to extract an acceptable, viable outcome from them.

It is especially significant that Beckett's review states this impasse so hard upon "the siege in the room," which, as I argue in the following chapter, produced work that extricated itself from that impasse in no more than form. "MacGreevy on Yeats" is also illuminating for what Beckett the reviewer chose to ignore in MacGreevy's book. In fact, *Jack B. Yeats* is more sophisticated than Beckett suggested and "less simple, and less delicious" than he allowed. The real core of MacGreevy's argument is a prognostic, an appreciation of Jack Yeats as a transitional figure, from political romanticism to a promised land of cultural nationalism — toward, that is, what Seamus Deane proposes as "new writing, new politics, unblemished by Irishness, but securely Irish." For MacGreevy, in his immediate time frame, the watershed is the end of the civil war.

> The Civil War ended in 1923.
> Since then, the sensitive minds that first reveal the direction in which a society is moving have shown two of the major tendencies that, in more settled countries than Ireland, were already identifiable and distinguishable one from the other. The first tendency is to use such liberty as has been achieved to attain to greater abundance of individual life, a subjective tendency. The second is to insist on the need for a definitive solution of Ireland's political and, more particularly, social problems which is a more objective tendency. (26)

With little adjustment, these two tendencies offer in brief the poles addressed at different times by Beckett and by the later Irish critics of their own culture cited here. The subject-object rupture is familiar from Beckett's work, most explicitly so in criticism, from the 1930s on. That tendency, "subjective," to freedom of formulations and to freedom from antecedents, in collision with that tendency, "objective," of precedence, context, and entrapment are central in Beckett's work from *Watt* on, though without the utile connotations of MacGreevy's formulation. They are central, too, to Frank O'Connor's problem in his 1942 programmatic essay "The Future of Irish Literature" with its theory of Irish writers' domination by material or distance from it. For MacGreevy, who without hesitation lauded Jack Yeats for his subjective tendency, "that Jack Yeats's work shows something of the subjective tendency should simply mean that he remains as Irish as ever, but as a mature man and artist, in a new Ireland realizing itself with less interference from outside" (28). MacGreevy, like the Irish cultural critics of the 1980s, was exacerbated by Ulster. The historical difference between MacGreevy's sentiment and those more recent ones is no more than alternative locations of origins of interference: in the 1940s, outside; in the 1980s, inside. Because the position and the debate are otherwise consistent across many years, there is some real pertinence now to Brian O'Doherty's dismissal of the MacGreevy of old as a "defrocked courtier lost in his own dream of Ireland" (80). There is also some interest in Thomas Flanagan's observation that we are fortunate to be able to overhear the debate. However, our fortune on rehearing the whole recurring debate, with its consistent conception of imminent liberation from inherited, restrictive formulations, may seem more bad than good. *Watt* reminds us of that possibility.

5

MAJOR FICTION AND DRAMA

MRS. ROONEY: It is suicide to be abroad. But what is it to
be at home, Mr. Tyler, what is it to be at home? A lingering dissolution.

— *All That Fall*

AN OBVIOUS CHARACTERISTIC of Samuel Beckett's major works — especially that series of works written in French in the late 1940s and
early 1950s — is the relative absence of references specific to Ireland
or, for that matter, to any particular locality. Beckett's *oeuvre* could be
organized by its systematic, generally chronological elimination of
known Irish landmarks, stereotypical characters, chestnuts of Irish
wit, and other clichés of literary production intended to be known as
unmistakably Irish, whether in general approval or disapproval of local culture. One essential characteristic of Beckett's major work is lack
of local specifications, identifications, and mannerisms. Vivian Mercier has noted this quality several times, most interestingly for a degree of personal identification in 1955 in "Savage Humor." "In
assimilating French language and culture, Beckett has not himself
become assimilated — an extraordinary achievement for an Anglo-
Irishman" (20). For others, such a quality leads logically enough to
the Beckett of minimalism, of the psychology of an unaccommodated
man, and of obliteration of accommodating literary convention.

Ample evidence from Beckett's works and helpful marginalia, in
conjunction with a phase of literary criticism intent on the interior of
the text, all led critical discourse on Beckett's works quite reasonably
to the literary representation of nothing. This emphasis served a number of admirable functions, academic and journalistic, and there have

143

been exceptions to this critical direction. But since the 1950s, literary criticism of Beckett's proximity to a metaphysical void, which treats the matter as if he were in the void instead of on the verge of it, has by reiteration become a rather exclusive reading. The gist of it had already been presented by 1952, when Richard Seaver introduced Beckett to English readers in advance of translations of "the French period." Then Seaver, complete with allusion to Democritus, still a stalwart of Beckett criticism, offered as conclusion, "The inevitable question remains to be asked, What does Mr. Beckett's work mean? The meaning, if there must be one, is perhaps latent in the lack of meaning. 'Nothing is more real than nothing,' says Malone" (79). This sort of speculation was prevalent enough to reappear a decade later as a matter of irony in *Happy Days:*

> Well anyway—this man Shower—or Cooker—no matter—and the woman—hand in hand—in other hands bags—kind of big brown grips—standing there gaping at me—and at last this man Shower—or Cooker—ends in er anyway—stake my life on that—What's she doing? he says—What's the idea? he says—stuck up to her diddies in the bleeding ground—coarse fellow—What does it mean? he says—What's it meant to mean?—and so on—lot more stuff like that—usual drivel—Do you hear me? he says—I do, she says, God help me—What do you mean, he says, God help you? (42–43)

About the time he finished *Watt* and began "the siege in the room," Beckett offered to Irish listeners of Radio Erin an address provocative in regard to the multiple attractions of the assimilated, the unassimilated, nothingness, and meaning. One 10 June 1946, Radio Erin broadcast a Beckett address, "The Capital of the Ruins" (McMillan 67–76), not published until forty years later. The occasion was a personal report on the Irish Red Cross installation at Saint-Lô, where Beckett served for about six months beginning in August 1945. The title was taken from a collection of photographs of Saint-Lô before and after the bombardment in June 1944. Beckett's radio address is moving in its description of ruins, a favorite image in the major works he was about to compose. The text was also a rebuttal to Dublin-based reports that Ireland's own volunteer efforts were underappreciated by the French. "These [Dubliners] are the sensible people who would rather have news of the Norman's semi-circular canals or resistance to sulphur than of his attitude to the Irish bringing gifts, who would prefer the history of our difficulties with an unfamiliar pharmacopia and system of mensuration to the story of our dealings with the rare and famous ways of spirit that are the French ways" (McMillan 74). As that passage suggests, the Beckett persona of the radio address was perceptive of the attractions of assimilation. "Many of us had never been abroad before," Beckett somewhat self-depreciatingly told the listeners of Radio Erin, and "some of those who were in Saint-Lô will come home realizing that they got at least as good as they gave" (75). The most explicit point in the address was that the Irish Red Cross facilities were adequate, "though painstaking anonymous attempts were made, in this country [Ireland], as recently I think as last winter, to prove the contrary" (73). The more generally provocative point was that the experience gave "a vision and sense of a time-honoured conception of humanity in ruins, and perhaps even an inkling of the terms in which our condition is to be thought again" (75 – 76). This statement leads to a quality fundamental to Beckett's major fiction and drama: a conception of humanism in opposition to a conception of relative conditions. That essential opposition, almost as a fillip, may lead, as Beckett suggests, to a rethinking of one, "our" (i.e., Irish) condition.

It is generally agreed that a primary power of Beckett's texts is their dynamic of constructing order and deconstructing it. Criticism is often drawn to Beckett's work for just this dynamic. For example, Wayne C. Booth, in *A Rhetoric of Fiction* argues a conservative thesis of the text in reference to Beckett: "Good literature can be produced based on radically limited and even downright erroneous views. The harm is done only when readers take the literature for philosophy and think that Beckett's marvelously funny and moving portraits of despair add real evidence to the case for nihilism, forgetting that the evidence before them paradoxically undermines its own claims" (262). Similarly, Wolfgang Iser, in *The Implied Reader: Patterns of Communication in Prose Fiction from Bunyan to Beckett,* finds Beckett's work an interesting example of antitheses left to be completed by the reader and so in its paradoxes and reflexive ironies useful evidence for his own more progressivist thesis on reading. Of *Molloy, Malone Dies,* and *The Unnamable,* Iser argues, "they resolutely resist all attempts at total comprehension, for this is the only way in which they can break down the barrier to the reader's contemplation of his own ideas. . . . If Beckett's novels stimulate us with reconsidering our own perceptions, then their intention can hardly be merely to represent the decadence of contemporary society" (177). Both otherwise contrary apologies for Beckett's alleged nihilism, then, ascribe the power of Beckett's texts to an oscillation of thesis and antithesis and attribute its positivism to the contribution of a reader. Both, too, imply that an effect of that dialectical rhetoric in Beckett's texts is a capacity for renewal, for reinterpretation, as in their own rebuttals to one period's widely circulating impressions of Beckett as prince of darkness and despair.

Criticism specific to Beckett has also been consistent on the presence of a dynamic of contraries and oppositions in his work. David H. Hesla's *Shape of Chaos: An Interpretation of the Art of Samuel Beckett* was an early and influential account of Beckett's major fiction and drama. Hesla argued that Beckett's "art is a Democritean art, energized precisely by the dialectical interplay of opposites—body and mind, the self and the other, speech and silence, life and death, hope and despair, being and non-being, yes and no" (10 – 11), and he concluded that "the shape of Beckett's mature art is the shape given it by the dialectic of action and reaction" (221). Much the same focus continues through later criticism on later examples of Beckett's work. Kateryna Arthur, for example, asserts in the 1980s about a 1980s Beckett work that "Beckett's novella *Company* exhibits more strikingly than any other of his later works a double impulse—towards order and coherence on the one hand and towards chaos and indeterminancy on the other. Associated with these poles are other antithetical positions between which the work moves" (136). At an early stage, Beckett criticism explicated even this focus of antitheses through source texts of the Great Books sort (Descartes, Augustine, Kierkegaard, etc.) and through close reading of internal imagery; both methods took on the aura of infallibility as exercised with prolixity increasing in direct proportion to the diminishing length of each new Beckett text. Of late, Beckett criticism more often contextualizes the work in a broader range of informing references: Arthur's application of a theory of schizophrenia from Deleuze and Guattari's *Anti-Oedipus* to *Company* is a representative example.

All of these—antithesis, reinterpretation, contextualization— legitimize the notion of the Irish Beckett. There is some encouragement in such reference to Ireland as exists in Beckett criticism when placed beside emphasis on dialectic. Lawrence Harvey's seminal biographical account, *Samuel Beckett: Poet and Critic,* suggested inclusion of the sense of place in the dialectical character of Beckett's early work: "Caught between the two impossibilities of domestication and exile and unfailing in filial devotion, he found return and departure almost equally painful — and equally desirable — alternatives" (67). In an early journalistic treatment of *The Unnamable,* Stephen Spender took the dialectic to be in itself specifically referable to modern Irish literature. "Samuel Beckett's theme," Spender wrote in 1958, "is the very Irish one in this century: the identity of opposites, a theme with which Yeats made so much play in his idea of 'Antinomes' [*sic*], and which is implicit in Joyce, where the subjective view of the world merges into its opposites, the objective and universal" (5). Later, in 1971, Marilyn Gaddis Rose updated that suggestion in a brief, selective illustration, "The Irish Memories of Beckett's Voice": "Beckett's fundamental antinomy, the systematic annihilation and reconstruction of self and its concomitants space, time, and matter, increases in comprehensiveness and import from *Murphy* through *How It Is*" (128). In 1977, Vivien Mercier constructed his book on Beckett around such antinomies, and the first of all dialectical formulations in *Beckett/Beckett* is "Ireland/The World." At this still later point in Beckett's publications, when the direction of *How It Is* or *Lessness* has been readjusted to that of *. . . but the clouds . . .* or *Company,* the presence in Beckett's work of a dialectic of self and place and the antinomies of home and abroad are considerably more evident. That operative word, *antinomies,* is Beckett's, too. In "The Calmative," collected in *Stories and Texts for Nothing,* the narrator speculates on the empirical differences between night and day and the likelihood of intervening subjectivity: "It is not my wish to labour these antinomies, for we are needless to say in a skull, but I have no choice but to add the following few remarks" (38). "The Calmative" was written in late 1946 (Bair 359), after *Watt* and "The Capital of the Ruins" radio address and immediately before *Molloy.*

Literary antinomies, obviously, have been an organizing principle in the preceding chapters on Beckett's early work. The great relevance of that early work to Beckett's more influential novels and plays is its indication of antitheses and antinomies as a fundamental element in Beckett's narrative and dramatic rhetorics and the origin of those antinomies in specifically Irish oppositions that are not exclusively philosophical or solely aesthetic. The antinomies of local social alternatives in *More Pricks Than Kicks,* local literary mythologies in *Murphy,* and local historical hypotheses in *Watt* are all subsumed in the trilogy of novels and in *Godot* and *Endgame* in the antinomies of being at home and of being abroad. In these three novels and two plays, one finds the preoccupations of Beckett's early works abstracted into a dynamics of home and away, provincialism and humanism, culture and self, and other antinomies. These are not the only significant dimensions of Beckett's major work, but they are a significant dimension of it. The idea of place in Beckett's work can be observed in transformation from the specific to the abstract in *Mercier and Camier.* The presence of a dynamics of home and away from home can be seen Beckett's trilogy of novels and first published plays. These texts are notable and representative examples of the dynamics of place that informs all of Beckett's *oeuvre.*

Awareness of the presence of Ireland or the representation of local concerns in Beckett's major works alters them, however slightly. Also, of course, that presence of Ireland or the representation of home in Beckett's major works has its importance in reference to Irish literature, Irish culture, and the ways that they are formulated and reformulated. As I discussed in earlier chapters, Beckett's works have the usefulness of anticipating and complicating cultural debate in Ireland. In 1988, Edna Longley, as part of a debate largely focused on the notion of an Irish Louis MacNeice, suggested that the antinomy of being away from home and being at home was the definitive problem in Irish poetry. The problem, according to Longley, is of great import because "besides personal factors it pinpoints historical, cultural, moral, environmental and linguistic conditions, together with intersecting literary traditions." These are the sorts of conditions that Beckett in his radio address in 1946 told Ireland to rethink. For Longley, in general and specific reference to Patrick Kavanagh and Louis MacNeice, the problem is that "the sometimes excessive preoccupation of Irish poetry with the ratio between home and away, with being in Ireland / not being in Ireland, being in Monaghan / not being in Monaghan, being in Belfast / not being in Belfast, may have fostered essential structures of imaginative inquiry" (77). Indeed it may. "A mere local phenomenon is something I would not have noticed," says Malone, "having been nothing but a series or rather a succession of local phenomena all my life, without any result" (*Three Novels* 234).

Mercier et Camier was written after Beckett, following up the 10 June radio address with the 24 June 1946 publication of the poem "Saint Lô" in the *Irish Times,* returned to France. The novel, or novella, was not published until 1970, and then, it is usually observed, "with some reluctance" (Knowlson and Pilling 132). It was not published in English translation until 1974. As in the case of many of Beckett's "trunk manuscripts," the general apprehension of the text derived as much from the date of publication as from the apparent date of composition. In the 1970s, *Mercier and Camier* appeared marginal to *The Lost Ones,* "uneven" compared to *Lessness,* or gross compared to *Enough.* Though circumstances made *Mercier and Camier* seem juvenilia in the 1970s, the shift in Beckett's work to an autobiographical vein and the return to the landscape of Dublin and its environs must lend additional significance to *Mercier and Camier* in the 1980s. From this later moment, the idea of reluctance in releasing a text like *Mercier and Camier* must be qualified by reference to *Not I* and *That Time,* plays about characters in and thinking about Ireland first performed in 1972 and 1976, respectively.

The narrator of *Mercier and Camier* shares with those of the trilogy of novels what Longley called a "perhaps excessive preoccupation" with being at home and being away. Having indicated his own presence in an opening sentence, the narrator of the novella offers an introductory summation.

Physically it was fairly easy going, without seas or frontiers to be crossed, through regions untormented on the whole, if desolate in parts. Mercier and Camier did not remove from home, they had that great good fortune. They did not have to face, with greater or less success, outlandish ways, tongues, laws, skies, foods, in surroundings little resembling those to which first childhood, then boyhood, then manhood had inured them. The weather, though often inclement (but they knew no better), never exceeded the limits of the temperate, that is to say of what could still be borne, without danger if not without discomfort, by the average native fittingly clad and shod. (7)

The characters are, nevertheless, "on a journey" and "not lightly launching out, into the unknown" (8). The unknown these characters confront, then, is at home. They principally differ from most of the characters of the later Beckett prose and drama only in that their traveling is done at home rather than abroad. The narrator and the characters can, on occasion, be authoritative on their locale: "The day was indeed fine, at least what passes for fine, in these parts, but cool, and night at hand" (100). In *Godot,* which derives patches of dialogue from *Mercier and Camier,* Vladimir, on the first appearance of the boy, has no such authority: "Are you a native of these parts? (*Silence.*) Do you belong to these parts?" (33). Though at home and amidst apparent sureties, Mercier and Camier are no better oriented than those later characters on journeys away from home, like Jacques Moran on his venture into the Molloy country. Their journey is, rather, a demonstration of dislocation at home, or, in a phrase from *The Unnamable,* in "that unfamiliar native land of mine" (314).

Their journey, or at least the narrator's version of it, is between city and country, much like *Watt.* Their route proceeds from a city center, along a canal towpath, to Helen's flat. The next day, they take "the slow and easy" (39), or the Dublin and South Eastern Railway, from a station of note for its architectural arch, clearly Harcourt Street Station, to the south. They disembark at a small town and lodge at an inn with a manager named Gall (or at least perceived as a Gall) and a barboy named Patrick. The next day, after sleep aided by a bottle of malt (in the French text, *"une bouteille de J.J."* [85]), they venture into the countryside, spend a night there, and then return to Helen's flat. From there they proceed to a city, visit rough pubs and scenes of Mercier's youth, and return to a city square, where they assault a constable. Presumably in flight, they appear next on a moor (in the French edition, the Old Military Road in the Wicklow mountains) and then, taking shelter among ruins along the way, they travel back to the city: "such roughly must have been the course of events" (107). In the city, they meet Watt, who says "my notoriety is not likely ever to penetrate to the denizens of Dublin's fair city, or of Cuq-Toulza" (111). Passing over the canal Lock Bridge, they sit and contemplate for a time a hospital for diseases of the skin before departing for their homes.

The preoccupation with place in *Mercier and Camier,* where the place is easily identified though usually unnamed, is one of disorientation, of viewing home as a traveler, and especially of loss, of dissociation of one from one's home. Enoch Brater, for one, connects this preoccupation with more cryptic texts, such as *Enough,* which, for Brater, "gives us a similar sense of loss [as *Mercier and Camier*], but without the realistic events to frame the sentiment" ("Beckett's *Enough*" 263). The antinomies of place in *Mercier and Camier* are attachment to it and repulsion from it, identification of self with place ruptured by distance of self from place, a familiar matter from much of modern Irish literature. Identification requires a far more accommodationist relation to place, to Dublin, than is common in Beckett's earlier works. Instead of the antagonistic imagery of *More Pricks Than Kicks* or the poems of "Echo's Bones," for example, *Mercier and Camier* offers a fonder evocation of place, as on the occasion of closing time at a pub.

> Most of them climbed aboard old high-slung Fords, others dispersed through the village in search of bargains. Others gathered talking in the rain which did not seem to incommode them. They were perhaps so pleased, who knows, for professional reasons, to see it fall, that they were pleased to feel it fall, wetting them through. Soon they would be on their several ways, scattered along the muddy roads shadowy already in the last gleams of niggard day. Each hastens towards his little kingdom, his waiting wife, his beasts snugly stalled, his dogs listening for the coming of their lord. (48–49)

The dialectic of place in *Mercier and Camier* also requires a contrary repulsion, which takes the form in this novella of ironic asides on intrusive literary conventions. The ironies of the narrator, such as "end of descriptive passage" (98) or "they advance into the sunset (you can't deny yourself everything)" (112), counter the possibility of a relation with place that is personal and free of antecedence. In the dialectics of place in *Mercier and Camier,* the attraction is the personal and individual identity of place and the repulsion is the oppressive, antecedent, literary identity of place. In such antinomies, one can at once be at home and away from home.

That predicament, particularly in generally unnamed settings, is entirely compatible with the criticism of Beckett's work that focuses on its critique of "conventional" fictional rhetoric. But a further oppressiveness of antecedence explicit in *Mercier and Camier* and implicit in the trilogy of novels is a local cultural identity inextricable from nationalism. The square or public garden where Mercier and Camier meet is dominated by a beech. The tree was ostensibly planted "by a Field Marshal of France peacefully named Saint-Ruth" (10), who is, reports Vivian Mercier in *Beckett/Beckett*, as "every Irish schoolboy knows" (42), Maréchal St. Ruth, Irish ally from France who died at the Battle of Aughrim in 1691. Such factors are among the prevailing controls on structures of imaginative inquiry that Mercier and Camier confront. Immediately after meeting, the two travelers at home encounter "the first of a long line of maleficent beings."

> His uniform, sickly green in colour, its place of honour rife with heroic emblems and badges, suited him down to the ground. Inspired by the example of the great Sarsfield he had risked his life without success in defence of a territory which in itself must have left him cold and considered as a symbol cannot have greatly heated him either. . . . Invalided out with a grudging pension, whence the sour looks of nearly all those, male and female, with whom his duties and remnants of bonhomie brought him daily in contact, he sometimes felt it would have been wiser on his part, during the great upheaval, to devote his energies to the domestic skirmish, the Gaelic dialect, the fortification of his faith and the treasures of a folklore beyond compare. The bodily danger would have been less and the benefits more certain. (13 – 14)

Beckett's representation of the burden or oppressiveness of such exterior forms of consciousness as these nationalistic antecedents follows no strict sectarian position. The self-sacrifice of St. Ruth or Sarsfield in the Stuart cause is countered by sarcasm at the expense of attempted preservation of the Gaelic folkloric tradition in sectarian alignment. Movement on nationalistic imperatives, like St. Ruth to Ireland or Sarsfield to Europe or this maleficent being to Flanders, is validated in this passage no more and no less than contentment with "the domestic skirmish." The antinomies here of going abroad and remaining at home, then, closely follow Mrs. Rooney's generalization in *All That Fall:* the first is suicide and the second is a lingering dissolution.

Though there are many historical and political allusions in *Mercier and Camier*, a single additional example may bring the matter to bear more clearly on the representation of local nationalistic ideology. Viewing a moor, "the travellers" chance upon a relic in a bog.

> It was the grave of a nationalist, brought here in the night by the enemy and executed, or perhaps only the corpse brought here, to be dumped. He was buried long after, with a minimum of formality. His name was Masse, perhaps Massy. No great store was set by him now, in patriotic circles. It was true he had done little for the cause. But he still had this monument. All that, and no doubt much more, Mercier and perhaps Camier had once known, and all forgotten. (98)

While Aughrim was a battle against the invading force of William of Orange and thus a defense of Ireland against Protestant colonization, this case has the added pertinence of being from the Irish Civil War of 1922 to 1923, which followed the establishment of the Free State of Ireland, or, as the text has it, a "domestic skirmish." The nationalist was Noel Lemass, a Republican in insurrection against the Free State forces. He was arrested on 3 July 1923, and his corpse was discovered in the Wicklow mountains at Glencree, where, Eoin O'Brien reports, the memorial stands (65). As it appears in *Mercier and Camier*, the suggestion is not of a particular ideological position but of a general confusion, sense of loss, and disorientation produced by an oppressive welter of exterior and antecedent forms of consciousness. The matter is murkier still, for a Huguenot would not likely be a Republican and, as Vivian Mercier notes in *Beckett/Beckett* with some personal authority, Lemass is a Huguenot name, as is Beckett, as is Camier, as is Mercier (42). These matters are the kind that "Mercier and perhaps Camier had once known, and all forgotten."

All this may be passed over in some readings of *Mercier and Camier* as "Beckett's little jabs against his native Ireland" (Levy 126); that is the reading of Eric P. Levy in pursuit of another context, a persuasive case for Dantean allusions. But in the Irish context, these examples constitute a consistent commentary of the text on matters not exclusively universal, literary, or philosophical. The sense of loss, to use Brater's term, in *Mercier and Camier* also has reference to a late phase of cultural nationalism, of which Ireland and Beckett's work are provocative instances. In a late chapter of *Nationalism and the State*, John

Breuilly turns to the sense of loss inevitable on obsolescence by success or altered circumstances of a sense of place formulated in nationalist ideology. As, Breuilly argues, nationalism is an ideology rather than a natural expression of collective identity, and as nationalism takes definitive shape in reflection of prior assumptions about social and political conditions, so "nationalist ideology actually brings into being an imitation of its own ideas." That is, so long as nationalist ideology functions as a program, it maintains "a more or less plausible connection with existing social arrangements and needs, with actual beliefs and with often widespread political grievances." Hence, insofar "as nationalism is successful it appears to be true" (343). Among other things, *Mercier and Camier* represents, in specific reference to Ireland, that sense of loss incurred by a society largely defined and organized by a nationalist ideology rendered obsolete by success and implausible by lack of connection with immediate social arrangements and needs. This loss might be particularly apparent to a Protestant author who was being educated in Fermanagh at the time of the partition of Ireland. The syndrome of the two travelers at home in *Mercier and Camier* is their inability to locate themselves with the only available formulations.

> Up who? said Camier.
> I heard Quin, said Mercier.
> That must be someone who does not exist, said Camier. (119)

In this predicament of inability to locate themselves in reference to place, Mercier and Camier closely resemble Vladimir and Estragon of *Godot*.

> Let us go home, said Camier
> Why? said Mercier.
> It won't stop all day, said Camier.
> Long or short, tis but a shower, said Mercier.
> I can't stand there doing nothing, said Camier.
> Then let us sit, said Mercier.
> Worse still, said Camier. (11)

The difference between the pairs of travelers in the texts of *Mercier and Camier* and *Waiting for Godot* is that the former are at loss amidst ample evidence of the cause, the latter are simply lost. The sense of place, of

Ireland, in *Mercier and Camier* is opposition between antecedent, obscure formulations and personal, individual coordinates. The much-noted void that Beckett's most influential works approach includes among its many suggestions, as *Mercier and Camier* helps demonstrate, the disjunction between a particular place and its preexisting identities, the gap between personal situation and antecedent cultural formulations of it. A preliminary work like *Mercier and Camier* and certain subsequent works help establish this dimension in the trilogy of novels and *Godot,* which are studiously enigmatic. As announced near the end of *Mercier and Camier:* "The whole question of priority, so luminous hithertofore, is from now on obscure" (103).

The trilogy of novels — *Molloy, Malone Dies,* and *The Unnamable* — along with the plays, *Godot* and *Endgame,* largely created and continue to fix the image of Beckett's work in twentieth-century literature. When read with full awareness of the identifiably Irish localities and cultural contexts in the earlier works, these, too, demonstrate the relevance of Ireland to Beckett's work and the relevance of Beckett's work to Ireland. All five works named above are versions of that preoccupation in modern Irish literature with home and away. Home and away is hardly the only preoccupation in Beckett's major works, but it is a significant one in them and a consistent one throughout the Beckett *oeuvre.* The novels, in particular, demonstrate with pronounced clarity a hermeneutics of place among their manifold provocations. That sense of place is evident even in the typically paradoxical and self-referential rhetoric of *The Unnamable.* "And the simplest therefore is to say that what I say, what I shall say, if I can, relates to the place where I am, to me who am there, in spite of my inability to think of these, or to speak of them, because of the compulsion I am under the speak of them, and therefore perhaps think of them a little" (*Three Novels* 301–2).

All three novels invite explication of place by identification of place. Michael Robinson was one of the first to elaborate this point. "The landscape that Malone describes in his story is clearly once again that of Molloy: the Irish countryside round Dublin. He portrays his hero lost on a plain between mountains and the sea, and rootless in the city of Dublin itself. Nearby is the asylum of St. John of God, the harbor of Dun Laoghaire from which the patients set out on their excursion, and the hills west of Carrickmines where the stonecutters live and about which the author and character enjoy their moment of Proustian remembrance" (174–75). One could add much more. There are references to Dublin's Butt Bridge and Tyler's Gate, to Cork and Killarney, and to blarney and blather. "Tears and laughter," says Molloy, "they are so much Gaelic to me" (37). On visiting Bally, in the domain of Ballyba, from his home in Turdy, hub of Turdyba, Jacques Moran reports: "no sooner did a tilth, or a meadow, begin to be sizeable than it fell foul of a sacred grove or a stretch of marsh from which nothing could be obtained beyond a little inferior turf or scraps of bog oak used for making amulets, paper-knives, napkin-rings, rosaries and other knickknacks" (134). Analogue to that topography is the presence in the novels of literary Ireland, inevitably that derived from Joyce and Yeats. Many have speculated on the relationship between the trilogy of Beckett's novels and the work of Joyce, from stream of consciousness to ironic mythic parallels, from linguistic-referential texts like Joyce's to a discourse on fiction most emphatically *not* like Joyce's, from allusions to the Count of Monte Cristo or Shelley to parodic use of texts like the Lord's Prayer or the song "I Dreamt I Dwelt." Fewer have speculated on the presence of Yeats, whose imperatives on taking life as theme accompany Moran's description of bog antiquities, whose "Meditations in Time of Civil War" feature one Jacques Mollay, and whose rather antiquarian *The Celtic Twilight* included a vagabond balladeer named Moran haunting Dublin bridges and skull thumping a degree more violent than Molloy's importunities to his mother.

The place of Beckett's work in Irish literary tradition is most evident in his plays, while the place of Ireland in Beckett's work is most evident in the novels. Of more interest than specific identifications, of Bally with Baile Atha Cliatha, for example, is the representation in the novels of a dynamics of place that is self-evidently derived from Ireland and abstracted into a new form of that attraction and repulsion from home manifested in more customary form, for example, in *Murphy*. Beckett's work is central to modern Irish literature for its elaboration of this preeminent topic, place, and for its evolution of that subject, from the stories in *More Pricks Than Kicks* through *Molloy* to his last works, to an abstract dynamic of that ambivalence to place more commonly represented in modern Irish literature with adequate signposts for provincial landmarks. In Beckett's work, the principal antinomies are those of *Mercier and Camier:* place and identity, antecedence and self, collective consciousness and individual desire. Of all the analogues for order that Beckett's trilogy of novels subject to chaos, that of place is preeminent. The opening words of the trilogy are "I am in my mother's room" (7).

If *Molloy* is taken as a single narrative, its principal parts appear to be in reverse: Jacques Moran, beginning at the midpoint of the text, assumes on conclusion the condition of Molloy at the opening. That condition, as Moran construes it, is "the long anguish of vagrancy and freedom" (132). If read for sense of place, the form of the novel appears to be an equivalent reverse: Molloy's return to home precedes Moran's departure from home. In this particular dialectic of home and away, devoted to consciousness of self, being at home is subordination of oneself to exterior forms of consciousness, and being away from home is what Moran refers to as vagrancy and freedom. The accompanying imagery is night and darkness for freedom, day and light for order. In his journey, which ends in a ditch on a spring morning, Molloy says, "at last I came out of that distant night, divided between murmurs of my little world, its dutiful confusions, and those so different (so different?) of all that between two suns abides and passes away" (15). Moran's journey, begun in his garden on a Sunday morning, ends at night, "Midnight perhaps" (174), though that was not necessarily the time he began to write his report. This imagery is reiterative throughout the three novels and Beckett's other works. Mother Peg in *Endgame,* for example, dies of darkness. Further, there are suggestive parallels in incidental comments: Alec Reid, in *All I Can Manage, More Than I Could,* attributes to Beckett the comment that *All That Fall,* the radio play that returns to an identifiable Irish setting, is "a text written to come out of the dark" (68).

Darkness is a compelling image in Beckett's work. In the trilogy, at least, it is also an imagery quite specific to place and the accommodating or frustrating appurtenances of place. Antithetical conceptions of place — fortifying or constricting — is, in large part, the fundamental distinction between Molloy and Moran in the dialectic of *Molloy*. Molloy's voices urge liberation from place: "I preferred to abide by my simple freedom and its voice that said, Molloy, your region is vast, you have never left it and you never shall. And wheresoever you wander, within its distant limits, things will always be the same" (65–66). Moran's voices are contrary: "it is within me and exhorts me to continue to the end the faithful servant I have always been, of a cause that is not mine, and patiently fulfill in all its bitterness my calamitous part, as it was my will, when I had a will, that others should" (132). Molloy's voice imagines a virtually limitless, ostensibly congenial, and fundamentally unchanging region. Moran's voice imagines defined territories and subdivisions, danger in other places, local knowledge in rapid obfuscation or obliteration. Molloy's voice posits the luxury of vagrancy without antecedent designations and inhibiting specifications, while Moran's is enamored of local distinctions and abhorrent of the abstract and generic. Molloy, then, tends toward the humanistic, Moran to the provincial, and *Molloy* to an intractable opposition of the two. The novel declines to validate either character's sense of place, origin, or worldview. The balance of a dialectic without synthesis is completed by the failure of either character's worldview to sustain its imaginative constructions. Molloy ends in his native town: "I longed to go back to the forest. Oh not a real longing. Molloy could stay, where he happened to be" (91). Moran ends without "the words that Moran had been taught when he was little and that he in his turn had taught to his little one" (176).

The dual narrators of *Molloy* adumbrate a dialectic of place that is fundamental to modern Irish literature and to literary representations of colonialism and postcolonialism. The model of exile, of aloofness to home, and of superiority to intellectual provincialism is, of course, that of Joyce and his work. The model of attachment to place, of establishment at home, and the use of imaginative provincialism is Yeats and his work. The dialectic continues: Edna Longley's articulation of an Irish literary preoccupation with place (stated in 1988 and so representative of that moment, as well as of the historical moments of the texts she analyzes) rests on the different models of relation to home represented by Louis MacNeice or by Patrick Kavanagh and John Hewitt. In Beckett's case, these antithetical directions, away from home or toward home, were evident from his early associations in Paris with George Reavey and Thomas MacGreevy. The biographical burden of association with Joyce, the hostile critique of Ireland in the early works, and the reduction of identifiable references to Ireland in his most influential works all combined to create an image of Beckett's work as an extension of one exemplary model of exile, Joyce's, to complete the superannuation of the sense of home. But the trilogy of novels opens with the failure of such an enterprise by Molloy. Like Molloy's voices, Beckett's work posits the premise of becoming Richard Ellmann's figure from *Four Dubliners:* "Nayman From Noland." But, as one feature of its poetics of failure, Beckett's work never quite achieves that status. The hermeneutics of place in *Molloy* extract instead the attractions of both home and away, the limits of both, and an impasse between those alternatives. To a certain degree, Beckett's work since the trilogy of novels validates or perhaps compels this reading of *Molloy*. After those most abstract texts, such as *How It Is* and *The Lost Ones,* Beckett's work returns, "to come out of the dark," to specifically Irish settings and frames of reference in such works as *That Time* and *Company*. That this direction should be less than formulaic and rigid should only confirm the final equivocation of *Molloy*. The predominantly hermeneutic treatment of place in his major work vitiates any simple sense of Beckett as an Irish writer. But the comprehensive treatment of antinomies of home and away from home in Beckett's work, the tendency in his work to represent the dialectic of both constructions of place and not to endorse either, gives Beckett's work in an Irish context a complex and central status.

Malone Dies reimagines that dialectic of place in more specifically ideological terms. One dimension of the centrality of Beckett's work to modern Irish literature is its exploitation of the analogical usefulness of the topography of Ireland. Malone makes frequent reference to "the island" as the designation of his home region, as do Molloy and the Unnamable. That identification has a general currency in modern Irish literature. One interesting example is provided by Elizabeth Bowen. In *Seven Winters and Afterthoughts,* Bowen describes how "her earliest pride of race" derived from that identification. "My most endemic pride in my own country was, for some years, founded on a mistake: my failing to have a nice ear for vowel sounds, and the Anglo-Irish slurred, hurried way of speaking made me take the words "Ireland" and "island" to be synonymous. Thus, all countries quite surrounded by water took (it appeared) their generic name from ours. It seemed fine to live in a country that was a prototype. England, for instance, was "an ireland" (or, a sub-Ireland) — an imitation" (13). She was, then, caught between the frames of reference of Molloy, with his vague, nearly limitless sense of region, and Moran, with his abhorrence of generic names. The difference between them, the gap between apparently natural and apparently ideological senses of place, Bowen usefully illustrates, have consequences in regard to perceived frames of reference. Beckett's work represents that gap without a corrective like Bowen's self-depreciation.

In *Malone Dies* that difference between the natural and the ideological is represented in the narrative alteration of the stories and in the revelations about the teller of those stories. In the novel, the stories originate as a means of distracting the teller from himself and of staving off rhetorical expiration. "I shall not answer any more questions. I shall even try not to ask myself any more. While waiting I shall tell myself stories, if I can" (180). But in the latest installment of the breakdown of the object under pressures of self-awareness initiated by Beckett in the 1930s, the stories inevitably lead back to the self and approach rhetorical failure in critical self-awareness. The stories Malone tells, or attempts to tell, consist of local phenomena, and he comments on the ubiquity of local phenomena. His narrative failures are lapses from local phenomena to "all this ballsaching poppycock about life and death" (225). That fatigue with an asymptotic approach to universal and humanistic preoccupations is an interesting irony from the author of *Godot* as that work is generally understood. It is reiterated in *The Unnamable,* where the narrator exclaims, "They must consider me sufficiently stupified with all their balls about being and existing. Yes, now that I've forgotten who Worm is, where he is, what he's like, I'll begin to be he. Anything rather than these college quips. Quick, a place" (348).

Malone's enterprise of discovering, or at least perpetuating, himself in stories has some specific significance in the Irish context. As liberating as it seems for him to shed the conventions of narrative fiction, the enterprise also entraps him in the culture-specific role of *seanachie,* or storyteller, and all the historical freight that comes with that designation. Maureen Waters, in *The Comic Irishman,* notes that a *seanachie* "usually exhibits a boldness in invention and narrative flair" that is "rooted in an oral tradition in which poet and storyteller played central roles, stimulating the minds of the people despite the severe hardships they endured" (79–80). The "invention and narrative flair" evident in *Malone Dies* is important in reference to Beckett's composition of the novel in French. "To write in French," according to A. Alvarez, "meant escaping from the whole weight of the Irish rhetoric Beckett had been born to, with its insidious cadences and genius for baroque linguistic flourish" (40–41). But in light of *Malone Dies,* with its cultural prototype for narrative role and residual "insidious cadences," that enterprise is scarcely more successful than Malone's own. On the survival of the *seanachie* role in modern Irish literature, Waters observes that the inheritance is a "dual sense of cultural identity." The modern Irish comic writer "tends to be suspicious of his rhetorical heritage and at the same time thoroughly capable of exploiting it" (80). In light of Beckett's trilogy of novels, one might add: and incapable of escaping it.

The local phenomena of Malone's stories are quite specific to Ireland and to its modern cultural identity. They begin with Saposcat, later renamed Macmann. His parents are professional in aspiration, and "he was struck each time by the vagueness of these palavers and not surprized that they never led to anything" (187). Saposcat is also struck by the inadequacy of exchange between rural and urban areas of his home, though Malone suspends attempt to generalize on this problem. In genuine curiosity or guilt, Saposcat turns to the peasantry, the Lamberts, in a scenario generally suggestive of the visits to unspoiled Gaels by Lady Gregory, Yeats, Synge, and innumerable other Protestant and roughly Anglo-Irish holiday refugees from bourgeois culture and contributors to the rhetorical invention of a nation. Malone promises that his stories "will not be the same kind of stories as hitherto" (180), and the Lamberts are indeed rendered differently from the usual figures of Kiltartan peasantry.

> Yes, at an age when most people cringe and cower, as if to apologize for still being present, Lambert was feared and in a position to do as he pleased. And even his young wife had abandoned all hope of bringing him to heel, by means of her cunt, that trump card of young wives. For she knew what he would do to her if she did not open it to him. And he even insisted on her making things easy for him, in ways that often appeared to her exorbitant. And at the least show of rebellion on her part he would run to the wash-house and come back with the beetle and beat her until she came round to a better way of thinking. (200)

Saposcat observes the Lamberts at work feeding hens, trading mules, and picking lentils, all the while leaving small gifts. The beneficiaries of the visits by Gregory, Yeats, Synge, and others are usually portrayed with preternatural dignity and absolute superiority to patronage. The Lamberts only protest briefly, "in the way tradition required" (205), before accepting the gifts. Malone's stories call into question, among other things, that venture of discovering an indigenous national culture fundamental to the Irish literary revival. The novel does indeed have among its preoccupations a decontextualized critique of narrative convention. But it also has among its textual elements the epistemology of local cultural nationalism. In *Nations and Nationalism*, Ernest Gellner points to the quality of nationalism essential to the stories of Saposcat and the Lamberts in *Malone Dies*. Nationalism has the capacity, famously used in the early twentieth-century formulation of a hidden Ireland, to invent a folk culture it ostensibly liberates. As Gellner argues, "Nationalism usually conquers in the name of a putative folk culture. Its symbolism is drawn from the healthy, pristine, vigorous life of the peasants, of the *Volk*, the *narod*. . . . If the nationalism prospers it eliminates the alien high culture, but it does not then replace it by the old local low culture; it revives, or invents, a local high (literate, specialist-transmitted) culture of its own, though admittedly one which will have some links with the earlier local folk styles and dialects" (57). For all its other implications, Beckett's work has the pertinent quality in modern Irish literature of exposing the assumptions of the revival: of exposing in its meditative narrators identity thinking. For all its formal novelty, *Malone Dies* reconstitutes a skepticism evident as a dissenting position contemporary with and following the revival. If, as Gellner and most other analysts of nationalism argue, cultural ideology is most frequently a complex intersection of *Volk* and political proponents, Beckett's representation of culture in modern Ireland is comprehensive for its attention to the folk and potential ideologues, to the Lamberts and to Saposcat, to the role of *seanachie* and enlightened inventors of a subculture in need of rescue.

The local phenomena of *Malone Dies* are not limited to the epistemologies of Irish cultural nationalism and its adjunct literature. They include as well the problematics of a nationalism that, in Gellner's phrase, prospers. In *Mercier and Camier*, the two travelers at home were baffled by the memorial to Noel Lemass. Though it was not quoted by Beckett, as related by Eoin O'Brien in *The Beckett Country*, that monument at Glencree has as its inscription a quotation from Terence MacSwiney. "He has lived a beautiful life and has left a beautiful field. He has sacrificed the hour to give service for all time. He has entered the company of the great and with them he will be remembered for ever [*sic*]" (66). Beckett has attended to such memorials before, in the confrontation of Neary with the statue of Cuchulain in *Murphy*, where the memorial was a source of frustration. Later, in *Mercier and Camier*, this memorial at Glencree is a source of puzzlement, confusion, and general alienation from a collective, public identity. Though such references call into question the premise of a "company of the great" being remembered forever, they also by their own existence in Beckett's work qualify suggestions of nationalist memorials' superfluity or irrelevance.

When Malone contemplates his loss of appetite, he refers to none other than Terence MacSwiney. "The Lord Mayor of Cork lasted for ages, but he was young, and then he had political convictions, human ones too probably, just plain human convictions. And he allowed himself a sip of water from time to time, sweetened probably. Water, for pity's sake! How is it I am not thirsty. There must be drinking going on inside me, my secretions. Yes, let us talk a little about me, that will be a rest from all these blackguards" (273). Lord Mayor MacSwiney, arrested in Cork in 1920 and transferred to Brixton, died there from a hunger strike of seventy-four days. Malone calibrates his own subsistence against dim memories of MacSwiney. The point of reference is ambiguous about whether political convictions are attributable to youth or to an earlier time, and it is ambiguous about the distinction between political convictions and human convictions. That opposition, of the historical and political against the personal ("Yes, let us talk a little about me") and the more generally humanistic, is part of Malone's dialectic of place and predicament between local and universal identifications. That is the predicament of place in Beckett's trilogy of novels, and it is a predicament in apprehension of Beckett's work.

When Saposcat transmutes into Macmann, Malone summons him. "He will therefore rise, whether he likes it or not, and proceed by other places to another place, and then by others still to yet another, unless he comes back here where he seems to be smug enough, but one never knows, does one?" (232). The place to which Macmann proceeds is St. John of Gods, Stillorgan. In *Murphy*, Wylie attempts to excuse Neary's assault on the buttocks of the GPO statue with the plea that Neary is a patient in that asylum. In *Malone Dies*, Macmann demands that a guard named Lemuel "state whether Saint John of Gods was a private insitution or run by the State, a hospice for the aged and infirm or a madhouse" (266). The question, unanswered, picks up a motif in Beckett's work most pertinent to a newly autonomous state, to a nationalism that prospers. In *Watt*, the occasion is the banning of the aphrodisiac Bando by "the State, taking as usual the law into its own hands" (170). In *First Love*, the occasion is the narrator's epitaph, "There is little chance unfortunately of its ever being reared above the skull that conceived it, unless the State takes up the matter" (12). In *Mercier and Camier*, it was the constable who served "in defense of a territory which in itself must have left him cold and considered as a symbol cannot have greatly heated him either" (13–14). The occasion in *Molloy* is Lousse's attempt to sway an angry crowd with the ethical appeal that her late husband died "in defense of a country that called itself his and from which in his lifetime he never derived the smallest benefit, only insults and vexations" (33). Moran, too, speaks of himself as "the faithful servant I have always been, of a cause that is not mine" (132).

All of these references to effective alienation of citizens from states indicate the substantial correlative of nationalism to the more often noted antitheses in Beckett's work between, say, the subjective and the objective, chaos and order, individual and conventional forms of discourse, among others. By almost any analysis, the general intention of nationalism is coherent reflection of a populace in its institutional state. As Gellner puts it, "nationalist sentiment is deeply offended by violations of the nationalist principle of congruence of state and nation" (134). A consensus theory of nationalism could be formed around the variety of ways that a congruence can be presumed, hypothesized, fictionalized, or decreed by parties to nationalism. John Breuilly, in *Nationalism and the State*, demonstrates a greater degree of sympathy than usual with the arbitrary qualities of a prospering nationalism. For Breuilly, "nationalist ideology is a pseudo-solution to the problem of the relationship between the state and society, but its plausibility derives from its roots in genuine intellectual responses to that problem" (349). And, a reader of Beckett's texts might add, its implausibility derives from instances of pseudo-relationships between state and society. Macmann's question to Lemuel in *Malone Dies* has that pertinence. Macmann's question, in a work following the rather comprehensive critiques of Irish cultural nationalism in *More Pricks Than Kicks*, *Murphy*, and *Watt*, demands that Lemuel *state* whether the institutional asylum is of the State. Like *Watt*, *First Love*, *Mercier and Camier*, and *Molloy*, *Malone Dies* adverts to the collapse of a pseudo-solution of the problem of society-state congruence into a pseudo-relationship. This relationship is one of many ways that Beckett's work opposes forms of individuality (literary, social, psychological, etc.) against exterior, antecedent, prescribed, and other customary forms of collective consciousness. In its own terms, the opposition in *Malone Dies* can be seen as derivative of Ireland; and in its paradigm, it can be seen as pertinent to Ireland.

Irish nationalism and the consequent nation-state of Ireland make a choice case study of problematic congruence of state and populace, and Beckett's work provides choice literary representations, Malone's stories among them, of that problem. D. George Boyce concludes in *Nationalism in Ireland* that the Irish nationalist movement "stressed the comprehensive nature of nationalism, its need to incorporate all Irishmen within its bounds, its inclusiveness, its non-sectarianism; but the popular appeal of nationalism, its emotional attraction, its sentiment, were derived, not from this ideology, but from a myth, a view of the past that was accepted whether it was true or false" (385). This myth, for Boyce, is "the contradiction of modern Irish nationalism" (384). The various lamentations about alienation from the state in Beckett's work expose that contradiction. Beckett certainly is not unique in Ireland for attention to this problem. But his work is most interesting for its indirect presentation of the problem and for presentation that if examined refuses to endorse the intentions of local cultural nationalism or revisionist counterargument. Though *Malone Dies* is best known for its psycho-dynamics of literary narrative, it is also remarkable and provocative for this preoccupation with place, with one island's dialectic of personal and collective forms of consciousness. "Yes, that's what I like about me, at least one of the things," says Malone, "that I can say, Up the Republic!, for example, or, Sweetheart!, for example, without having to wonder if I should not rather have cut my tongue out, or said something else" (236).

The matter of Ireland is not the sole significance of Beckett's trilogy of novels, but its own degree of significance has to do with the general understanding of Beckett's texts and with the literary-cultural identity of Ireland. *The Unnamable,* at first thought to be perhaps the least promising text for a reading of the Irish Beckett, is a useful indication that the dialectics of place is essential to Beckett's most abstracted, most self-referential texts. The novel is a re-representation of antinomies familiar from Beckett's previous works. Though the narrators of the trilogy proceed from the lame to the bedridden to the legless and bottled, the Unnamable, nevertheless, remains a reluctant traveler ("you're tired, you want to stop, travel no more, seek no more, lie no more, speak no more" [400]); perplexed by place ("Did I wait somewhere for this place to be ready to receive me? Or did it wait for me to come and people it?" [296]; and plagued by antecedence ("My family. To begin with it had no part or share in what I was doing. Having set forth from that place, it was only natural I should return to it, given the accuracy of my navigation" [322]). The trilogy of novels shifts emphasis from stories, to stories mixed with exegesis of the teller, to exegesis of the teller. The Unnamable, however, remains to some degree a storyteller: "Then my voice, the voice, would say, That's an idea, now I'll tell one of Mahood's stories, I need a rest" (309). While the capacities for travel, away from home and toward home, and story telling diminish from *Molloy* to *Malone Dies* and to *The Unnamable,* some residual sense of place and compulsion to stories remain in the last of the three novels. For all its proximity to a hypothetical void and condition of perfect meaninglessness, *The Unnamable,* by its own internal premise, cannot reach that place and that condition: "Ah if only the voice could stop, this meaningless voice which prevents you from being nothing, just barely prevents you from being nothing and nowhere" (370).

The proximity to a void and meaninglessness has been the preoccupation of critical commentaries on *The Unnamable,* no doubt in part because of the prominence upon publication of Beckett's obliteration of familiar conventions of narrative fiction. Attention to the novel once quite understandably focused on obliteration. Hence, an influential early commentary such as H. Porter Abbott's *Fiction of Samuel Beckett: Form and Effect,* emphasized that in *The Unnamable,* "Gone is all sense of place, all rooms, all limbs, specificity as to the number of toes, possessions, creations" (128). But *a* sense of place does remain in *The Unnamable* and does indeed survive in unconventional and diminished form even in reference to body, physical location, and metaphorical situation. The text demands consideration of *what* sense of place may be "gone" and *what* sense of place remains. Though the Unnamable laments his inability to be nowhere, the striking quality of the text has been taken to be his degree of success. The focus on what apparently has been obliterated continues to prevail in Iser's *Implied Reader*. "The nameless narrator refers to no normal, external objective reality at all. . . . In *The Unnamable* such relics of an outside world have disappeared altogether." This, of course, is the narrator whose euphemism for death is going "to Killarney" (359). The result, an interesting one for Iser, is that readers of the trilogy must grasp at such internal references as do exist, and so in *The Unnamable,* following *Molloy* and *Malone Dies,* "the theme of this novel evolves out of the self-dissection of the first two" (170), all of which helps establish the enterprise of Beckett criticism as *explication de text,* publication of drafts and notebooks, word counting, and variorum annotation to a degree unequaled by criticism of any other mid-century author during his life.

But the narrator's degree of failure—the extent to which his failure is qualified, the extent to which he is unable to rid himself of the burdens of place and so unable to be nowhere—is also striking. Alternatively, a reading can locate the Beckett narrator on the brink between somewhere and nowhere in reference to the former rather than the latter. This currently unfashionable reading of Beckett has enough history to include its own problematics. One important objection to the exclusively formalist approach to modernist literature, including Beckett, is Georg Lukács's *Meaning of Contemporary Realism* and its well-known, if seldom wholly admired, introductory chapter, "The Ideology of Modernism." In general, and with useful reference to the usual critical enthusiasm for the ingenious proximity to a void in Beckett's novels, Lukács castigates the exclusively internal reading: by "concentrating on formal criteria, by isolating technique from content and exaggerating its importance, these critics refrain from judgement on the social or artistic significance of subject-matter" (34). Lukács refers explicitly only to *Molloy,* though surely his pique would rise on encounter with *The Unnamable*. One of Lukács's dissatisfactions with literary modernism is its "attenuation of reality" (25), its unconstructive subjectivity, its relegation of potentiality to abstraction:

that attenuation of reality "is carried *ad absurdum* where the stream of consciousness is that of an abnormal subject or an idiot—consider the first part of Faulkner's *Sound and {the} Fury* or, a still more extreme case, Beckett's *Molloy*" (26). In distinguishing between constructive and other attenuation of reality, between concrete and abstract potentiality, Lukács looks to Beckett for the worst. "Lack of objectivity in the description of the outer world finds its compliment in the reduction of reality to a nightmare. Beckett's *Molloy* is perhaps the *ne plus ultra* of this development. . . . He presents us with an image of the utmost human degradation — an idiot's vegetative existence" (31). Any literary failure to uncover a social character in psychopathology, for Lukács, is perforce "perverse in the manner of Beckett" (32).

The apprehension of Beckett's narrators as degradation of man has been rebutted countless times since TCD in 1959 took up the task of praising Beckett for "compassion and humanity" (Bair 504), and the Nobel Prize committee caught up with TCD a decade later. The many formalist expositions on the ennobling qualities of these narrators, including narrators following *The Unnamable,* have adequately stated the case for the dramatization in Beckett's work of imagination. But Lukács's contention that Beckett's work is symptomatic of modernism's ontology of solitude and ahistorical confinement to the limits of personal experience cannot be dismissed in formalist fashion, which, as Lukács argued, rests on isolation of interior technique and so inevitably confirms the suspicion of an ontological view without external reference.

Attention to the local Irish contexts of Beckett's novels indicates that their ontological view is social and is historical, even in such a text as *The Unnamable.* The attenuation of reality in the novel, however ingenious its technique of approaching a metaphysical void and condition of meaninglessness, is incomplete. The progressive obliteration of place over the span of the trilogy of novels effectively highlights a residual sense of place, with concomitant social and historical contexts. The dynamics of place from *Molloy* and the stories of *Malone Dies* survive in *The Unnamable.* "To tell the truth — no, first the story. The island. I'm on the island, I've never left the island, God help me. I was under the impression I spent my life in spirals round the earth. Wrong, it's on the island I wind my endless ways" (326–27). All the stories to which the Unnamable reverts on proximity to silence are, however vegetative, also historical. The narrator resists, but must acknowledge, attempts "to produce ostensibly independent testimony in support of my historical existence" (319). In its strenuous attempt to be nowhere, *The Unnamable* represents as inevitable the resilience of someplace, with its social and historical entanglements. In concluding efforts to be nowhere, *The Unnamable,* near suspension in final words about going, reverts to a particular reiterative rhetoric about being away: "I who am far" (403); "I am far, far, what does that mean, far, no need to be far, perhaps he's here, in my arms" (404); "as if I were somewhere else, there I am far again" (413). In this verge on "the silence, full of murmurs" (413), the narrator's language is social and historical, derived from Thomas Moore's *Irish Melodies.* The language on the verge of a void reverts, of course, to Moore's "She Is Far From the Land," the song about nationalist Robert Emmet, captured by the British in 1803, celebrated in fancy for his doomed preflight visit to his beloved Sara Curren, and celebrated in fact for his speech from the dock before execution. Moore's poem centers on Curren.

> She is far from the land where her young hero sleeps,
>   And lovers are round her, sighing:
> But coldly she turns from their gaze, and weeps,
>   For her heart in his grave is lying.
>
> She sings the wild song of her dear native plains,
>   Every note which he loved awaking;
> Ah! little they think who delight in her strains,
>   How the heart of the Minstrel is breaking.
>
> He had lived for his love, for his country he died,
>   They were all that to life had entwined him;
> Nor soon shall the tears of his country be dried,
>   Nor long will his love stay behind him.
>
> Oh! make her a grave where the sunbeams rest,
>   When they promise a glorious morrow;
> They'll shine o'er her sleep, like a smile from the West,
>   From her own loved island of sorrow.

(333–34)

The allusion could be counted as a rhetorical gesture to *Ulysses,* but Beckett's works are equally informed by this kind of delicious cultural debris. Another of the later lives of the poem is its appearance as almost remembered by Joxer in Sean O'Casey's *Juno and the Paycock.* The matter of this single allusion in the crucial concluding passages is of interest as a gesture in the text to material shared by denizens of a State where nationalism prospered and to antecedent forms of cultural consciousness reverted to on proximity to no place. Nor is Moore's text, with its weepy celebration of home and away from home, with its serene confidence in rhetorical evocation of home, with its personal and topographical islands, and with its own blunt dialectic of the personal and the national, wholly irrelevant to *The Unnamable.* Like allusion to nationalist memorials, Beckett's allusion to a high-sentimental example of *Irish Melodies* extracts in reference to an object of negative critique a textual equivocation. In its attempt to obliterate social and historical ontology, *The Unnamable* ends by confirming it.

Entrapment in cultural context is a feature of Beckett's earlier works: in the capitulation to social expectations in *More Pricks Than Kicks,* in the paralysis between prevailing literary antinomies in *Murphy,* and in immobility before alternative historical hypotheses in *Watt.* The dialectic of being home and being away from home in *Molloy* and the intrusion of historical inheritance in the putative personal stories of *Malone Dies* rework those conditions of inaction in more abstracted situations. The antinomies of self and place, of self and antecedence, and of individual awareness and exterior forms of consciousness remain central in *The Unnamable.* "I have my faults," says the narrator of the last of the trilogy of novels, "but changing my tune is not one of them" (335).

The significance of the Irish Beckett for both critical apprehension of Beckett's work and its continuing relevance to Irish culture is that, contrary to the opinion of Lukács, the ontological view in these works is social and historical. Thus, these works could, but do not, admit concrete potentiality. Immobility before a dialectics of place, inability to establish place, and inability to escape place, are all part of the impasse generally recognized by Beckett critics but in culturally neutral terms. The novels are fully equipped with rhetorical ironies, as most criticism indicates. But they are also consistent in social, specifically Irish, analogues for these ironies. The novels "offer nothing affirmative," as Iser says in deference to Lukács. But they do not abrogate that problem. They could offer something affirmative, because they are sufficiently social and historical, but they do not. For that reason, the Irish Beckett, recently admitted or readmitted to the national literary canon, scarcely serves the positivistic aims for which it is often, of late, summoned. Beckett as Irish may cheer some, but the Ireland in Beckett may dismay many.

   When *Waiting for Godot* was in its first productions, the matter of its universal and humanist or local and Irish import was an issue. Expectation of local import was as axiomatic then as the humanistic image of Beckett is now. In Dublin, the issue was of some particular interest because of the author's Irish portfolio and the general configuration of Irish drama in the 1950s around privileged regionalism, a.k.a. Peasant Quality. The case was not closed, as it has been since. *Godot* had affinities with modern Irish drama that were apparent to frequenters of the Abbey. But the play had come from an author who in their memory had been branded in court a bawd and a blasphemer from Paris, and the play left them, like others, with the enigma of Godot.

   A. J. Leventhal, who years later could be more decisive, presented the case without verdict in the *Dublin Magazine* on the occasion of the Pike Theatre's Dublin premiere of *Godot* in 1956. Familiar with the previous Paris and London productions, Leventhal took up the issue because "the real innovation in the Irish production lies in making the two tramps (Austin Byrne and Dermot Kelly faithfully efficient) speak with the accent of O'Casey's Joxer tempered by Myles na gCopaleen's 'Dubalin' man." Locally, at least, Leventhal wrote with the authority of personal familiarity: years later Denis Johnston, a notable omission from Beckett's memory of Dublin's drama of the late 1920s, would always refer to Leventhal as Beckett's secretary, as Beckett had been Joyce's. Perhaps with support or upon instruction by the author, Leventhal responded to the "Dubalin" accents somewhat imperiously: "It seemes [*sic*] evident that the author had in mind a universal rather than a regional application of his vision of mankind in perpetual expectation, desperately endeavouring to fill the haitus between birth and death" ("Dramatic Commentary" 52). His sole printed rationale for that claim was that the names of the four characters indicate different nationalities. (It is interesting to note that Siegfried Unseld reports a luncheon with Theodor W. Adorno, who proposed the same theory of names in *Endgame*, and Beckett, who denied any such use of names in that play [Unseld 93].) Responding to local hearsay, much as Beckett had in "The Capital of the Ruins," Leventhal observed in his review of the Dublin production of *Godot* that

> Mr. Beckett's origin has caused the view to be widely accepted that the whole conception of *Waiting for Godot* is Irish, a fact which the original French has been unable to conceal, it is claimed. The Pike Theatre production lends support to this view, and it may well be that *Waiting for Godot* will go down in the local records as a lineal descendant of the works of the high literary kings of the Irish dramatic renascence. It is understood that there is a proposal to translate the play into Irish which would assist in bringing about a general acceptance here of this theory. Indeed later literary historians might align Mr. Beckett with George Moore who, in his efforts to help in the revival of the Irish language, suggested that he might compose his work in French which could be translated into English for the convenience of the Gaelic Leaguers who would then, in their turn, have little difficulty in turning the text into Irish. (52–53)

In 1956, Leventhal only offered by way of verdict the speculation that "the point might be made that the effective use of local idiom would also be a proof of the universal applicability of the play since its intrinsic quality would lose nothing by the change" (52). That opinion is wholly ambiguous, of course, if the point was made: if local idiom was a change, then it would prove little about the intrinsic quality of the play. In any case, the assumption of the strictly universal contexts of *Godot,* argued somewhat uneasily by Leventhal in 1956, eventually became as axiomatic in Ireland as elsewhere.

That axiom, though, needs examination. Production lore is replete with incidental evidence of Beckett's working links with Irish drama. A number of works were written for Irish actors, Beckett's favorite actors included a string of Irish ones, and Roger Blin's qualifications for the first Paris production of *Godot,* however universal its intention, seems to have included his previous appearance in a French production of *The Playboy of the Western World* (Bair 404). Irish actors, if they thought Beckett not Irish, thought he was something other than universal. Jack MacGowran was performing O'Casey's *Shadow of a Gunman* in London when he was recruited for the BBC taping of *All That Fall*. "I didn't know then who Beckett was," MacGowran said. "I'd never heard of him. I thought he was a Frenchman whose work had been translated into English" (Young 52). Beckett, though, knew what to make of an Irish character actor like MacGowran. Beckett adds to these suggestive links his multiple tributes to Irish dramatists, his willing information about his formative encounters with productions of plays at the Abbey and Gate theatres, and even the use of fundamental local images in works like *Not I*. "'I knew that woman in Ireland,' Beckett said, 'I knew who she was—not 'she' specifically, one single woman, but there were so many of those old crones, stumbling down the lanes, in the ditches, beside the hedgerows. Ireland is full of them. And I heard 'her' saying what I wrote in *Not I*. I actually heard it'" (Bair 622).

None of this discussion is to suggest that Samuel Beckett was aspiring to be an Abbey Theatre playwright. His relationship to the Irish theater in the 1950s was as impatient and as antagonistic as his dudgeon on Irish censorship had been in the 1930s. His attitude was clear enough when he withdrew mimes from the 1958 Dublin Theatre Festival as part of a dispute provoked by the Archbishop of Dublin's disapproval of O'Casey's *Drums of Father Ned* and of a stage adaptation of *Ulysses*. O'Casey and others managed to shut down the festival because of perceived censorship. Beckett's mimes were not generally missed, but he extended his own ban to productions of any of his works in Ireland. That self-inflicted boycott lasted until 1960: "it is now time I fell off my high Eire moke" (Murray 108). A relationship of antagonism is a relationship nonetheless. In his formidable study, *The Intent of Undoing in Samuel Beckett's Dramatic Texts,* S. E. Gontarski takes as his problem the principle that "Beckett is unable to slough his literary past, the culturally coded forms of literature, as easily as he would like. As much as Beckett might resist the notion, he finds himself already written into the text of Western literature. In much of his creative process, he struggles to undo himself" (xiv). This passage is instructive and useful. There are niches of cultural forms within Western literature, though, and Gontarski's persuasive theory of Beckett's plays, undoing, also has reference to literary pasts and cultural codes more specific than Western literature.

In his "French period," Beckett's dramatic productions are, in a decade: two plays in French, *En attendant Godot* and *Fin de Partie*, which he translated into English; two plays in English, *Krapp's Last Tape* and *Happy Days*, which he translated into French; and a pivotal radio play, *All That Fall*, in English, set in Ireland, and only translated into French by another's hand. Beckett's novels, roughly contemporary with the same "period," are, as I argue, consistently about place and more often than not about Ireland. Drama differs from the maieutics of Beckett's narrative fiction in easy effacement of specific locale: it is more conducive, in the phrase of the narrator of *Watt*, to very interesting exercises. Those plays most effaced of geographically identifiable setting nevertheless do refer to Ireland's features, for example, Connemara in *Godot* and Connaught in *Krapp*. As do Beckett's novels, these plays also draw on more personal, autobiographical material, always Irish, like the revelation on the pier in Dun Laoghaire in *Krapp*.

But such connections as have been made about Beckett's plays and Irish drama are often glosses of the sort that, at this time of heightened awareness of the mechanics of cultural relativity, can be taken as patronizing. Katherine Worth in *The Irish Drama of Europe from Yeats to Beckett*, for example, adds to the national definitions of Beckett: "an Irishman who lives in France, writes with equal facility in French and English, regularly translates himself from one to the other and always keeps in his English an Irish lilt" (241). In 1983, Hugh Kenner wrote that Beckett "is not Irish as Irishness is defined today by the Free State," that Beckett is instead "willing to be the last Anglo-Irishman" (*A Colder Eye* 270).

Argument for the "Irishness" of Beckett's plays might take two tacks. The first would examine the Irish material in Beckett's plays, including the helpfully flagged vision of the Irish crone in *Not I* and also the less obvious representations of action constructed in and refined out of local material. The second would examine the place of Beckett's plays in Irish drama, of, in Gontarski's terms, the plays' relations to culturally coded forms of distinctly Irish literature. The latter seems more useful to this study's more detailed examination of Beckett's early prose and fiction, and there is interesting secondary evidence for this argument. When the Irish-language version of *Godot* promised by Leventhal finally materialized for two nights in 1971, the

Irish Times reviewer of *Ag Fanacht Le Godot* offered the opinion, in Irish, "Until I saw *Godot* in Irish I didn't properly understand how exactly Beckett takes hold of the Irish literary heritage" (Murray 107 n9) — the literary heritage, that is, rather than the general cultural heritage. This perspective may usefully augment the treatment of Ireland in Beckett's "French period" fiction with treatment of Beckett's drama of the same "period" in Irish dramatic contexts. Though only provisional, and relying on *Godot* and *Endgame* as representative evidence, this tack is most valuable here for its relevance to the question of rehabilitation of Beckett's work in a local literary tradition.

Contemporary with the admission of such Beckett works as *More Pricks Than Kicks* into Irish studies was an Irish Theatre Company production of *Godot* in 1982, which was accompanied by revivals of *On Baile's Strand* by Yeats and *The Well of the Saints* by Synge. The artistic director of the company announced his thesis that "these plays show Irish drama as firmly rooted in the European tradition" (Murray 121). The subject of Katherine Worth's book was a strain in modern Irish drama derived from the Continent, usually in circumnavigation of England, as represented by Wilde, Synge, Yeats, and O'Casey, all leading to Beckett. This listing is selective and it has in mind certain examples of their works, but it is a provocative selection. Synge, Yeats, and O'Casey are the names most prominent in Beckett's own memories of the Abbey Theatre in his student days. For James Knowlson's gallery catalog, *Samuel Beckett: An Exhibition,* Beckett offered to Knowlson the information that the Irish dramas most vivid in his memory were "several" of O'Casey's plays; Yeats's plays, including but not limited to two Sophoclean "versions"; "most" productions by Synge in the late 1920s; and two plays by Lennox Robinson (22–23). Shaw appeared in Beckett's comments as a negative aside, and Beckett's well-known response to a request for a tribute to Shaw, mentioned earlier in reference to Murphy's chosen resting place, and also recorded in Knowlson's catalog, brought forth again a preference for specific works by Yeats, Synge, and O'Casey: "What I would do is give the whole unupsettable applecart for a sup of the Hawk's Well, or the Saints', or a whiff of Juno, to go no further" (23).

As he was selective in his praise for Yeats's poetry and the state of Irish writing in "Recent Irish Poetry" in 1934, so Beckett was selective on these later dates in reference to Irish drama. Those names—

Yeats, Synge, O'Casey—may at this time seem a fairly comprehensive compendium, but a reading of Joseph Holloway's theater diaries from the late 1920s gives a corrective sense of the great mass of productions that go unmentioned by Beckett. Certainly, those recollections owe something to the moment of the question, which as posed by Knowlson was forty years or so after the fact. But they also point to the degree to which Beckett's plays constitute an extension of one strain in Irish drama, a strain most antithetical to a local dramatic "realism," and a strain generally ignored by the Abbey Theatre in the years between the first productions of that trinity of Irish playwrights and those of Beckett. That gap in time, between the 1920s and the 1950s, helps account for the interesting local effect of Beckett's dramatic works as a retroactive influence. Beckett's plays help extricate a strain in the national drama for a time obscured. That retroactive action is evident in the new proposals for ideal programs of Irish plays lately offered by many critics. John Rees Moore would join *The Cat and the Moon* (Yeats) with *Godot* (246); Worth would join *Godot* with *The Well of the Saints* or *At the Hawk's Well* (Synge) with *Endgame* (260); Robin Skelton would join *The Shadow of the Glen, Juno and the Paycock* (O'Casey), and *Godot* (63). For better or worse, these groupings shift the canon of Irish drama, alter the sense of individual plays, and suggest that the exclusively universal "application," as Leventhal said, of *Godot,* for example, may be arbitrary.

In 1984, Christopher Murray provided in *Irish University Review* the kind of summary of Beckett productions in Ireland that was (in its own publication—in a special issue about Beckett—as well as in its content) indicative of the change in appreciation of Beckett in Ireland. Murray opens with the note that "*Waiting for Godot* was the winning play in the all-Ireland amateur drama festival in 1980, a fact which contrasts sharply with the trend twenty years earlier, when conventional Irish plays were usually the festival winners" (103). By the 1980s, Beckett's plays had become conspicuous elsewhere, too. In Ireland, though, the manner in which *Godot* was produced is of some pointed interest as a sequel to the Pike Theatre "Dubalin" production of 1956. For by the 1960s, the question of universal or local applications was clearly settled in favor of the former, which is an application not often given to other native writers. As Murray reports, Edward Golden had directed Beckett's *Play* and *Come and Go* at the smaller "experimental" Peacock Theatre of the Abbey, and Golden saw the endeavor as problematic: "After all the Abbey was born in a welter of realism and naturalism, theatric idioms very different to that created by Beckett." At the time of the 1969 Abbey Theatre production of *Godot,* when the theater sought newness to go with its new building, Micheál Ó hAodha, a noted historian of Irish theater and at the time a member of the board of directors, argued in rather stronger terms that Beckett's work differed from local theatrical idioms: "Beckett is the first dramatist of the space-age. In his plays set on the edge of nowhere, society does not exist and man is in a void. The dramatic astronaut views life on earth with a wry sadness through vistas of space" (Murray 115). Thus Ireland, by producing Beckett, would presumably be moving closer to a new technological age. But this sort of rhetoric was not singular to Ireland. What is singular is that the idea that the theatrical idioms of Beckett's plays were alien to Abbey tradition was one idea Beckett's plays helped correct. Beckett's plays revive in their way a national drama not at all a welter of realism, though that may have seemed to short-term memory in 1969 the sole tradition.

Twenty years after those statements, Beckett's theatrical idioms are more pervasive and the sense of place in *Godot* — concerned like the trilogy of novels with the dialectic of being home and being away from home — can be seen as more concerned with the "edge" than with the "nowhere." Like the narrators of the novels, Vladimir and Estragon are away from home, travelers with memories of the Eiffel Tower, Mâcon, and the Rhone. The scene is that situation generalized by D. E. S. Maxwell in *A Critical History of Modern Irish Drama, 1891 – 1980* as common to *Godot, Endgame, Krapp's Last Tape,* and *Happy Days.* "Beckett's first four main plays are in part about surrounding landscapes. Within their precisely delimited compass the characters try to locate themselves/their selves" (197). As strangers, Vladimir and Estragon attempt to locate themselves against a usable if flimsy substitute for the informing certainties available at home. "What are we doing here, *that* is the question," Vladimir says. "And we are blessed in this, that we happen to know the answer. Yes, in this immense confusion one thing alone is clear. We are waiting for Godot to come" (51). Other than that apparently self-defined purpose, the two travelers are left to preoccupy themselves with manners of waiting, for "nothing is certain when you're about" (10). Their disorientation is one of place and also one of time. The two acts obscure the certainties of time for the audience, as well as for the characters. Vladimir and Estragon are unable to confirm their apparent immediate history upon the reappearance of Pozzo and Lucky or of the boy, and the audience, too, is left with the apparent sequence and consequence changed into enigma. The pair of travelers in *Godot* remain on the brink of situating themselves in regard to place and to time, and so the situation of these "strangers" (15) is distinct from that of Pozzo and the boy, who are at home, and that of Lucky, whose performance of thinking cannot even imitate the manner of situating oneself in reference to an assemblage of coordinates that includes Connemara, Berkeley, and camogie. The universalist application — birth astride a grave — is evident to Vladimir and Estragon but insufficient for their purposes.

That the two tramps waiting for "your man" (14) have locally identifiable origins is a tantalizing suggestion. "The world they inhabit," writes James Knowlson in his essay on Beckett and Synge, "their lineage and the less identifiable 'feel' of the characters — in the French as well as in the English text — is unmistakeably Irish" (Knowlson and Pilling 261). The action of attempting to situate oneself against poles of home and away also have a centrality in modern Irish literature. *Godot* even gestures toward prominent literary exemplars in reference to Yeats's *Wind Among the Reeds* collection and Joyce's Shelley motif of "pale for weariness" in *Portrait*.

As Beckett was so articulate about O'Casey in "The Essential and the Incidental" in 1934, O'Casey's dramatic knockabout has been a principal point of local reference for *Godot*. In several works, David Krause has pointed to parallels between *Godot* and *Juno and the Paycock*. Krause takes as the link the knockabout principle of disintegration, which Beckett stated in reference to *Juno*. Thus, in *The Profane Book of Irish Comedy*, Krause argues that "at the conclusion of *Juno* and *Godot*, for example, no solidities remain, not a scrap of furniture on the bare stage, only the slumping couples in their final spasm of comic disintegration and dissociation" (273). Leventhal also noted the resemblance to *Juno* in the first Dublin production of *Godot*, though he was less satisfied with it. O'Casey himself, in the same year as the Pike Theatre production of *Godot* and at the same time as Patrick Kavanagh's endorsement of *Godot*, saw less connection between his work and Beckett's. O'Casey, in "Not Waiting for Godot" praised Beckett's play for being "a rotting and remarkable play" but decried its absolute lack of optimism: there is "nothing in it but a lust for despair, and a crying of woe, not in a wilderness, but in a garden" (51). O'Casey's distinction between his work and Beckett's alerts one to the fact that *Juno* does preface Captain Boyle's final lament of the world in a state of "chasis" with Juno Boyle's own final speech of resolve and that the setting, Dublin in 1922, does admit historical conflicts at least conceivably resolvable.

In the 1970s Seamus Deane wrote of contrary representations of place in Irish drama around the poles of "O'Casey and Yeats: Exemplary Dramatists." At that time, for Deane, just that specificity of setting in *Juno* limited O'Casey's contemporary pertinence: "He is a provincial writer whose moment has come again in the present wave of revisionist Irish history, itself a provincial phenomenon" (*Celtic Revivals* 122). For Deane, at that moment in the 1970s, the limitations of O'Casey came under the general heading of belonging "to the Abbey Theatre Yeats tried not to have." That is, O'Casey's drama was provincial in reiterating the specific forms of local sectarianism. "For the theatre in Ireland," Deane continued, "by its rejection of Yeatsian forms of drama, by its repudiation of those gestures of body, colour, form and speech which he [Yeats] alone revivified in the early part of the century, has joined with the dull reaction of the thirties, both right and left wing, against all that was important and innovative in the modern arts." Thus it is "that Yeats is a more profoundly political dramatist than O'Casey, that it is in his plays that we find a search for the new form of feeling which will renovate our national consciousness" (122). In this argument, that strain of Irish drama exemplified by Yeats is in need of revivification for effect on a continuing sectarianism in Ireland approaching stalemate. Beckett, though Deane is silent on his plays, would seem to be a useful agent for that revivification. Resemblances of Beckett's plays to that other pole, O'Casey and such connections as exist between *Godot* and *Juno,* are an extraneous dimension of Beckett's drama in the local context. To apply Gontarski's terms to the details of a local niche of Western literature, the O'Casey parallel is a culturally coded form of drama that Beckett admirably struggles to undo.

Yeats himself is quite useful on this distinction. The relevance of his ideas may have been helped by virtue of his having been an Irish playwright in Paris long before Beckett arrived. In the 1890s, especially, one finds Yeats interested not only in the *Cathleen Ni Houlihan* vein, but also in Villiers de L'Isle-Adam's *Axel*, in Alfred Jarry's *Ubu roi*, and in Maeterlinck. In "The Theatre," written at the turn of the century, he announed the plan for an Irish Literary Theatre, which would be a theater of art, for plays that are "remote, spiritual, and ideal," for departure from "the stupefying memory of the theatre of commerce" (*Essays and Introductions* 166). His practical priorities were stage language unlike "something out of the newspapers," abolition of "meretricious landscapes, painted upon wood and canvas," and costume devoid of the supposed "magnificence of velvet and silk and on the physical beauty of women" (168–69). Though his works on occasion departed from these ideals, and though indeed his differences with O'Casey could be construed as contradiction with all of his plans, the intentions remained intact at the end of Yeats's life. In "An Introduction For My Plays" in 1937, Yeats wrote, "When I follow back my stream to its source I find two dominant desires. I wanted to get rid of irrelevant movement—the stage must become still that words might keep all their vividness—and I wanted vivid work" (*Essays and Introductions* 527). His argument then was for that paring away of theatrical conventions now most commonly associated with Beckett, whose directorial attention to language and minimization of movement are well known. In that late essay, Yeats acknowledged that his enterprise did not find its audience, which favored others, including O'Casey. Implicitly, of course, he hoped that it would, in his own works and in works generated by compatible dramaturgic priorities.

This is the strain in Irish national drama revived later in the century by Beckett. Various affinities between the plays of Yeats and Beckett have been pointed out before: spare settings, tramp characters, masks, dance, curtailment of physical movement, and strategic emphasis on language. It is, however, particularly in Yeats's *Purgatory* that one finds a striking dramatic parallel to *Godot*. Yeats specifies as the setting "A ruined house and a bare tree in the background" (*Collected Plays* 430). Beckett specifies "A country road. A tree" (6). In Yeats's play, a pair of characters view a pair of ghosts. In Beckett's play, a pair of characters meet Pozzo and Lucky and later a boy. The principal characters in both plays are keeping appointments: in *Purgatory*, an anniversary assignation with relations; in *Godot*, a meeting with a figure who may provide sustaining relation. The old man in *Purgatory* attempts to obliterate the consequences of historical event and personal misdeed by killing the boy. But the attempt only extends the pattern of reliving the past, which gives the play its metaphor of purgatory. Beckett, who spoke of purgatorial metaphor in his first published words on Joyce and who adumbrated his own purgatorial metaphor in *More Pricks Than Kicks*, in *Godot* has characters repeating actions without knowing why, without knowing whether they are, and without any real opportunity to change their circumstances. Yeats's play concludes with the old man lamenting that "Mankind can do no more. Appease / The misery of the living and the remorse of the dead" (436). Beckett's play begins with the comment "Nothing to be done" (7) and ends with the stage direction "They do not move" (60). Though Yeats's play has some indication of historical context, such as Georgian Big House and the marriage of an ascendancy woman and a Catholic groom, Beckett is rather vague on the antecedents of Vladimir and Estragon. In a 1938 interview, Yeats offered explanations for his play that resemble Beckett's for *Godot* in denial of allegory, denial of meaning other than what happens in the play, and, in a statement that parallels the premise of Beckett's "Recent Irish Poetry," assertion that "the problem is not Irish, but European, though it is perhaps more acute here than elsewhere" (Torchiana 358). Donald Torchiana, who included this interview in *W. B. Yeats and Georgian Ireland,* concludes that "modern Ireland, its past and future, is the essential material for *Purgatory*" (359). Apart from authorial intention, one could argue in agreement that *Godot* in its close parallel to Yeats's play also has modern Ireland as essential material for its highly stylized representation of a hermeneutics of place and time.

Godot, as parallel to *Purgatory,* demonstrates much the same relationship to local literary precedent as the story "A Case in a Thousand" did as parallel to Joyce's "A Painful Case" or as "A Wet Night" did as parallel to "The Dead." As Marilyn Gaddis Rose has pointed out in an essay on "The Purgatory Metaphor of Yeats and Beckett," positivistic opportunity—what Georg Lukács would call concrete potentiality—has in Beckett's play "been more nearly obliterated than in Yeats. . . . The quests of all of [Beckett's characters] are more insecure, almost ontologically insecure, and hence, more dubious. For example, the Old Man of *Purgatory* can give God, who alone can intervene in purgatorial consequences, a kind of reality by praying to Him. But Beckett, beginning where Yeats ends, affirms only the uncertainty" (39). Thus, in reference to Yeats as to Joyce, Beckett has the relevance of reiteration of preestablished cultural, literary, and historical dilemmas without positive revision. However much Beckett's *Waiting for Godot* may be in an Irish context a revivification of that Yeatsian form of drama described by Seamus Deane, that extrication of a dramatic tradition from a pervasive local convention of Abbey "realism" does not in itself offer a renovation of the natural consciousness. It is of some interest here that the connotation of *renovation* for Deane is the formulation of something new, while the connotation of *renovations* in Beckett's *Proust* is an endless "comedy of substitution" (16).

A final representative illustration may serve to corroborate this dimension of *Godot*. *Endgame* shares with *Godot* that quality of extricating a particular strain of modern Irish drama that could be construed as having the most potential and extracting from it instead an impasse. This dimension of local literary history is compatible with the generalized sense of termination in Beckett's work argued by Theodor W. Adorno. Adorno used *Endgame* in specific rebuttal to Georg Lukács, in general examination of the failures of literary existentialism, and in praise of Beckett's representation of historical moment. While history in literary modernism must for Lukács take the form of potential progression, modernism's literary historicity for Adorno must take the form of reflection and representation rather than partisanship. Hence, Adorno's response in "Trying to Understand *Endgame*," "that Lukács's objection, that in Beckett humans are reduced to animality, resists with official optimism the fact that residual philosophies, which would like to bank the true and immutable after removing temporal contingency, have become the residue of life, the end product of injury" (125). For Adorno, the historical pertinence of Beckett's work — dismissed by Lukács and others for lack of potentiality, constructivity, and any capacity for a condition of becoming — is the literary representation of a static condition. In *Endgame*, "what would be called the *condition humaine* in existentialist jargon is the image of the last human, which is devouring the earlier ones — humanity" (123), and the material for such an image is "the reified residue of education" (121).

In *Endgame,* evocation of the residue of a past is one form of the terminal maneuvers suggested by its title. As is often the case in Beckett's drama, *Endgame* offers only suggestions of the past of its characters, a past rather more accommodating than their present, and a past, imagined or not, with some historical relevance to Ireland.

> HAMM: And your rounds? When you inspected my paupers. Always on foot?
> CLOV: Sometimes on horse. (8)

Like many characters in Beckett's drama, those in *Endgame* are travelers. Nagg and Nell, at least, have passed through the Ardennes and Sedan and Lake Como before assuming their stationary positions; and the predicament of Hamm and Clov begins with recognition that "there's nowhere else" (6). Away from home they are destitute of order, the sustenance of place. "How easy it is," says Clov, locked in that dialectics of place that makes flight attractive when at home and return attractive when abroad. "They said to me, That's friendship, yes, yes, no question, you've found it. They said to me, Here's the place, stop, raise your head and look at all that beauty. That order!" (80). Away from home, Hamm and Clov cannot rid themselves of it, their past, its order. As Hamm quite carefully enunciates the matter; "I love the old questions. (*With fervour.*) Ah the old questions, the old answers, there's nothing like them" (38). In *Endgame,* Hamm and Clov, lacking alternatives, pass the final moments of the play looking back to the past, to the residue of their experience.

The residue of the past in *Endgame* also includes that particular theater of art that Beckett's plays resemble and that Beckett counts as inspiration. *Endgame* has some affinities with the plays of Yeats. The opening and closing flourishes of Hamm's handkerchief are conspicuously like the curtain cloths, ideally of Edmund Dulac design, in *At the Hawk's Well.* But those Irish adaptations of miracle play also suggest a third, Synge's *Well of the Saints.* These plays were those that Beckett linked as preferable to Shaw's. Synge, too, is another example of an Irish playwright in Paris. Katherine Worth's *Irish Drama of Europe* points out the arbitrary quality of reading Synge's mission to Aran entirely in terms of where he went instead of what he left: "For a long time after he was recalled to Aran by Yeats, he continued to divide his year between Ireland and Paris, and to write book reviews and articles for French journals like *L'Européen*. He spoke and wrote in French with enough ease to be thought of as bilingual, translated Villon, was always slipping into French in his notebooks; his notes on *The Well of the Saints* are half in French, half in English. No wonder if Beckett in his turn feels at ease with Synge" (122). In addition, after his own early articles in specific dissatisfaction with antiquarianism, Beckett would also feel at ease with the marginalia of Synge, such as "Deaf Mutes for Ireland," a satire of deanglicization that proposes resurrection of a dead language by advocacy of a deaf mute society, and "National Drama: A Farce" on the contrivances of an ideological theater. Beckett referred to Synge's plays as early as *Dream of Fair to Middling Women*, though there in effective parody.

"Haven't we had enough of that in this festering country. Haven't we had enough Deirdreeing of Hobson's weirds and Kawthleens in the gloaming hissing up petticoats of sorrarrhoea? Haven't we had enough withered pontiffs of chiarinoscurissimo." "The mist" she sneered "and it rollin' home UP the glen and the mist agin an' it rolling' home DOWN the glen. Up, down, hans arown . . Merde. Give me noon. Give me Racine." (Harvey 336)

As already noted, Arland Ussher in 1942 found some affinity between *Murphy* and *The Well of the Saints*. In addition to incidental references to Synge in later published comments, Beckett responded in 1972 to James Knowlson, as reported by Knowlson and Pilling in *Frescoes of the Skull;* "in answer to a somewhat bold question relating to the most profound influences that he himself acknowledged upon his dramatic writing, Beckett referred me specifically to the work of J. M. Synge" (260). Knowlson also presents a number of points of comparison between the plays of Synge and Beckett, to similarities of situations, to resemblances of characters, and to comparable settings, though warning all the while against overstatement of these correspondences.

Conjunction of *The Well of the Saints, At the Hawk's Well,* and *End-game* is of interest apart from direct or indirect influence. The "old questions" that *Endgame* raises as residue, as static representation of cultural debris, helps bring Adorno's sense of Beckett to bear on the local context. The outcomes of the plays are one indication of that bearing. In *The Well of the Saints*, two tramps, Mary and Martin Doul, have their miracle, the return of their sight, but prefer and have restored their condition of aspiration in blindness, of potentiality in liability. Whatever their condition, the final words of the play stress that they have chosen it. This was the element of the play that Yeats stressed in his well-known preface to the play in *Essays and Introductions:* "Mr. Synge, indeed, sets before us ugly, deformed or sinful people, but his people, moved by no practical ambition, are driven by a dream of that impossible life" (304).

Synge's penultimate stage direction, that Martin and Mary Doul go out, is of course contrary to Beckett's final stage direction in *Godot*. In *At the Hawk's Well*, slightly more than a decade after Synge's play and Yeats's preface to it, Yeats qualifies the affirmative stage direction: his young man and old man are deprived of the miracle they seek but do go out during a song on the bitterness of life. That is, they do go out, and persevere in their hope of renewal, despite the chorus' final song about their idiocy. In *Endgame*, the possibilities of a miracle or even of imagining miracles are moot. As Hamm says, "But what in God's name do you imagine? That the earth will awake in spring? That the rivers and seas will run with fish again? That there's manna in heaven still for imbeciles like you?" (53). Instead, choice is replaced by a passive consciousness that something is taking its course, which is the significance of *Endgame* that Adorno construes in global terms. In addition to the essay devoted to the play, Adorno makes the same argument, again with some references to Lukács, in "Reconciliation Under Duress." "The primitivism with which [Beckett's] works begin so abruptly represents the final phase of a regression, especially obvious in *Fin de Partie*, in which, as from the far-distant realm of the self-evident, a terrestrial catastrophe is presupposed" (161). By reference to Synge and Yeats, one can see in local dramatic representations some progress toward that final phase evident in *Endgame*.

The relevance of Ireland to Beckett's drama does not rest entirely on suppositions or selected parallels that could be attributed to coincidence. *All That Fall* is an explicit extension of Beckett's poetics of futility and a regression to a precisely identified Ireland. It is a pointed application of Beckett's exposure of sustaining, positivistic illusions of a modern, partitioned Ireland. "What kind of a country is this," Mrs. Rooney asks, "where a woman can't weep her heart out on the highways and byways without being tormented by retired bill-brokers!" (42 – 43). In *Krapp's Last Tape,* the monologue sets out to ascertain "those things worth having" (15), begins with a Miss McGlome of Connaught, and ends with Crogan of the Wicklow mountains. Christopher Murray reports from an interview with Cyril Cusack, who played the part of Krapp in Ireland in 1960, that Cusack chided Beckett that *Krapp* "appeared as a 'piece of Irish-Protestant sentimentality' and Beckett quipped back: 'That is what it is intended to be'" (111). In *Happy Days,* the detritus informing the monologue includes not only the oft-cited allusion to the opening line of *At the Hawk's Well* but also, as identified in S. E. Gontarski's "Literary Allusions in *Happy Days,*" the little-known Irish poet Charles Wolf. Beckett's later plays *Not I* and *That Time* were excavated from an earlier manuscript known as *Kilcool.* Also, as confirmation that Beckett's plays re-represent preoccupations already central to at least one strain of modern Irish drama and as confirmation of the place of Beckett's plays in a local tradition, one can look to the retroactive influence of Beckett's drama on the three men most present in Beckett's incidental comments and in his plays: Yeats, Synge, O'Casey. In their essays that hope to give new life to Yeats's plays, both Ruby Cohn, in "The Plays of Yeats Through Beckett-Coloured Glasses," and Andrew Parkin, in "Similarities in the Plays of Yeats and Beckett," look to Beckett for support. Robin Skelton's study *The Writings of J. M. Synge,* which proposes Synge as precursor to Beckett, could not have taken its final shape without Beckett as epigone. In 1988, even journalistic coverage of a Gate Theatre's acute production of *Juno and the Paycock* was unanimous that, with help from the company, their power to reinvent O'-Casey was thanks to their general awareness of Beckett and to their simultaneous production of *Godot.* The question of which sort of renovation that may be—something new or a comedy of substitution—gives Beckett's plays their particular relevance to modern Ireland.

Beckett's prose text *Company,* written in English and published in 1980, brings into purview a resolution of antinomies, a synthesis of an entire corpus of dialectical oppositions. The text's gathering of past images gives it a recapitulative quality: the situation in the dark and the name of the Unnamable, the meadow strewn with sheep placentae from *More Pricks Than Kicks,* and, as if in final closing of an account, the precarious perch on a diving board from the early poem "For Future Reference." The novella's oppositions of self and company, of individual and place, of imagination and context, all bring to the foreground those paradigms of antitheses isolated in this study's reading of the Beckett *oeuvre.*

Company also offers local reference with familiar irony. Its image of the exterior, the other, is "speech in Bantu or in Erse" (10). It supplants the universal form of a problem with the local form: "Nowhere in particular on the way from A to Z. Or say for verisimilitude the Ballyogan Road. That dear old back road. Somewhere on the Ballyogan Road in lieu of nowhere in particular" (23). In addition, *Company* reverts to a collection of private, autobiographical references, including Connolly's Stores, a doctor named either Hadden or Haddon, and a family De Dion Bouton automobile. Near its closing, *Company* offers an image with which this study began: "Having covered in your day some twenty-five thousand leagues or roughly thrice the girdle. And never once overstepped a radius of one from home. Home!" (60). All these images of place are antithetical to the self in *Company,* a novella about such sustenance, such company, as old forms might offer: "a certain activity of mind however slight is a necessary adjunct of company" (9). Here, activity is not validated by any objective standard; it is, rather, a devising of the self for such company as activity itself may create. But in closing — rhetorically and metaphorically — the text ends the possible negotiation of self and company. Having presented the possibility of a new, renovated relation of self and company, having constructed that possibility in affectionate terms, and having created a literary dimension of company in "fabling," the text terminates that renovation in its abrupt final word: "Alone" (63).

All of Beckett's work has this capacity to suggest a newly renovated relation of self to contextual adjuncts of self, and all his work rejects that possibility. The terminal quality of Beckett's work has been noted many times before in celebration of technique, as in James Atlas's "The Prose of Samuel Beckett: Notes From the Terminal Ward." However, that terminal quality and persistent pessimism also complicate, though they certainly do not inhibit, the uses of Beckett's work. At that time, when Beckett was awarded the Nobel Prize, James Mays wrote in the Irish journal *Hibernia* that some recognition of "Beckett's Irishness" would "enhance his achievement" and so make "it appear less as a purely technical *tour de force,* and more of a human one" (14). How does Beckett's "Irishness" meet new literary cultural demands of "Irishness?" As might be expected, given the record thus far in *The Irish Beckett,* the results are equivocal.

The local terms for examination have been put into useful form most recently by Seamus Heaney, in "The Pre-Natal Mountain: Vision and Irony in Recent Irish Poetry," the inaugural Richard Ellmann Lecture in Modern Literature in 1988. Though Beckett is seldom mentioned, Heaney's title coincidently alludes to Beckett's own statement on the topic, "Recent Irish Poetry," and so is an interesting update half a century later. The lecture is far more forthright in regard to his personal work, as well as to the national cultural debate, than any of Heaney's more widely circulated essays. It addresses such issues as the costs of formalism, the alternative attractions of cosmopolitan and local frames of reference, and the apprehension of apparent intractability, all central to Beckett. For Heaney, the cost of formalism, by which literary texts are "distinguished *qua* art from rhetoric or sentiment," includes absorption in an evasive solitude that has "been embraced by many as the condition proper to our times, and — if the place be Ireland — proper to our place" (466). In this reflection on broad issues in local context, the cost of formalism also includes evasion of social criteria by inflation of formal ("*qua* art") criteria: "With the outbreak of civic violence in Belfast and Derry, Irishism was perceived to be not only a manifestation of ethnic kitsch but potentially a code that spelled loyalty to the aims and (by extension) the methods of the IRA." That is, under the present influence of formalism (for Heaney the business of poets, here principally the business of critics), any literary expression by an author known to be from Ireland that was apparently cognizant of politics and did not take the course of bemoaning the existence of politics, is perforce inhumane and also just plain bad taste. Finally, the cost of formalism in a local sphere has been, for Heaney, its own campaign "to confine the operations of imaginative writing to a sanitized realm that might include the ludic, the ironic, the parodic, the satiric, the pathetic, the domestic, the elegiac, and the self-inculpatory but which would conscientiously exclude the visionary prophetic, the patriotic witness, the national epical" (467).

Heaney refers particularly to Louis MacNeice in reference to Paul Muldoon's "Introduction" to *The Faber Book of Contemporary Irish Poetry*, which was a transcription of MacNeice's dismissal on radio in 1939 of F. R. Higgins's premise of the fundamental relations of writer to home. MacNeice's assertion, as Heaney phrases it, was of "the cosmopolitan over the national, the lightness of detachment over the heaviness of attachment." But in MacNeice's work, Heaney finds "troublesome complexities" (471) that he takes to be characteristically Irish. "By acknowledging the drag back into the demeaning actualities of Ulster, MacNeice's poetry remains more problematically burdened than his rather brisk critical pronouncements would suggest; it is certainly not partisan, not what we would dare call 'Unionist poetry' or 'Nationalist poetry,' yet it engages the 'particular historic complex' upon which these caricatured poetic divisions are predicated" (474). For Heaney, those same brisk critical pronouncements and the resistance to the drag back are indications of a shrewd distance from the "particular historic complex" (Heaney elsewhere attributes the phrase to David Jones). This distance Heaney takes to be utile: "what is intractable when wrestled with at close quarters becomes tractable when addressed from a distance. The longer the lever, in fact, the less force is necessary to move the mass and get the work going" (476).

With some minor modifications, Heaney's description of MacNeice, though not the deductions from it, fit the Irish Beckett rather well: by acknowledging the drag back to the home country, Beckett's work remains more problematic than his or others' critical pronouncements would suggest; his work is certainly not partisan, not revivalist or revisionist, yet it engages a "particular historic complex." Beckett's work, set against criticism of it, provides a striking demonstration of the sanitizing effects of a critical formalism whose lightness of detachment has extended to subordination of the "social reality" of a body of contemporary work to an obscure subsection in obligatory consideration of juvenilia and marginalia. The uses of Beckett have been generally relegated in academic criticism to enthusiasm for technique, happily aloof to troublesome complexities, and to proof of a universality that, as W. J. McCormack said about Yeats in

Ascendancy and Tradition, Platonizes the author out of existence (296). Beckett is, as I hope these chapters show, an author whose own critical pronouncements are in local context less exceptional than central and whose fiction and drama represent in explicit terms or in abstract codes matters of a particular historic complex.

In Ireland, Beckett's *oeuvre* has the pertinence of participating in a debate of local cultural dilemma in the first half of this century and in the recurrence of the debate in the second half. Criticism of Beckett's work, not Beckett's work, is the predominant factor in the creation of a condition in which, as Heaney observed, "even to canvas the idea of connection between founded nation and a founded poetic voice is in danger of being judged old-fashioned, if not downright retrograde" (468). Beckett's work offers Ireland as predicament, as "troublesome complexities," and without partisanship, all as Heaney would prefer. For these complexities and equivocations, far more than for dismissal of the local in favor of the universal, Beckett's work is suitable for Irish revisionist use.

However, Beckett's work is also useful for correcting easy reaction to a variety of long-standing predicaments. Beckett's work read in local context certainly serves to correct the impression lamented by Heaney that literary engagement in the troublesome complexities of place necessarily ends in "collusion with the business of elevation, exhortation, and expostulation" (467). Beckett's work does demonstrate that representation of cultural issues is also compatible with the business of pessimism, passivity, and inertia. However, Beckett's work from the 1930s to the 1980s also exposes the arbitrary assumption that the cost of sanitizing the literary intelligentsia was the exclusion of "the visionary prophetic, the patriotic witness, the national epical." Beckett's work is a corrective reminder that the excluded may also be negative critique, patriotic despair, and national dirge. Finding the local context of Beckett's work might seem to open the way to prophetic positivism, but attention to the local contexts of Beckett's work reveals instead a pessimism that may encourage in Irish as well as in Anglo-American criticism some Platonizing. Beckett's work deconstructs a local revivalism confident of the sureties of place and collective consciousness. But his work does not, as easy reaction would have it, consequently construct a positive revisionism. His lever may be the longest on record, but it does not make the intractable tractable or by exhortation "move the mass and get the work going." From both object of critique and evident alternative, Beckett's work consistently extracts, rather, a further intractability. His renovations have his connotations: an endless comedy of substitution. For this reason Beckett's work is unsuitable for revisionist use.

The operative question in much Beckett criticism is, as it should be, that of *Happy Days:* "What does it mean? What's it meant to mean?" The answer in regard to the Irish Beckett is that Beckett's work elaborates a paradigm of orientation and disorientation, of place and individual, and of context and imagination that is analogous to, among other things, the particular historical complex of modern Ireland and other comparable complexes of affiliation and self-determination in personal and collective forms. The Irish Beckett offers no easy reduction. It does not suggest, for example, the view facetiously reported by A. J. Leventhal that "the whole conception of *Waiting for Godot* is Irish." But attention to the Irish contexts does indicate that Beckett's work is consistently grounded in a particular local *Irish* cultural predicament, that the predicament as represented in Beckett's work is of a broader scope than the narrow chronological and topical bounds of the Irish literary revival, and that Irish cultural self-examination has been a more sophisticated if less progressive form of identity thinking than is usually suggested. Further, the Irish Beckett places his work on a verge at the end of the literary revival, from which it looks back and recapitulates more than it looks forward in prophetic-visionary fashion. In all its ample Irish materials, Beckett's work has the means, the historic materials, to offer positivistic outcomes, but it does not. Such small consolation as *Company* offers for this troublesome *oeuvre* is that "Confusion too is company up to a point" (26).

 WORKS CITED
INDEX

WORKS CITED

Abbott, H. Porter. *The Fiction of Samuel Beckett: Form and Effect*. Berkeley: U of California P, 1973.

Acheson, James. "Chess with the Audience: Beckett's *Endgame*." *Critical Essays on Samuel Beckett*. Ed. Patrick A. McCarthy. Boston: G. K. Hall, 1986. 181–92.

Adorno, Theodor W. "Reconciliation under Duress." *Aesthetics and Politics: Theodor Adorno, Walter Benjamin, Ernst Bloch, Bertold Brecht, George Lukács*. London: Verso, 1980. 151–77.

———. "Trying to Understand *Endgame*." Trans. Michael T. Jones. *New German Critique* 26 (1982): 119–50.

AE (George Russell). "An Essay on the Character in Irish Literature." *The Wild Bird's Nest: Poems From the Irish*. By Frank O'Connor. Dublin: Cuala, 1932. N.p.

———. *Homeward: Songs by the Way*. Dublin: Whaleys, 1894.

———. "Nationality and Cosmopolitanism in Literature." John Eglinton, et al. *Literary Ideals in Ireland*. London: T. Fisher Unwin, 1899. 79–88.

Alvarez, A. *Samuel Beckett*. New York: Viking, 1973.

Arthur, Kateryna. "Texts for *Company*." *Beckett's Later Fiction and Drama: Texts for Company*. Ed. James Acheson and Kateryna Arthur. New York: St. Martin's, 1987. 136–44.

Atlas, James. "The Prose of Samuel Beckett: Notes from the Terminal Ward." *Two Decades of Irish Writing: A Critical Survey*. Ed. Douglas Dunn. Cheshire: Carcanet 1975. 186–96.

Bair, Deirdre. *Samuel Beckett: A Biography*. New York: Harcourt Brace Jovanovich, 1978.

Banville, John. *Birchwood*. New York: Norton, 1973.

Beckett, Samuel. *All That Fall. Krapp's Last Tape and Other Dramatic Pieces.* New York: Grove, 1960. 33–91.

———. "Assumption." *Transition* 16–17 (1929): 268–71.

———. *. . . but the clouds. . . . Ends and Odds: Nine Dramatic Pieces.* New York: Grove, 1976.

———. "A Case in a Thousand." *Bookman* 86 (1934): 241–42.

———. "Che Sciagura." *T.C.D.: A College Miscellany* 14 Nov. 1929: 42.

———. *Collected Poems in English and French.* New York: Grove, 1977.

———. *Company.* New York: Grove, 1980.

———. *Disjecta: Miscellaneous Writings and a Dramatic Fragment.* Ed. Ruby Cohn. New York: Grove, 1984.

———. *Endgame: A Play in One Act.* New York: Grove, 1958.

———. *First Love and Other Shorts.* New York: Grove, 1974.

———. *Fizzles.* New York: Grove, 1976.

———. *Happy Days.* New York: Grove, 1961.

———. *How It Is.* New York: Grove, 1964.

———. *Krapp's Last Tape and Other Dramatic Pieces.* New York: Grove, 1960.

———. *Lessness.* London: Calder and Boyars, 1970.

———. *The Lost Ones.* New York: Grove, 1972.

———. *Mercier and Camier.* New York: Grove, 1975.

———. *Mercier et Camier.* Paris: Editions de Minuit, 1970.

———. *More Pricks Than Kicks.* New York: Grove, 1972.

———. *Murphy.* New York: Grove, 1957.

———. *Not I. Ends and Odds: Nine Dramatic Pieces.* New York: Grove, 1976. 13–23.

———. *Proust.* New York: Grove, n.d.

———. *Stories and Texts for Nothing.* New York: Grove, 1967.

———. *That Time. Ends and Odds: Nine Dramatic Pieces.* New York: Grove, 1976. 27–37.

———. *Three Novels by Samuel Beckett.* New York: Grove, 1965.

———. *Waiting for Godot: A Tragicomedy in Two Acts.* New York: Grove, 1954.

———. *Watt.* New York: Grove, 1959.

Beckett, Samuel, et al. "Poetry Is Vertical." *Transition* 21 (1932) 148–49.

"Beckett Wins Nobel for Literature." *New York Times* 24 Oct. 1969: 1, 3.

"Book Libel Suit." *Irish Press* 23 Nov. 1937: 2, 12.

Booth, Wayne C. *The Rhetoric of Fiction.* Chicago: U of Chicago P, 1961.

Bowen, Elizabeth. "The Big House." *Collected Impressions.* New York: Knopf, 1950. 195–200.

_____. *Bowen's Court*. London: Longman, Green, 1942.

_____. *The Last September*. New York: Knopf, 1929.

_____. *Seven Winters and Afterthoughts*. New York: Knopf, 1962.

Boyce, D. George. *Nationalism in Ireland*. Baltimore: Johns Hopkins UP, 1982.

Bradford, Roy. *The Last Ditch*. Belfast: Blackstaff, 1981.

Brater, Enoch, ed. *Beckett at 80: Beckett in Context*. New York: Oxford UP, 1986.

_____. "Why Beckett's *Enough* is More or Less Enough." *Contemporary Literature* 21 (1980): 252–66.

Breuilly, John. *Nationalism and the State*. New York: St. Martin's, 1982.

Brooke-Rose, Christine. "Samuel Beckett and the Anti-Novel." *London Magazine* 5 (12 Dec. 1958): 38–46.

Brown, Malcolm. *The Politics of Irish Literature: From Thomas Davis to W. B. Yeats*. Seattle: U of Washington P, 1972.

Brown, Terence. "Edward Dowden: Irish Victorian." *Ireland's Literature: Selected Essays*. Totowa, N.J.: Barnes and Noble, 1988.

_____. *Ireland: A Social and Cultural History 1922–85*. London: Fontana, 1985.

Bruck, Jan. "Beckett, Benjamin, and the Modern Crisis in Communication." *New German Critique* 26 (1982): 159–71.

Büttner, Gottfried. *Samuel Beckett's Novel "Watt."* Trans. Joseph P. Dolan. Philadelphia: U of Pennsylvania P, 1984.

Chalker, John. "The Satiric Shape of *Watt*." *Beckett the Shape Changer*. Ed. Katherine Worth. Boston: Routledge and Kegan Paul, 1979. 19–37.

Clarke, Austin. *Collected Poems*. Dublin: Dolmen, 1974.

Clissmann, Anne. *Flann O'Brien: A Critical Introduction to His Writings*. New York: Barnes and Noble, 1975.

Cohn, Ruby. "The Plays of Yeats Through Beckett-Coloured Glasses." *Threshold* 19 (1965): 41–47.

_____. *Samuel Beckett: The Comic Gamut*. New Brunswick, N.J.: Rutgers UP. 1962.

Corkery, Daniel. *The Hidden Ireland: A Study of Gaelic Munster in the Eighteenth Century*. 1924. Dublin: Gill and Macmillan, 1979.

_____. *Synge and Anglo-Irish Literature: A Study*. 1931. New York: Russell and Russell, 1965.

Costello, Peter. *The Heart Grown Brutal: The Irish Revolution in Literature, from Parnell to the Death of Yeats, 1891–1939*. Totowa, N.J.: Rowman and Littlefield, 1978.

Cullen, Louis M. *The Hidden Ireland: Reassessment of a Concept.* 1969. Mullingar: Lilliput, 1988.

Dangerfield, George. *The Damnable Question: One Hundred and Twenty Years of Anglo-Irish Conflict.* Boston: Little, Brown, 1976.

Darnton, Robert. *The Great Cat Massacre: And Other Episodes in French Cultural History.* New York: Vintage, 1985.

Deane, Seamus. *Celtic Revivals: Essays in Modern Irish Literature 1880 – 1980.* Winston-Salem, N.C.: Wake Forest UP, 1987.

———. *Heroic Styles: The Tradition of an Idea.* Derry: Field Day Theatre Company, 1984.

———. "Irish Poetry and Irish Nationalism." *Two Decades of Irish Writing.* Ed. Douglas Dunn. Cheshire: Carcanet, 1975. 4 – 22.

Devlin, Denis. *Intercessions.* London: Europa, 1937.

Donoghue, Denis. "Afterword." *Ireland's Field Day.* London: Hutchinson, 1985.

———. "The State of Letters." *Sewanee Review* 84 (1976): 129 – 33.

———. *William Butler Yeats.* New York: Viking, 1971.

"Dr. Gogarty's Book." *Irish Press.* 23 Nov. 1937: 6.

Driver, Tom F. "Beckett by the Madeleine." *Columbia University Forum* 4.3 (1961): 21 – 25.

Edgeworth, Maria. *Castle Rackrent.* Dublin: Browne and Nolan, n.d.

Eglinton, John. "What Should Be the Subjects of a National Drama?" John Eglinton, W. B. Yeats, George Russell, and William Larminie. *Literary Ideals in Ireland.* London: T. Fisher Unwin, 1899. 9 – 13.

Eliot, T. S. "Tradition and the Individual Talent." *Selected Essays.* New York: Harcourt Brace Jovanovich, 1950. 3 – 11.

———. "Tradition and the Practice of Poetry, with an Introduction and Afterword by A. Walton Litz." *Southern Review* 21 (1985): 873 – 88.

———. "*Ulysses,* Order, and Myth." *Dial* 75 (1923): 480 – 83.

Ellmann, Richard. *Four Dubliners: Wilde, Yeats, Joyce, and Beckett.* New York: George Braziller, 1988.

———. *James Joyce.* New York: Oxford UP, 1959.

Fanning, Ronan. "The Meaning of Revisionism." *Irish Review* 4 (Spring 1988): 15 – 19.

Federman, Raymond. *Journey into Chaos: Samuel Beckett's Early Fiction.* Berkeley: U of California P, 1965.

Federman, Raymond, and John Fletcher. *Samuel Beckett: His Works and His Critics: An Essay in Bibliography.* Berkeley: U of California P, 1970.

Fennell, Desmond. "Against Revisionism." *Irish Review* 4 (Spring 1988): 20–26.

Fitch, Noel Riley. *Sylvia Beach and the Lost Generation: A History of Literary Paris in the Twenties and Thirties.* New York: Norton, 1983.

Flanagan, Thomas. "Afterword." *Ireland's Field Day.* Notre Dame: Notre Dame UP, 1986. 107–17.

Fletcher, John. *The Novels of Samuel Beckett.* London: Chatto and Windus, 1964.

Foucault, Michel. "What Is an Author?" *Language, Counter-memory, Practice: Selected Essays and Interviews.* Ed. and trans. Donald F. Bouchard. Ithaca, N.Y.: Cornell UP, 1977. 113–38.

Friedman, Melvin J. "The Novels of Samuel Beckett: An Amalgam of Joyce and Proust." *Comparative Literature* 12.1 (1960): 47–58.

Geertz, Clifford. *Local Knowledge: Further Essays in Interpretive Anthropology.* New York: Basic, 1983.

Gellner, Ernest. *Nations and Nationalism.* Ithaca, N.Y.: Cornell UP, 1983.

Gilbert, Stuart. "Transition Days." *Transition Workshop.* Ed. Eugene Jolas. New York: Vanguard, 1949.

Gogarty, Oliver St. John. *As I Was Going Down Sackville Street.* New York: Harcourt, Brace & World, 1937.

———. *Tumbling in the Hay.* New York: Reynal & Hitchcock, 1939.

Gontarski, S. E. *The Intent of Undoing in Samuel Beckett's Dramatic Texts.* Bloomington: Indiana UP, 1985.

———. "Introduction: Crritics and Crriticism: 'Getting Known.'" *On Beckett: Essays and Criticism.* Ed. S. E. Gontarski. New York: Grove, 1986.

———. "Literary Allusions in *Happy Days.*" *On Beckett: Essays and Criticism.* Ed. S. E. Gontarski. New York: Grove, 1986.

Gregory, Lady Isabella Augusta. *Our Irish Theatre: A Chapter of Autobiography.* 1913. New York: Oxford UP, 1972.

Guggenheim, Peggy. *Out of This Century: The Informal Memoirs of Peggy Guggenheim.* New York: Dial, 1946.

Hanly, David. *In Guilt and in Glory.* New York: William Morrow, 1979.

Harmon, Maurice. *Sean O'Faolain: A Critical Introduction.* Notre Dame, Ind.: U of Notre Dame P, 1966.

Harvey, Lawrence. *Samuel Beckett: Poet and Critic*. Princeton: Princeton UP, 1970.

Hassan, Ihab. *The Literature of Silence: Henry Miller and Samuel Beckett*. New York: Knopf, 1967.

Hayman, David. "A Meeting in the Park and a Meeting on the Bridge: Joyce and Beckett." *James Joyce Quarterly* 8 (1971): 372–84.

Heaney, Seamus. "The Pre-Natal Mountain: Vision and Irony in Recent Irish Poetry." *Georgia Review* 42 (1988): 465–80.

Henn, T. R. *The Lonely Tower: Studies in the Poetry of W. B. Yeats*. 2d ed. London: Methuen, 1965.

Hesla, David H. *The Shape of Chaos: An Interpretation of the Art of Samuel Beckett*. Minneapolis: U of Minnesota P, 1971.

Higgins, Aidan. *Languishe, Go Down*. New York: Grove, 1966.

_____. "Tired Lines, Or Tales My Mother Told Me." *A Bash in the Tunnel*. Ed. John Ryan. Brighton: Clifton, 1970. 55–60.

Higgins, F. R. *Arable Holdings*. Dublin: Cuala Press, 1933.

Holloway, Joseph. *Joseph Holloway's Irish Theatre: Volume One 1926–1931*. Ed. Robert Hogan and Michael J. O'Neill. Dixon, Calif.: Proscenium, 1968.

Hoult, Norah [N. H.]. "Caviare to the General." *Dublin Magazine* 9.3 (July–Sept. 1934): 84–87.

Hutchinson, John. *The Dynamics of Cultural Nationalism: The Gaelic Revival and the Creation of the Irish Nation State*. London: Allen and Unwin, 1987.

Rev. of *Intercessions*, by Denis Devlin. *Times Literary Supplement* 23 Oct. 1937: 786.

Iser, Wolfgang. *The Implied Reader: Patterns of Communication in Prose Fiction from Bunyan to Beckett*. Baltimore: Johns Hopkins UP, 1974.

Joyce, James. *The Critical Writings of James Joyce*. Ed. Ellsworth Mason and Richard Ellmann. New York: Viking, 1959.

_____. *Dubliners: Text, Criticism, and Notes*. Ed. Robert Scholes and A. Walton Litz. New York: Viking, 1969.

_____. *Finnegans Wake*. New York: Viking, 1959.

_____. "*A Portrait of the Artist as a Young Man*": *Text, Criticism, and Notes*. Ed. Chester G. Anderson. New York: Penguin, 1977.

_____. *Selected Letters of James Joyce*. Ed. Richard Ellmann. New York: Viking, 1975.

————. *Ulysses*. New York: Random House, 1961.

Joyce, Stanislaus. *My Brother's Keeper: James Joyce's Early Years*. Ed. Richard Ellmann. New York: Viking, 1958.

Kavanagh, Patrick. *Collected Poems*. London: Martin Brian and O'Keeffe, 1972.

————. *The Green Fool*. Harmondsworth: Penguin, 1975.

————. "Some Notes on *Waiting for Godot*." *Sacred Keeper: A Biography of Patrick Kavanagh*. By Peter Kavanagh. The Curragh, Ireland: Goldsmith, 1979. 296–98.

Kearney, Richard. "Beckett: The Demythologising Intellect." *The Irish Mind: Exploring Intellectual Traditions*. Ed. Richard Kearney. Dublin: Wolfhound, 1985. 267–93.

————. *Transitions: Narratives in Modern Irish Culture*. Dublin: Wolfhound, 1988.

Kennedy, Sighle. *Murphy's Bed: A Study of Real Sources and Surreal Associations in Samuel Beckett's First Novel*. Lewisburg, Penn.: Bucknell UP, 1971.

————. "Spirals of Need: Irish Prototypes in Samuel Beckett's Fiction." *Yeats, Joyce, and Beckett: New Light on Three Modern Irish Writers*. Ed. Kathleen McGrory and John Unterecker. Lewisburg, Penn.:Bucknell UP, 1976. 153–66.

Kenner, Hugh. *A Colder Eye: The Modern Irish Writers*. New York: Knopf, 1983.

————. *Flaubert, Joyce, and Beckett: The Stoic Comedians*. Boston: Beacon, 1962.

————. *A Reader's Guide to Samuel Beckett*. London: Thames and Hudson, 1973.

Kiberd, Declan. "Beckett and Kavanagh: Comparatively Absurd?" *Hermathena* 141 (1986): 45–55.

Kinsella, Thomas. "The Irish Writer." W. B. Yeats and Thomas Kinsella. *Davis, Mangan, Ferguson? Tradition and the Irish Writer*. Dublin: Dolmen, 1970. 57–66.

Knowlson, James. *Samuel Beckett: An Exhibition*. London: Turret, 1971.

Knowlson, James, and John Pilling. *Frescoes of the Skull: The Later Prose and Drama of Samuel Beckett*. New York: Grove, 1980.

Krause, David. *The Profane Book of Irish Comedy*. Ithaca, N.Y.: Cornell UP, 1982.

————. *Sean O'Casey: The Man and His Work*. New York: Macmillan, 1975.

Leventhal, A. J. "Dramatic Commentary." *Dublin Magazine* ns 31.1 (1956): 52–54.

Levy, Eric P. "*Mercier and Camier:* Narration, Dante, and the Couple." *On Beckett: Essays and Criticism.* Ed. S. E. Gontarski, 1986. 117–30.

Le Fanu, Joseph Sheridan. *Uncle Silas.* Oxford: Oxford UP, 1981.

Lewis, Wyndham. *Time and Western Man.* London: Chatto and Windus, 1927.

Longley, Edna. "Putting on the International Style." *Irish University Review* No. 5 (1988): 75–81.

Lukács, Georg. "The Ideology of Modernism." *The Meaning of Contemporary Realism.* Trans. John Mander and Necke Mander. London: Merlin, 1963. 17–46.

Lyons, F. S. L. *Culture and Anarchy in Ireland 1870–1939.* Oxford: Clarendon, 1979.

———. *Ireland since the Famine.* London: Collins, 1973.

———. "Yeats and the Anglo-Irish Twilight." *Irish Culture and Nationalism, 1750–1950.* Ed. Oliver MacDonagh, et al. London: Macmillan, 1983: 212–38.

Lyons, J. B. *Oliver St. John Gogarty: The Man of Many Talents.* Dublin: Blackwater, 1980.

McCormack, W. J. *Ascendancy and Tradition in Anglo-Irish Literary History from 1789 to 1939.* Oxford: Clarendon, 1985.

———. *The Battle of the Books: Two Decades of Irish Cultural Debate.* Mullingar, Ireland: Lilliput, 1986.

———. "Seeing Darkly: Notes on T. W. Adorno and Samuel Beckett." *Hermathena* 141 (1986): 22–44.

MacDonagh, Oliver. *States of Mind: A Study of Anglo-Irish Conflict, 1780–1980.* London: Allen and Unwin, 1983.

MacGreevy, Thomas. "Homage to James Joyce." *Transition* 21 (1932): 253–55.

———. *Jack B. Yeats: An Appreciation and an Interpretation.* Dublin: Victor Waddington Publications, 1945.

———. *Poems.* London: Heinemann, 1934.

McHugh, Roger, ed. *Jack B. Yeats: A Centenary Gathering.* Dublin: Dolmen, 1971.

MacManus, Francis. "The Literature of the Period." *The Years of the Great Test: 1926–39.* Ed. Francis MacManus. Cork: Mercier, 1967. 115–26.

McMillan, Dougald. "Beckett at Forty: The Capital of the Ruins and 'Saint-Lô.'" *As No Other Dare Fail: For Beckett on His Eightieth Birthday by His Friends and Admirers.* New York: Riverrun, 1986. 67–76.

MacNeice, Louis. *The Poetry of W. B. Yeats.* New York: Oxford UP, 1941.

Mahon, Derek. "MacNeice in England and Ireland." *Time Was Away: The World of Louis MacNeice.* Ed. Terence Brown and Alec Reid. Dublin: Dolmen, 1974. 113–22.

Matthews, James. *Voices: A Life of Frank O'Connor.* New York: Atheneum, 1983.

Maxwell, D. E. S. *A Critical History of Modern Irish Drama 1891–1980.* New York: Cambridge UP, 1984.

Mays, J. C. C. "Beckett and the Irish." *Hibernia* 23 (7 Nov. 1969): 14.

———. "Introductory Essay." *Brian Coffey Special Issue. Irish University Review* 5.1 (1975): 11–29.

———. "Mythologized Presences: *Murphy* in Its Time." *Myth and Reality in Irish Literature.* Ed. Joseph Ronsley. Toronto: Wilfred Laurier, 1977. 197–218.

———. "Young Beckett's Irish Roots." *Irish University Review* 14.1 (1984): 18–33.

Mercier, Vivian. *Beckett/Beckett.* New York: Oxford UP, 1977.

———. "Savage Humor." *New Republic* 19 Sept. 1955: 20–21.

Miller, Liam. *The Noble Drama of W. B. Yeats.* Dublin: Dolmen, 1977.

Monnier, Adrienne. "James Joyce." *Mercure de France* 326 (Jan. 1956): 122–24.

Mood, John J. "'The Personal System'—Samuel Beckett's *Watt.*" *PMLA* 86 (1971): 255–65.

Moore, John Rees. *Masks of Love and Death: Yeats as Dramatist.* Ithaca, N.Y.: Cornell UP, 1971.

Moore, Thomas. *The Poetical Works of Thomas Moore.* Boston: Philips, Sampson, 1854.

Morse, J. Mitchell. "The Ideal Core of the Onion: Samuel Beckett's Criticism." *French Review* 38 (1964): 23–29.

Muldoon, Paul, ed. *The Faber Book of Contemporary Irish Poetry.* London: Faber and Faber, 1986.

"Murphy." *Dublin Magazine* 14.2 (Apr.–June 1939): 98.

Murray, Christopher. "Beckett Productions in Ireland: A Survey." *Irish University Review* 14.1 (1984): 103–25.

O'Brien, Conor Cruise. "Irishness." *Writers and Politics.* New York: Pantheon, 1965. 97–100.

O'Brien, Eoin. *The Beckett Country: Samuel Beckett's Ireland.* Monkstown, Co. Dublin: Black Cat, 1986.

O'Brien, Flann. *At Swim-Two-Birds.* London: Longmans Green, 1939.

O'Casey, Sean. "Not Waiting for Godot." *Blasts and Benedictions.* London: Macmillan, 1967. 51–52.

————. *Windfalls: Stories, Poems, and Plays.* New York: Macmillan, 1934.

O'Connor, Frank. "The Future of Irish Literature." *Horizon* 5 (Jan. 1942): 55–63.

————. *Guests of the Nation.* London: Macmillan, 1931.

————. "Joyce: The Third Period." *Irish Statesman* 14 (1930): 114–16.

————. "Synge." *The Irish Theatre: Lectures Delivered During the Abbey Theatre Festival Held in Dublin in August 1938.* Ed. Lennox Robinson. London: Macmillan, 1939. 31–52.

————. *The Wild Bird's Nest.* Dublin: Cuala, 1932.

O'Connor, Ulick. *Oliver St. John Gogarty: A Poet and His Times.* London: Jonathan Cape, 1964.

O'Conor, Norreys Jephson. "The Trend of Anglo-Irish Literature." *The Bookman* 86 (1934): 233–34.

O'Doherty, Brian. "Jack B. Yeats: Promise and Regret." *Jack B. Yeats: A Centenary Gathering.* Ed. Roger McHugh. Dublin: Dolmen, 1971. 77–91.

O'Faolain, Sean. "Daniel Corkery." *Dublin Magazine* 12.2 (1936): 49–61.

————. "Emancipation of Irish Writers." *Yale Review* 23 (1934): 485–505.

————. *The Finest Stories of Sean O'Faolain.* Boston: Little, Brown, 1957.

————. "Four Irish Generations." *Commonweal* 9 (1928–29): 751.

————. "Irish Poetry Since the War." *London Mercury* 31 (1934–35): 545–52.

————. "Literary Provincialism." *Commonweal* 17 (1932–33): 214–15.

————. *Midsummer Night Madness and Other Stories.* London: Jonathan Cape, 1932.

————. "Style and the Limitations of Speech." *Criterion* 8 (1928): 67–87.

Our Exagmination Round His Factification for Incamination of Work in Progress. London: Faber and Faber, 1929.

Parkin, Andrew. "Similarities in the Plays of Yeats and Beckett." *Ariel* 1 (July 1970): 49–58.

Pearse, Padraig. *Collected Works: Political Writings and Speeches.* Ed. Desmond Ryan. Dublin: Maunsel, 1924.

Perloff, Marjorie. "Between Verse and Prose: Beckett and the New Poetry." *Critical Inquiry* 9.2 (1982): 415–34.

Power, Mary. "Samuel Beckett's 'Fingal' and the Irish Tradition." *Journal of Modern Literature* 9.1 (1981–82): 151–56.

Putnam, Samuel. *Paris Was Our Mistress: Memoirs of a Lost and Found Generation.* New York: Viking, 1947.

Putnam, Samuel, et al., eds. *European Caravan.* New York: Brewer, Warren, and Putnam, 1931.

Reid, Alec. *All I Can Manage, More Than I Could.* Dublin: Dolmen, 1969.

————. "Test Flight: Beckett's *More Pricks Than Kicks.*" *The Irish Short Story.* Ed. Patrick Rafroidi and Terence Brown. Lille: Publications de L'Université de Lille, n.d 227–35.

"Review of *Intercessions.*" *Times Literary Supplement* 23 Oct. 1937: 786.

Robinson, Michael. *The Long Sonata of the Dead: A Study of Samuel Beckett.* New York: Grove, 1969.

Rose, Marilyn Gaddis. "The Irish Memories of Beckett's Voice." *Journal of Modern Literature* 2 (1971): 127–32.

————. "The Purgatory Metaphor of Yeats and Beckett." *London Magazine* 7 (Aug. 1967): 33–46.

Rosen, Stephen J. *Samuel Beckett and the Pessimistic Tradition.* New Brunswick, N.J.: Rutgers UP, 1976.

Ryan, Noelle. *Samuel Beckett: Early Days in Foxrock.* Foxrock: Local History Club, 1982.

Seaver, Richard. "Samuel Beckett: An Introduction." *Merlin* 1.2 (1952): 73–79.

Senneff, Susan Field. "Song and Music in Samuel Beckett's *Watt.*" *Modern Fiction Studies* 10.2 (1964): 137–49.

Shaw, Bernard. *The Matter with Ireland.* Ed. David H. Greene and Dan H. Laurence. London: Hart-Davis, 1962.

Shenker, Israel. "Moody Man of Letters." *New York Times* 6 May 1956: sec. 2; 1, 3.

Skelton, Robin. *The Writings of J. M. Synge.* Indianapolis: Bobbs-Merrill, 1971.

Somerville, E. Œ., and Martin Ross. *The Big House of Inver.* London: Heinemann, 1925.

————. *The Real Charlotte.* London: Longmans Green, 1911.

Spender, Stephen. "Lifelong Suffocation." *New York Times Book Review* 12 Oct. 1958: 5.

Stuart, Francis. *Things to Live For: Notes for an Autobiography.* London: Jonathan Cape, 1934.

Synge, John M. *The Complete Plays of John M. Synge*. New York: Random House, 1935.

———. "Deaf Mutes for Ireland." *Collected Works*. Vol. 3. Ed. Anne Saddlemyer. Washington, D.C.: Catholic U of America P, 1982. 218–19.

———. "A Landlord's Garden in Country Wicklow." *Collected Works*. Vol. 2. Ed. Alan Price. Washington, D.C.: Catholic U of America P, 1982. 230–33.

———. "National Drama: A Farce." *Collected Works*. Vol. 3. Ed. Anne Saddlemyer. Washington, D.C.: Catholic U of America P, 1982. 220–26.

Thomas, Dylan. "Documents: Recent Novels." 1938. *James Joyce Quarterly* 8 (1971): 290–92.

Torchiana, Donald. *W. B. Yeats and Georgian Ireland*. Evanston, Ill.: Northwestern UP, 1966.

Trilling, Lionel. *Beyond Culture: Essays on Literature and Learning*. New York: Viking, 1968.

Unseld, Siegfried. "To the Utmost: To Samuel Beckett on His Eightieth Birthday." *As No Other Dare Fail: For Samuel Beckett on His Eightieth Birthday by His Friends and Admirers*. New York: Riverrun, 1986. 91–95.

Ure, Peter. *Yeats and Anglo-Irish Literature: Critical Essays by Peter Ure*. Ed. C. J. Rawson. New York: Barnes and Noble, 1974.

Ussher, Arland. "The Contemporary Thought of Ireland." *Dublin Magazine* 22 (July–Sept. 1947): 24–30.

———. *The Face and Mind of Ireland*. Old Greenwich, Conn.: Devin-Adair, 1950.

Waters, Maureen. *The Comic Irishman*. Albany: State U of New York P, 1984.

Watson, Francis. Rev. of *More Pricks Than Kicks*. *Bookman* 86 (1934): 219–20.

Watson, G. J. *Irish Identity and the Literary Revival: Synge, Yeats, Joyce, and O'Casey*. New York: Barnes and Noble, 1979.

West, Rebecca. *The Strange Necessity: Essays by Rebecca West*. New York: Doubleday, Doran, 1928.

White, Terence de Vere. "Social Life in Ireland 1927–1937." *The Years of the Great Test 1926–39*. Ed. Francis MacManus. Cork: Mercier, 1967. 19–29.

Wood, Michael. "Comedy of Ignorance." *New York Review of Books* 30 Apr. 1981: 49–52.

Worth, Katherine. *The Irish Drama of Europe from Yeats to Beckett*. Atlantic Highlands, N.J.: Humanities, 1978.

Yeats, Jack B. *The Amaranters*. London: Heinemann, 1936.

Yeats, William Butler. *The Autobiography of William Butler Yeats*. New York: Macmillan, 1953.

————. "The Censorship and St. Thomas Aquinas." *The Uncollected Prose of W. B. Yeats*. Ed. John P. Frayne and Colton Johnson. Vol. II. New York: Columbia UP, 1976. 480–85.

————. *The Collected Plays of W. B. Yeats*. New York: Macmillan, 1953.

————. *The Collected Poems of W. B. Yeats*. New York: Macmillan, 1956.

————. *Essays and Introductions*. New York: Collier, 1961.

————. *Explorations*. Selected by Mrs. W. B. Yeats. New York: Collier, 1973.

————. ed. *Fairy and Folk Tales of The Irish Peasantry*. New York: Collier, 1986.

————. *Mythologies*. London: Macmillan, 1962.

————. *Uncollected Prose by W. B. Yeats*. Ed. John P. Frayne. 2 vols. New York: Columbia UP, 1970–76.

————. *A Vision*. New York: Collier, 1966.

Young, Jordan R. *The Beckett Actor: Jack MacGowran, Beginning to End*. Beverley Hills, Calif.: Moonstone, 1987.

INDEX

THE IRISH BECKETT

was composed in 12 on 13 Garamond No. 3 on a Mergenthaler Linotron 202
by Partners Composition;
with display type in Garamond Open;
printed by sheet-fed offset on 50-pound, acid-free Glatfelter Natural Hi Bulk,
Smyth-sewn and bound over binder's boards in Holliston Roxite B,
and with dust jackets printed in two colors and laminated
by Braun-Brumfield, Inc.;
designed by Sara L. Eddy;
and published by
SYRACUSE UNIVERSITY PRESS
SYRACUSE, NEW YORK 13244-5160

Richard Fallis, *Series Editor*

Irish Studies presents a wide range of books interpreting important aspects of Irish life and culture to scholarly and general audiences. The richness and complexity of the Irish experience, past and present, deserves broad understanding and careful analysis. For this reason, an important purpose of the series is to offer a forum to scholars interested in Ireland, its history, and culture. Irish literature is a special concern in the series, but works from the perspectives of the fine arts, history, and the social sciences are also welcome, as are studies that take multidisciplinary approaches.

Selected titles in the series are: